War, Industry, and Society
the Midlands, 1939–45

David Thoms

ROUTLEDGE
LONDON AND NEW YORK

First published 1989
by Routledge
11 New Fetter Lane, London EC4P 4EE
29 West 35th Street, New York, NY 10001

© 1989 David Thoms
Disc Conversion in Baskerville by Columns of Reading
Printed in Great Britain by TJ Press (Padstow) Ltd,
Padstow, Cornwall

British Library Cataloguing in Publication Data

Thoms, David.
War, Industry, and Society: the Midlands 1939–1945
1. England. Midlands. Industries 1939–1945
I. Title
338.09424

ISBN 0–415–02272–X

Library of Congress Cataloging in Publication Data

Thoms, David.
War, Industry, and Society: the Midlands 1939–1945/David Thoms.
p.   cm.
ISBN 0–415–02272–X ✓
1. World War, 1939–1945 – England – Midlands. 2. Midlands (England)
– Industries. 3. Midlands (England) – Social conditions.
I. Title.
D760.8.M53T47   1989
942.4′084–dc19   88–36770

To Kate, Rachel, and Hugo
for their patience and support

Contents

Tables

Preface

The official histories are an invaluable guide to economic and social change in Britain during the Second World War. However, in recent years a number of studies have appeared which have supplemented or challenged our knowledge and interpretation of domestic events during this period, many of them employing distinctive methodologies to investigate fresh areas of enquiry, particularly in social history. Yet there remain relatively few detailed local or regional studies against which to test and modify macro assessments. The purpose of this book is to help redress the balance through an investigation of selected themes within the particular context of the Midland region. Prior to 1939, few government departments, with the exception of the Ministry of Labour, had a regional organization, but this changed with the outbreak of war as a substantial bureaucracy was created based on twelve civil defence regions, of which the Midlands was one. This region, which covered an area of some 5,000 square miles and included the counties of Staffordshire, Shropshire, Warwickshire, Worcestershire, and Herefordshire, was predominantly rural in character, but its hub in terms of the war effort was based upon the industrial complex which radiated out from Birmingham. Engineering dominated the local economy and during the period of rearmament and war the manufacture of aero engines, airframes, wheeled and tracked vehicles, and munitions came to dominate its output and employment structures. The Midlands is therefore a particularly useful region for the consideration of the mobilization, organization, and effectiveness of the industrial war economy, while its changing social profile raised issues of a different but nevertheless important kind. This study does not attempt to cover the whole of the region but concentrates upon the key locality of the Birmingham–Coventry axis. Similarly, it is not a general economic and social history, but rather an analysis of themes selected for their wider importance and controversial nature.

I am indebted to many individuals and institutions for making this study possible. In particular, I should like to acknowledge the help provided by library and other staff at the Coventry Record Office, the Modern Records Centre at the University of Warwick, the Public Record Office, the Imperial War Museum, the universities of Cambridge and Sussex, the Museum of British Road Transport, and Coventry Polytechnic. I am also grateful to the British Motor Industry Heritage Trust for permission to consult a number of important sources deposited by them at the University of Warwick. I must record my appreciation of those people, too numerous to name individually, who kindly shared with me their recollections of the war period. Finally, a special note of thanks to Steven Morewood and Tom Donnelly who not only read and commented upon parts of the manuscript but also gave me the benefit of their own research work in this field. I am, of course, responsible for any errors or weaknesses which remain.

1

Prelude to war:
the creation of the aircraft shadow
factories

By the mid-1930s the strengthening of Britain's air capability had assumed a high military priority so that between 1936 and 1938 the Air Ministry, with Treasury support, moved from last to first place among the defence departments in terms of its share of public expenditure.[1] In July 1934 the Cabinet adopted Scheme A, the first of a series of programmes designed to expand the air force. This was only a modest beginning but Germany's increasingly menacing foreign policy, together with its rearmament drive, enabled the Ministry to capitalize on Baldwin's commitment to the Commons in March 1934 for Britain to maintain parity with any air power within striking distance of its shores. By September 1939 the RAF had still not achieved numerical equality with the Luftwaffe but Britain did possess a larger and modernized air force as well as the industrial capacity to support further growth.[2] This expansion demanded significant additions to factory space and plant since on the eve of rearmament the aircraft industry was a relatively small scale operation and in many respects technically and organizationally backward.[3] This was achieved in part through the creation of a series of shadow factories to supplement the existing facilities of the professional aircraft industry. The first, and some of the most important, of these were located in the Midlands and gave the region its first real experience of preparing for war.

The application to aircraft manufacture of the shadow factory principle was first discussed towards the end of the 1920s, though the term itself appears to have been introduced by the Weir Committee which reported in 1934 on ways of raising munitions output. The scheme's participants were paid an agency fee for managing additional productive capacity in the form of government owned factories and plant. The initial contracts were placed outside the aircraft industry, but with the acceleration of rearmament from 1938 the agency scheme was extended to the professional firms and by the period of peak wartime production they were responsible for the majority of the shadow factories.[4] The possible contribution of the motor vehicle industry to any emergency expansion of aircraft production was discussed as early as 1927, but it was not until the implementation of Scheme F nine years later that the Air Ministry took positive steps to activate these contingency plans. Scheme F was the first large scale development of the RAF, taking the number of front line aircraft and reserves to over 8,000, more than double the number envisaged by its immediate predecessor.[5] In order to help facilitate this growth the secretary of state for air, Lord Swinton, recruited Austin and Rootes for the construction of the Fairey Battle and Bristol Blenheim airframes respectively, while these two and another five firms – Wolseley, Daimler, Standard, Singer, and Rover – were approached in connection with the manufacture of aero engines. The Singer company and Wolseley, which was part of the Nuffield organization, subsequently dropped out of the scheme, though in 1938 the latter was given responsibility for establishing what became one of the most important of all the aircraft factories, the giant Castle Bromwich works on the edge of Birmingham. This became famous for its output of Spitfire fighter aircraft, though only after control had passed to Vickers-Armstrong. Metropolitan Vickers and English Electric were the only other firms to become involved in the construction of airframes under the pre-war shadow scheme, while it was not until 1939 that the government went beyond the motor companies for additional aero engine capacity.[6]

The minutes of Lord Swinton's weekly progress meetings with the Air Council reveal that both he and his influential advisor, Lord Weir, were highly supportive of the shadow factory arrangement. Yet it was evident from the spirited nature of the debate within the Air Ministry that a powerful body of opinion favoured limiting expansion to the professional industry, while a number of important criticisms were also voiced over the detailed operation of the plan. Some of the most serious organizational problems associated with the shadow scheme thus became apparent only when the Air Ministry was committed to its implementation and negotiations with the motor vehicle firms had begun. Swinton and Weir were frequently placed on the defensive. One example of this, which reflected the Minister's personal discomfort, surfaced in a minute of 26 April 1936 when, in reply to the suggestion that the Bristol Aeroplane Company rather than the motor firms should satisfy the government's order for additional aero engines, Swinton retorted sharply that he 'did not think that we could possibly contemplate going back on a major decision of this kind at this stage of the proceedings'.[7]

Following their meeting with Swinton on 7 April 1936, the representatives of the seven motor car firms formed their own co-ordinating committee, and at their first session, held at the Standard works in Coventry, elected Herbert Austin chairman. It was this group which decided the particular form the first shadow scheme would take, namely the manufacture by individual firms of selected components, with the Bristol and Austin companies alone responsible for assembling complete engines. One of the most persistent critics of this arrangement was Colonel H. A. P. Disney, the Ministry's head of aeronautical production. Disney argued that the scheme was unduly complex and that if efficiency was the goal the best solution would be for the Bristol company to have sole responsibility for the additional 4,000 engines required under Scheme F by March 1939. He also believed that to entrust the as yet untested car makers with such an important order involved exceptionally high defence risks.[8] If a split system of production was to be employed, Disney's own preference was for three of the seven firms to erect shadow factories for the manufacture of engine parts, and to assemble and test the finished products, with the remaining companies providing minor components on a subcontract basis.[9] This proposal had certain advantages. In particular, it meant that the skills of the more efficient firms could be maximized, relegating the weaker units to the less important work. It also complied with the educative principle which, according to Swinton and Weir, was one of the main arguments in favour of the shadow scheme as a whole. Disney continued to press his case with Weir and senior defence staff but was reluctantly obliged to accept a policy which in practice was foisted upon the Ministry by its own inadequate planning and the obduracy and self-interest of the motor manufacturers, and Herbert Austin in particular.

As the debate on the shadow scheme unfolded during the spring of 1936, Swinton came to recognize the weaknesses of the split system of engine manufacture favoured by the motor firms and changed his position so radically that he later publicly recorded his disappointment at the co-ordinating committee's inflexibility.[10] Ministry officials pointed out that the dispersal of components production between a number of units multiplied the threat of interruptions to the supply of completed engines through the vulnerability of individual firms to air attack, labour strikes, and poor workmanship. Swinton suggested that the best protection against sub-standard workmanship was the self-policing role of the group itself through its own co-ordinating committee.[11] Air attack was regarded as a serious risk but it was felt that there were ways in which this could be minimized, while the strike issue received relatively little attention, perhaps because the motor industry was not characterized by strong trade unions or excessive labour unrest. What Swinton and his officials appear to have under-estimated was the degree to which production schedules could be thrown into confusion by the failure of one or more firms to meet their targets simply because they were less efficient, and this problem came eventually to undermine the credibility of the split system of manufacture as it was formulated in 1936.

A consensus evolved within the Air Ministry that the most effective way of ensuring delivery of the order for 4,000 aero engines was the creation of a shadow complex managed by the Bristol Aeroplane Company. This was encouraged by growing speculation that the motor companies would find it difficult to meet their production commitment. For example, Lord Weir was concerned that 'The "shadow" engine firms were not making sufficient allowance for the difference in manufacturing processes between motor car and aero engines.'[12] In fact when Wolseley dropped out it was decided that BAC should manage a new shadow factory at Filton. Nevertheless, Swinton was anxious to persevere with the motor companies, even though it involved resolving a number of difficult problems. Part of the explanation for this was financial since he believed that further orders placed with the Bristol Company would encourage other aircraft firms to demand similar treatment, with the danger of a ratchet-like escalation of costs. Since the motor firms were to act as agents rather than principals it was reasonable to assume that their investment and other expenses would be minimized. In fact the car makers were less generously remunerated than the aircraft manufacturers, perhaps in part because, unlike them, they negotiated their fees with the government individually rather than through their trade association. More importantly, however, Swinton and Weir shared the belief that in the longer term a shadow complex which went beyond the professional firms was the only practical device for accumulating sufficient capacity and expertise to meet wartime production requirements, a view that was reinforced by the manifest inadequacies of the air force and aircraft industry. Indeed Weir went so far as to suggest in January 1936 that 'the problem of remedying our present deficiencies was so serious that it would probably engage the whole manufacturing resources of the country'.[13] Sir Christopher Bullock, the Air Ministry's senior civil servant until his premature departure in the summer of 1936, took a similar view, arguing that 'as at present organized' the aircraft industry was incapable of meeting the government's expansion targets.[14] The educative, or work experience, value of distributing government contracts beyond the professional aircraft firms was therefore strongly emphasized by Swinton and his principal advisors. One of the ironies of the first shadow aero engine scheme was that its arrangement actually weakened the Ministry's own case for the programme as a whole since it restricted the engineering experience gained by the participating firms to the production of a limited range of components. It remains doubtful whether Swinton was ever fully committed to the work experience argument. The motor firms were obliged to follow specifications established by the aircraft companies and Herbert Austin made it clear in the early stages of his negotiations with the Air Ministry that in his view it would be most unwise to tinker with the Bristol design team's work.[15] An indication of Swinton's private thoughts on the educative principle emerged at one of his weekly progress meetings towards the end of April 1936 when he insisted that since the motor firms 'were all sound engineering concerns' they should be permitted to organize ·manufacture in their own way.[16] Indeed, to have argued differently would have vitiated one of the main arguments for utilizing the talents of the car makers, namely their experience of mass production techniques. In the event, however, they were compelled largely to follow the practices of a company whose methods had already resulted in serious shortfalls in the Air Ministry's aero engine programme.

Despite the limitations of the work experience rationale, it was a sensible public justification for the shadow factory scheme and a valuable negotiating point with the professional aircraft companies. When discussions opened with Bristols it soon became clear that the company's senior management was reluctant to yield trade secrets to possible future competitors. Their anxiety was understandable since the highly competitive nature of the motor industry in the 1930s, together with the growth of aircraft manufacture envisaged by the rearmament programme, was almost certain to tempt some of the car firms into aeronautical engineering. Wolseley and Alvis had already moved in that direction by 1936, while Standard and Daimler soon made clear their wish to participate in the Air Ministry's expansion plans.[17] There was also the recent memory of the First World War when several motor companies became closely involved in supporting the infant aircraft industry and, in the case of Siddeley-Deasy, continued after the Armistice to develop this side of their business. The German reoccupation of the demilitarized Rhineland zone at the beginning of March 1936 which signalled Hitler's intention to overthrow the Treaty of Versailles by force meant that Bristols had little alternative but to co-operate with the Air Ministry's shadow scheme. However, the company's management expressed a wish to choose their own partners from among the motor manufacturers but this was rejected on the grounds that the allocation of firms had already been fixed by government on a department-wide basis. Swinton assured the company that unless the international situation deteriorated the award of aircraft contracts to the motor firms would be regarded as a bridging operation and that it was not intended to become a permanent feature of government supply policy.[18] He did acknowledge that as part of the educative process certain aspects of aero engine technology would inevitably be taken up by the car makers. In practice this threat was tempered by the split system of components manufacture which limited the expertise gained by any one firm, and there is no doubt that Bristols' management would have been more intransigent had the Ministry insisted upon the complete engine method of production. Their resistance to the idea of Alvis making complete Bristol engines is a clear indication of this. The inclusion of the motor companies in the shadow factory scheme did help to spread the risk of over-expansion at a time when it was still unclear whether the aircraft industry was to be placed on a permanent war footing and this consideration probably calmed a few frayed nerves in the Bristol boardroom.

One of the most interesting features of the early shadow factory arrangement concerned Herbert Austin's role as chairman of the engine group from its inception in the spring of 1936 until his departure in May 1940, and in particular his part in the introduction of the split components form of manufacture. Swinton was very keen to secure Austin's co-operation in meeting the Air Ministry's defence requirements. Towards the end of 1935 he wrote to Sir Maurice Hankey, the secretary of the Imperial Defence Committee, expressing concern that as part of the rearmament programme the facilities of the Austin company had reputedly gone to the War Office while those of the Nuffield organization had been allocated to the Air Ministry. Although this was not in fact the case, the incident reveals Swinton's enthusiasm for a link with Austin and his distinct coolness towards Lord Nuffield. Swinton expressed confidence that Nuffield would work well with the War Office but added, 'We, on the other hand, would probably find him a difficult partner.' This soon proved to be a perfectly accurate forecast.[19]

It was argued in 1936 and later that the motor vehicle firms were themselves responsible for the particular structure which characterized the first shadow aero engine scheme. Swinton recorded in his autobiography that the motor entrepreneurs were anxious to avoid the wasteful duplication of equipment and the delays which would inevitably follow from each firm being required to compete for the scarce resources necessary for the manufacture of complete engines.[20] Production efficiency was certainly high on the agenda at the Minister's first meeting with the car firms in April 1936. Reginald Rootes suggested that specialization was the only practical way of achieving really large increases in output.[21] However, doubts were voiced over the ability of the group system to harness effectively the skills of a number of independent manufacturing concerns, each with their own particular strengths and weaknesses. In particular, it was felt that some difficulty might be experienced in securing the fine tolerances required in the construction of aero engines.[22] A shortage of skilled engineering

7

labour in the West Midlands was also regarded as a potentially serious problem, though there was general agreement that this 'might be less intense if different firms were working on different components'.[23] A further advantage of the split system of engine manufacture was said to be the minimal disruption which it would cause to normal commercial operations, while at the same time limiting the danger of over-expansion by any one firm. Yet, significantly, the minutes also reveal that Spencer Wilks and John Black, from Rover and Standard respectively, would have preferred to build complete engines.[24] In addition, Wolseleys were represented by Leonard Lord, who supported the split system of manufacture, rather than Lord Nuffield, who soon expressed his disapproval of it by withdrawing his organization from the shadow factory scheme. Lord's resignation as managing director of Morris Motors in 1936 was largely the consequence of a financial disagreement with Lord Nuffield, though the row over the shadow engine project was almost certainly a contributory factor. He returned to the motor industry with Austin in 1938, played a leading part in the company's rearmament programme, and eventually became its managing director and chairman.[25]

In their early negotiations with the Air Ministry members of the co-ordinating committee expressed a willingness to consider alternatives to the split system of production, but by May their attitude had apparently hardened and Swinton was forced to report that 'the firms could not guarantee delivery of the 4,000 engines required by March 1939, unless they were allowed to make them in 7 units, each manufacturing one part of the engine'.[26] Although a general consensus may have evolved among the motor companies in favour of this arrangement, there are reasons for thinking that they took their lead from Austin, as at least one Ministry official claimed. For example, when Swinton and Weir met Austin at the end of April to discuss production methods he remained unwilling to consider any form of compromise, even though in attending the meeting alone he was under no immediate pressure from other members of the co-ordinating committee.[27] As one of the world's leading pioneers of volume car production, Austin enjoyed a particular status in the industry which was reflected in his election as chairman of the shadow engine group. In addition, Austin's authority with the Ministry which, because of the Fairey Battle contract, was already very considerable, was enhanced by Nuffield's withdrawal from the shadow scheme, which also made Swinton personally more dependent on his co-operation. Whatever the merits of the split system of engine manufacture, it suited Austin well because his company emerged as the sole member of the group to secure the technical and financial advantages which flowed from the assembly of complete engines. This was important since, according to Lord Weir, Austin had been 'thinking of ultimately entering the field of aero engine manufacture in a permanent capacity as a designer or constructor'.[28] Contact between Herbert Austin and the Bristol Aeroplane Company had already been established by the beginning of 1936 and Swinton believed that one of the purposes of this was the creation of some form of long-term association.[29]

The motor firms' absorption into the Air Ministry's rearmament programme appeared perfectly logical since their engineering expertise was closely allied to that of the aircraft companies. Apart from a common interest in power units, both industries were concerned with the construction of body frames, and by the mid-1930s most of the car firms had made significant progress in the application of metal fabrication techniques. It was also expected that there would be an organizational spin-off involving the transfer of volume production methods associated with the leading car manufacturers, such as Austin and Morris, to the aircraft industry which was more familiar with generating its output in limited batches. One of the particular attractions of Austin, for example, was said to have been the company's substantial experience in the construction and operation of machine shops geared towards mass production techniques. In this respect aircraft manufacture would benefit from the management skills accumulated by the motor companies and supposedly in short supply among the professional firms. Similarly, the motor industry, and Coventry in particular, had a reputation for the skill of its engineering labour force, while the slow process of unionization may have been another factor which influenced government officials in allocating military contracts. In a speech to the Trades Union Congress in September 1938, Arthur Deakin of the Transport and General Workers' Union claimed that whenever diversification of industrial development occurred 'the drive is towards the Midlands of this country – an area prolific in providing workers who are outside the pale of the Trade Union Movement'.[30]

Although the motor industry escaped the worst ravages of the world depression of the late 1920s, the sales performance of a number of firms slumped dramatically so that spare manufacturing capacity became available. The industry picked up as the general recovery gathered pace, but this experience may have helped to persuade some government officials that any productive slack could be accommodated within the Air Ministry's programme and that in time of war this form of manufacturing adjustment could be introduced on a broader basis. This had the attraction of economy and efficiency but failed to recognize several important differences between the construction of motor car and aero engines. It was only at his weekly progress meeting on 7 April 1936 that Swinton finally grasped this point and acknowledged the inevitability of a separate shadow provision. As he said at the time, if the motor companies 'had to clear out most of their own machinery and put in new plant it would be essential for them to put up new factories if we were to get any real output from them during the first six months of war'.[31] It was a serious indictment of the Ministry's forward planning that Swinton should have been debating such a fundamental aspect of the shadow scheme on the very day that representatives of the motor companies arrived at the Ministry to discuss its implementation.

The First World War enabled the motor industry to demonstrate its technical versatility when several leading firms became involved in different aspects of aircraft manufacture. Herbert Austin's Longbridge plant produced over 2,000 aeroplanes and a sizeable quantity of aero engines,[32] while Coventry, because of the number of firms involved, achieved recognition as a particularly important centre of aeronautical engineering. Humber, which was assimilated into the Rootes group in 1929, was one of the country's pioneer aircraft manufacturers and during the First World War produced the Bentley BR1 and BR2 rotary engines at its Coventry works.[33] Daimler was another early entrant to the industry and during the course of the war progressed from the manufacture of engines to that of complete aircraft. This necessitated considerable extension to the company's Radford complex, including construction of a private airfield, and some eighty aircraft eventually came to leave the works monthly, which made it one of the government's principal suppliers in the industry.[34] The first aircraft contract won by Standard was for fifty tubular framed BE12s. Other orders followed, including work on the famous Sopwith Pup, so that by the Armistice the firm's output totalled around 16,000 aircraft.[35]

Siddeley-Deasy was the only motor manufacturer to retain a strong presence in the aircraft industry after 1918 when a number of its own designs proved commercially viable. Although Daimler became associated with the Bristol Aeroplane Company in the manufacture of aero engine cylinders, connecting rods, and other parts, it was on a relatively small scale and for only a short period of time.[36] However, the experience of the war years helped to make the company an obvious candidate for inclusion in the rearmament plans of the 1930s. The same could be said of Standard and Austin. In order to accommodate its aircraft and other contracts, Standard negotiated the purchase of a thirty acre site at Canley in 1925 and this was followed three years later by the acquisition of a further hundred acres adjacent to the new works.[37] The North and West works at Longbridge were constructed with government money in order to provide Austin with the capacity to satisfy Ministry of Munitions contracts, with the company having the option to purchase the plant and buildings at the end of the war.[38] These links with aircraft manufacture provide part of the explanation for the readiness with which Austin, Daimler, and Standard participated in the Air Ministry's development programme of the mid-1930s. The First World War publicly demonstrated the engineering links between the motor vehicle and aircraft industries and also helped to provide the means and incentive to re-establish the relationship once the need to expand the air force became apparent.

Lord Weir claimed that the motor companies contributing to the first shadow factory scheme were chosen on the basis of their reputation for efficient production,[39] though there is no evidence of any systematic pre-selection evaluation of their respective capabilities. Ministry officials possessed some knowledge of each firm but this tended to be of a fairly general nature and it was not until late June 1936 that Colonel Disney presented a detailed assessment of their individual strengths and weaknesses. Although the interwar period was a time of very considerable growth for the motor industry as a whole, the manufacturing and financial performance of its different elements varied enormously and even the most successful companies experienced periods of market failure. By 1935, when Britain produced over 300,000 cars, sales were dominated by Nuffield, Austin, and Ford, with Rootes, Standard, and Vauxhall collectively responsible for a little over 20 per cent of total output.[40] Since the Wolseley aero engine plant at Wolverhampton was the sole constituent of the Nuffield empire allocated to the Air Ministry it was logical that Austin should assume a leading role in Swinton's rearmament plans. This was strengthened, of course, by the personal animosity which existed between Lord Nuffield and the Minister. Swinton enjoyed a friendly relationship with Austin, at least in the early stages of their negotiations before they became enmeshed in the structure and financial implications of the shadow factory programme, but it was C. R. Engelbach, the company's works director since 1922, who appears to have made the greatest impression. Engelbach was an experienced engineer of high repute who had successfully reorganized the Longbridge plant in 1927 to accommodate volume production, and it was this achievement which seems to have made a particular impact upon Swinton and Weir. However, despite the company's profitability in the 1930s, its development was inhibited by an ageing management, which came to be reflected in a poor record of design innovation, a weakness not remedied until the recruitment of Leonard Lord towards the end of the decade.

To begin with, Reginald Rootes was reluctant to commit Humber to the shadow factory scheme, preferring instead to concentrate the firm's resources upon the development of its motor vehicle business, but an appeal by Swinton on behalf of the national interest secured his co-operation, together with that of his brother, William.[41] William Rootes, in particular, became closely identified with the rearmament programme and in 1940 he was appointed chairman of the Joint Aero Engine Committee, which was responsible for the two shadow schemes then operating. Through a series of judicious take-overs, which included the Humber, Hillman, Commer, and Sunbeam companies, the Rootes brothers constructed a large motor manufacturing combine which, by the late 1930s, ranged from commercial vehicles to both specialist and mass produced cars. The broad scope of the group's engineering experience, including Humber's work on aircraft during the First World War, was probably one of the most important factors in its selection by the Air Ministry in connection with the implementation of Scheme F.

Rootes' success in the 1930s was based upon a number of shrewd business deals while that of the Standard Motor Company was largely due to the production engineering flair of John Black. After service in the Great War, Black joined Hillmans, another Coventry car firm, where he remained until it was acquired by the Rootes brothers in 1928. He was then recruited by Standard to help reverse the financial problems which had taken the company to the edge of bankruptcy. The assembly shops at Canley were reorganized to facilitate volume production. This helped to bring a long-term improvement in productivity and profit levels so that by 1939 the company's output of cars was almost seven times greater than at the beginning of the decade, while the size of the labour force had hardly changed.[42] This success brought Black's elevation to managing director following the death of Reginald Maudslay, Standard's founder, in 1934. Black had first expressed an interest in producing aero engines for the Air Ministry at this time, an approach that was politely rebuffed. When Black renewed his offer early in 1936, having heard of the possibility of a shadow engine scheme, the Air Ministry was much more accommodating. Colonel Disney reported in June 1936 that Black was 'to all intents and purposes in sole control of the business',[43] and was clearly impressed by the company's achievements, suggesting that it 'is capable of undertaking anything we ask, either airframes or engines'.[44] Standard's contribution to rearmament and to the war effort itself was substantial and Black's part in this was formally recognized when he was honoured with a knighthood in 1943. Standard's reputation was rising within the Air Ministry even before the shadow scheme began and at one time was discussed as a possible third supplier of airframes.[45] With the benefit of hindsight, it seems likely that the company would have performed a valuable service in this role and that the practical talents of John Black could have been employed on a broader front.

The success enjoyed by Rootes and Standard was paralleled in reverse by the decline of Singer which slumped from the country's third largest car manufacturer in 1929 to a position of relative insignificance a decade later. This was largely the result of a succession of poor management decisions which undermined the company's viability as a volume producer. The firm was saved in the mid-1930s by a major financial reconstruction and kept going during the war with government support, but it remained commercially fragile until its absorption by the Rootes group in

1953.[46] Colonel Disney was scathing in his criticisms of Singer's managing director, William Bullock, claiming that 'his views on any subject are not worth consideration'. He described the company's Birmingham works as 'dirty and badly arranged' and with much of its machinery being out of date.[47] In fact Singer only became involved in the shadow scheme as a late entrant and its financial disasters, coupled with Disney's report, ensured that its participation was brief. Moreover, with the exception of Austin, the other participants in the scheme were not anxious to see Singer involved, fearing that the company would almost certainly hold up production. The fact that the Singer company was included in the shadow programme at all is another indication of the Air Ministry's poor industrial intelligence at that time.

Daimler and Rover, the remaining members of the first shadow engine group, had sound engineering pedigrees but the interwar period proved an anti-climax as both companies failed to capitalize on their early promise. Daimler, which became part of BSA in 1911, specialized in high powered quality vehicles, the market for which was limited and highly competitive. The company was starved of capital during the 1920s so that its technology and production methods became increasingly antiquated and its products over-priced. In the following decade a change of policy saw Daimler enter the market for smaller vehicles with the purchase of Lanchester of Birmingham in 1931, while various economies were also introduced to help save the firm from liquidation.[48] The Daimler management, anxious to seek an outlet for their unemployed resources, courted the Air Ministry's favour by drawing attention to the company's distinguished wartime production record and experience in the armaments field. Despite its financial traumas, the Daimler reputation for quality remained high and Colonel Disney reported that the firm was quite capable of making complete engines, and had the capacity to do so, but that its management needed strengthening.[49] Management failure also characterized Rover during the 1920s with boardroom disputes creating a climate of instability which almost brought the company down. Recovery coincided with the appointment of Spencer Wilks as managing director, a man of wide experience in the motor industry, including a period at Hillmans with John Black. His careful regulation of output, together with the introduction of a new range of cars, was instrumental in placing

Rover on a sound financial basis with a significant, if unspectacular, niche in the quality end of the market. Moreover, it was Wilks's reputation as the British motor industry's leading engine manufacturer which first brought him to the attention of Lord Weir. The company's chequered history was reflected in Disney's report for while he regarded Rover as a 'sound unit' capable of making components for the Bristol aero engine, he also felt that the 'assembly arrangements are well out of date and generally the factory is not really well organised'.[50] However, under Wilks's direction, the two Rover shadow engine factories and the firm's own works emerged as crucial elements in the motor industry's contribution to the war effort.

The rift between Swinton and Lord Nuffield, one of Britain's premier industrialists, introduced a personal note into the creation of the shadow factory scheme. Within a month of his joint meeting with the motor manufacturers, Swinton was informed by Wolseley's senior management that the firm now wished to make complete engines rather than selected components. This caused confusion and bad feeling within the Air Ministry with accusations of deviousness and even dishonesty being levelled against the company. When the matter was discussed at the Minister's weekly progress meeting, Swinton expressed the view that

> while the Bristol Company would in any case probably refuse to let Wolseleys have their designs for this purpose, if the proposal were put to them, the real answer to the letter was that if we had wanted to get the 4,000 engines made other than as an educative order, we should undoubtedly have asked Bristols themselves, rather than a rival engine firm, to make them.[51]

The issue was further complicated because it was the Wolseley motor company which was earmarked for inclusion in the shadow engine scheme and yet it seemed patently obvious that it was the aero engine division which was seeking Air Ministry orders. This situation was starkly illustrated at Swinton's second meeting with the motor manufacturers when two representatives from Wolseley were present, one from the motor and another from the aero engine division. The rejection of Wolseley's offer generated a series of meetings and a large volume of correspondence between Ministry officials and the Nuffield organization. As chairman of the shadow engine co-ordinating committee, Herbert Austin was employed as an intermediary to help resolve the dispute and it was under the auspices of this body that in late July 1936 Wolseley was invited to replace the ailing Singer company and to take over some of the aero engine work previously allocated to Daimler.[52] Leonard Lord, Wolseley's managing director, telephoned Disney on 7 August to convey his acceptance of the offer, which he confirmed in writing a week later.[53] Events were then overtaken by Lord's resignation on 24 August for within two days his replacement, Oliver Boden, informed the Ministry that the Nuffield organization was discontinuing its own manufacture of aero engines and also withdrawing from the shadow scheme.[54] The affair received wide publicity a few weeks later when Lord Nuffield issued a press statement accusing the Air Ministry of shabby treatment and pointing out that he had always opposed the present shadow engine scheme because in 'aero engine manufacture unity of control is in my judgment essential'.[55] This prompted the government to take the unusual step of issuing a White Paper explaining the nature and purposes of the shadow programme and setting out some of the correspondence between the disputants. When the matter was debated in the House of Lords Swinton apologized for any personal injustice which Nuffield felt he had suffered, but privately seems to have believed that his own position had been fully vindicated.[56]

This extraordinary episode at the start of Britain's rearmament programme demonstrates the uncertain relationship between government and industry at that period but also reveals a clash of temperament as well as policy between the two main protagonists. The critical point came in July 1935 when Nuffield's request for a meeting with Philip Cunliffe-Lister, later Lord Swinton, to discuss future government contracts was turned down on the grounds that the Minister was already heavily engaged at the time suggested. Although his excuse was perfectly genuine, Nuffield was deeply angered by this rebuff, recalling later that it was the first time that a request by him for an interview with a Cabinet Minister had been rejected.[57] The ill feeling generated by this incident was exacerbated when Cunliffe-Lister's notes of explanation failed to offer Nuffield an alternative appointment. In practice, however, Nuffield's grievance with the Air Ministry had simmered for some years and was related to the failure of the Wolseley aero engine plant to secure government contracts since its establishment in 1929. The Ministry's supply policy appears in this instance to have been governed by the restricted capacity of Wolseley engines which rendered them unsuitable for service use, together with the limited production facilities at the firm's Wolverhampton works which Colonel Disney described as a first-class laboratory but 'not worth consideration' for other purposes.[58] Nuffield's failure to expand significantly the aero engine part of his business empire soured his attitude towards the shadow engine programme as it evolved during April and May 1936 and increased his general mistrust of politicians, particularly since this side of Wolseley's activities was under his own private ownership. The nature of Wolseley's withdrawal from the shadow engine scheme also highlights policy disagreements within Nuffield's management. While Leonard Lord supported the company's involvement, Boden did not, and the Ministry's files suggest that he was the person primarily responsible for persuading Nuffield to leave the engine group for a second and final time. The reason for this is unclear, though Lord claimed that Boden was simply not capable of handling the additional responsibility, and knew it.[59] This was probably indicative of a degree of professional jealousy between the two men, and a more likely explanation, especially in view of Boden's contribution to the establishment of the Castle Bromwich works, is that the new managing director was keen to harness the Nuffield organization's scarce management resources to the task of reviving the car side of the business following the problems and policy changes of the early 1930s.

The introduction of a second shadow group in 1939, as the international situation deteriorated markedly following Hitler's annexation of Czechoslovakia in March, was intended to help redress the serious under-provisioning of aero engines which had become apparent by that time.[60] The group comprised Daimler, Rootes, Rover, and Standard, but not the Austin Motor Company. According to E. L. Payton, Austin's deputy chairman, the reason for this omission was that the company declined to become involved in another major new scheme when it was already heavily committed to the Air Ministry and when labour supply in the Birmingham area was extremely tight.[61] In fact, however, the Austin company was offered a role in the second stage of the aero engine shadow programme but only as a joint partner in one of the four new factories, and it may well be that this implied decline in status was more than the company was prepared to accept. The terms applied to Austin's involvement in the new scheme perhaps reflected concern within the Air Ministry at the company's problems in meeting production targets. One example of this surfaced in May 1937 when Colonel Disney insisted that the company's senior staff should be strengthened by the appointment of a manager specifically responsible for aero engine manufacture. He acknowledged that this would be expensive, but added pointedly that 'we pay and we want him appointed'.[62] By the beginning of 1939, however, the company was finding it difficult to maintain the levels of engine production achieved by Standard, Daimler, and Rover and doubts were voiced within the Ministry over the Austin company's capacity for further large scale expansion.[63] This situation was highly ironic since Austin had been recruited in the first instance because of the firm's record in mass production techniques of manufacture. This reversal of roles – Austin being outstripped by the competitors it was dominating in the car market – could hardly have been envisaged in 1936.

The organization of the second shadow scheme differed from its predecessor in that the four firms worked in two pairs to produce complete engines. Management of the two groups was rationalized and made more flexible in May 1940 when their supervision was transferred to a joint committee under the chairmanship of William Rootes. According to Hornby, the purpose of the new manufacturing structure was to reduce the danger of interruptions to output from air attack,[64] but this was only part of the explanation since the split system continued to leave the programme vulnerable to enemy raids. More importantly, the operation of the initial shadow scheme revealed that efficiency varied significantly between firms and that this could seriously depress overall production levels. For example, it was clear by the beginning of 1939 that Standard was outstripping the other members of its group so that, incredibly, Ministry pressure was applied to reduce the 'pace of its production by avoiding night and Saturday shift working and reducing overtime'.[65] The understandable desire to remove such a politically embarrassing and strategically damaging situation appears to have been the decisive influence behind the introduction of the paired structure, which eradicated the possibility of one firm undermining the pace of shadow engine production as a whole.

The shadow engine programme was paralleled by the creation of a similar facility for airframes, though initially only two firms were involved when the scheme was devised in 1936. These were Rootes and Austin who were contracted to supply 600 Blenheim and 900 Fairey Battle medium bombers respectively. Herbert Austin had expressed a preference for the Blenheim, probably because of his developing links with its designers, the Bristol Aeroplane Company, but this was vetoed personally by Swinton because in his view Austin's management, and Carl Engelbach in particular, 'would be of great value in helping to put Messrs Fairey, whose production capacity was at the moment far from satisfactory, on a more efficient footing'.[66] The second member of the airframe shadow team was the subject of some debate within the Air Ministry. Daimler's experience in the aircraft industry and its existing spare capacity made it Weir's first choice, but the decision eventually moved in favour of Rootes with particularly strong support from Christopher Bullock who pointed to Humber's alleged production efficiency and the personal characteristics of William Rootes who was said to be 'a really live wire'.[67] The pre-war expansion of the airframe side of the aircraft industry proved hardly less controversial and difficult for Ministers and their officials than the shadow engine scheme. Apart from deep personal antipathy between Austin and William Rootes, the latter's decision to manufacture the Blenheim at White Waltham, near Reading, provoked immediate opposition when it was announced by Swinton in January 1937.[68] Concern was expressed at the area's vulnerability to air attack, though the more persuasive argument, in view of Rootes' subsequent switch to Speke in Lancashire, was that the original location did nothing to alleviate Britain's regional unemployment problem. The Air Ministry had itself voiced these objections together with the Chancellor, Neville Chamberlain, but Rootes' threat to withdraw altogether from the shadow scheme led to his proposals being accepted. A number of other difficulties surrounded the implementation of the shadow airframe scheme so that when plans were next introduced for a major expansion of capacity in 1938 it was decided so far as possible to draw upon existing facilities. English Electric thus became responsible for suplementing Handley Page's output of Halifax bombers, while another electrical engineering firm, Metro-Vickers, were manufacturing agents for A. V. Roe's Manchester bomber. Of more immediate relevance to this study, however, was the fifth and final shadow airframe scheme involving Lord Nuffield and the Castle Bromwich works.[69]

Nuffield's elevated status as one of Britain's leading industrialists meant that his withdrawal from the shadow engine group was an acute embarrassment to the government and pressure soon developed to secure his renewed involvement with the Air Ministry's rearmament programme. A suitable opportunity for this arrived in 1938 with the proposed expansion of the shadow scheme, while Swinton's resignation in May of that year removed one of the chief obstacles to an agreement. Lord Nuffield was assigned the important task of strengthening Britain's fighter aircraft capability through the manufacture of the new Spitfire. This reflected the Cabinet's decision of December 1937 to switch priority within the air programme to fighter production, both on the grounds of cost and because the development of radar offered, for the first time, the prospect of a successful defence against bombers. Swinton's intention had been to allocate responsibility for the new works to Vickers, the parent company managed by his old friend, Sir Charles Craven. However, Nuffield's experience of mass production techniques, together with a feeling within the Ministry that Vickers' ambitions needed to be curbed, helped to swing the decision of the new Secretary of State, Kingsley Wood, in his favour.[70] The urgency of the fighter programme was also instrumental in securing Nuffield's co-operation, for it enabled him virtually to dictate his own terms to the Air Ministry. The speed, secrecy, and scope of the deal, which directly involved the Prime Minister but not the Cabinet, earned Kingsley Wood a stiff rebuke from the Chancellor of the Exchequer who objected to the Treasury's exclusion from the negotiations.[71] Chamberlain's personal role in the affair explains why another major public row involving Lord Nuffield was avoided and the Air Minister's inexperience in his new post also allowed the Treasury to escape the impression that its authority had been eroded.

Nuffield's control of the Castle Bromwich project was short lived for in May 1940 supervision of the works was transferred to Vickers. This drastic measure reflected a lack of confidence in the factory's ability to meet output targets and growing frustration at the level of finance required to make it operational. Opinion within the Air Ministry was divided at the end of 1939 on the seriousness of the problem at Castle Bromwich, though there appears to have been general agreement that Nuffield's management had underestimated production difficulties and that Spitfire deliveries would be later than originally planned. It was not only the delays themselves which angered Ministry officials but also the fact that 'Nuffield have consistently refused to produce a definite delivery programme.'[72] When he met Kingsley Wood on 12 March 1940, Lord Nuffield blamed delays in output on the poor quality of information which he claimed was supplied by the parent company.[73] At the Minister's request, Sir Charles Craven met with Nuffield a short time later and expressed Vickers' willingness to assume responsibility for the project. Nuffield, however, denied that there was any real cause for concern and reiterated his belief that design modifications had caused his staff a number of major problems and held back the appearance of the factory's first aircraft. Craven was surprised at this response and reported to Kingsley Wood, 'I was somewhat taken aback when Lord Nuffield assured me that he was not late in his deliveries of "Spitfires" and that he thinks his people have done very well in the progress they have made.'[74] In Craven's view, Nuffield's management had been seriously depleted by the recent death of Oliver Boden and simply did not possess the depth of talent necessary to organize the project effectively. One possible solution to this dilemma would have been for Vickers to have seconded staff to Castle Bromwich, but this was rejected by Craven on the grounds that since they would be under the control of the existing management they would lack 'freedom of action' and would not 'have the right to call in Vickers' organization for help when required'.[75] Although Craven's remarks appear convincing, he was hardly an independent observer and his personal influence as Kingsley Wood's emissary was one of the factors responsible for the downfall of the Nuffield regime.

The Air Ministry's criticism of the Castle Bromwich operation was partly a reaction to attacks from the Treasury at its own rather ineffectual control of development expenditure. When the Ministry belatedly received Nuffield's building plans in the middle of 1939 it became clear that the works would cost just over £4 million, more than double the original estimate.[76] As construction proceeded it also became clear that management supervision of the project was weak, and although this information filtered through to the Ministry, officials were slow to respond. As one of them later admitted, 'There has been little Departmental control over expenditure at Castle Bromwich, and we have felt concern as to the efficiency and economy with which the work has been carried out.'[77] The matter eventually became the subject of an enquiry by the Parliamentary Select Committee on National Expenditure and this raised the problem for the Air Ministry as to whether 'we are to continue our attempts to bolster up Lord Nuffield's activities or whether we should frankly admit that we have known little of the financial implications until the change of management let us in'.[78] The whole Castle Bromwich affair placed the Ministry in a very awkward position since Kingsley Wood had previously guaranteed Lord Nuffield minimum intervention in setting up the works, the implications of which were to sour relations with the Treasury and render the Ministry highly vulnerable to public criticism when the project began to go wrong. Sir Charles Craven and Vickers provided the Ministry with an escape route, while Nuffield had little alternative but to accept the change of management, despite protesting vigorously to Churchill. In some respects Lord Nuffield was unfortunate, for the row over Castle Bromwich emerged just before the factory began to demonstrate its capabilities and at a time when aircraft production had been placed under the political control of Lord Beaverbrook who remained impervious to the threats which the car magnate hurled at him.[79]

The implementation of the shadow engine and airframe programmes involved substantial additions to plant which left a permanent imprint upon the industrial landscape of the West Midlands. The initial aero engine scheme involved the construction of two additional manufacturing units within the Standard complex at Canley, the No. 1 factory for engine work and another for the production of Claudel-Hobson carburettors to supplement production at the parent works in Wolverhampton which had fallen behind in its deliveries to the shadow engine factories. The firm's No. 2 shadow engine factory, which formed part of the Ministry's 1939 expansion plan, was at nearby Banner Lane and involved the conversion of a greenfield site of some 80 acres into the largest shadow works in Coventry, incorporating three machine shops each with a roof span of 250 feet.[80] The first Daimler and Rootes shadow engine factories were also built near to their parent works, but Rover, restricted by lack of space at its Coventry plants in Helen Street and Parkside, was offered accommodation at Acocks Green on the southern outskirts of Birmingham and only a short distance from its own components factory at Tyseley. Rover's No. 2 shadow engine factory was much larger than the Acocks

Green works and was erected on some 60 acres of farmland near Solihull, though on its own initiative the company acquired almost 200 acres of additional land surrounding the engine complex.[81] Although Daimler's management was also anxious to develop outside Coventry, the company was instructed to build its No. 2 factory within five miles of Standard's Banner Lane works, its partner in the new joint production scheme of the late 1930s. Rootes' second engine plant was located at Ryton on Dunsmore, some four miles to the south of Coventry, and was the last of the shadow factories to be constructed in the city.

The Birmingham shadow factories at Cofton Hackett and Castle Bromwich were built to accommodate the assembly of complete aircraft and so were rather different in appearance from those in Coventry. Austin's Cofton Hackett works was built on farmland adjoining the Longbridge plant and eventually included engine shops, an airframe factory, flight shed, and airfield facilities. Although the airframe factory was erected for the manufacture of the Fairey Battle, it was also designed to take larger machines and was later used for production of the Stirling bomber. One interesting feature of the works was the construction in 1942 of an underground tunnel measuring 25 feet by 600 feet which was used to house components manufacture but also doubled as an air raid shelter with accommodation for 11,000 people.[82]

The Castle Bromwich works was constructed on land which had been sold to Birmingham Corporation by the Dunlop Rubber Company. Restrictive covenants governing the use of the site, which had been intended for local authority housing to serve the needs of Dunlop employees, were waived in the national interest and almost certainly as the result of government pressure. There was a suggestion that the plant ought to have gone to an area of high unemployment but, as part of his deal with the Air Ministry, Nuffield had the final word on its location. His choice of Birmingham seems to have been influenced by the availability of skilled engineering labour and also, perhaps, because he perceived some advantage in strengthening his manufacturing base in the West Midlands. Castle Bromwich was planned as the largest of the shadow factories and involved the massive task of turning a building site of 345 acres into a working complex which finally came to house more than 52 acres of buildings.[83]

Construction of the shadow factories generated a number of

problems relating to architectural design, and the pace and cost of building work. The application of mass production techniques to the manufacture of aero engines and airframes raised several new issues which affected factory design and led, in the case of the Castle Bromwich project, to an investigation of Continental building practices, including, ironically, those adopted in Germany. The urgency of the rearmament programme meant that special efforts were made to obtain and prepare suitable building sites as quickly as possible and to proceed with the work until it was finished. Bad weather created serious transport difficulties in Coventry during the winter of 1939–40 and delayed completion of the Rootes complex at Ryton, while at the same time one of the sub-contractors at Standard's No. 2 shadow engine factory risked damage from frost by laying one of the concrete floors before the roof of the building was in place.[84] Work was held back at Cofton Hackett because the roads adjoining the site were too narrow for the heavy lorries which were required to bring in building materials so that it became necessary to install a railway siding.[85] Another problem here, but one which was probably repeated elsewhere, concerned the different speeds at which the various sub-contractors functioned so that, for example, delays in fitting rain water pipes retarded the laying of floors and hence completion of the main structure.[86] Services had to be provided to meet the various demands of the factories and their personnel. The Rootes plant at Ryton gave rise to an unusual requirement for its rather isolated location necessitated the building of a sewage farm specifically to accommodate its needs. Less surprisingly, perhaps, was the introduction of subsidized bus services to transport employees to and from outlying towns and villages, and the provision of a works canteen with seating for some 4,000 people.[87]

The introduction of the shadow factory scheme generated several other important issues which are discussed in subsequent chapters. Labour had to be recruited, machinery and raw materials acquired, and suitable production methods developed, while the partial suspension of the normal rules of commercial enterprise and the increasingly interventionist role of government raised fundamental questions concerning the relationship between state and industry. Another aspect of the shadow factory provision was its particular contribution to the war effort, which was undoubtedly immense, though there are reasons for believing that this investment of the nation's resources could have yielded even greater returns. It is also evident that even before the outbreak of war Swinton's initiative in 1936 had a broad and significant impact upon the economic and social balance of the Midland region and that this continued well beyond 1945.

2

The growth of manufacturing production

By the outbreak of the war the Midlands had an international reputation for the scope and pervasiveness of its light engineering industries, particularly motor vehicles and their components, but also aircraft, machine tools, electrical goods, and a multiplicity of small metal wares. Some firms, such as Austin, Lucas, and GEC, were already among the country's largest employers in 1939, while a number of others had workforces which ran to several thousands, but the Birmingham area in particular was also the home of hundreds of small engineering concerns, many of which enjoyed a high reputation for their specialist expertise. These characteristics ensured that the Midlands played a major role in the creation of an industrial base geared to the needs of modern warfare in which the rapid transfer of men, armaments, and information was of the utmost importance. The presence of ICI, Courtaulds, and Cadburys gave the Midlands a relatively diversified industrial structure, but in order to keep within manageable limits this analysis concentrates mainly upon the metal engineering sector, which represented the region's principal contribution to the war effort.

With the exception of Spitfire production at Castle Bromwich, the Midlands is perhaps less easily identified with the aircraft industry than some other parts of the country. Yet the region was responsible for around 16 per cent of all aircraft manufactured in Britain during the war, together with a huge number of parts, including aero engines.[1] The indigenous airframe industry was represented by Armstrong-Whitworth in Coventry and Boulton Paul at Wolverhampton, with the former being the more important because of its output of Whitley, Lancaster, and Stirling bombers. The Whitley medium bomber was selected as part of the Air

26

Ministry's expansion plan of 1936 and by the time production ceased in 1943, 1,824 aircraft of this type had been manufactured by the group. Thereafter attention switched to the Lancaster heavy bomber designed by staff at A. V. Roe's works in Manchester and in the following year 550 of these machines were manufactured in Coventry, together with 106 Stirlings. Some 300 Lancasters were also produced at Castle Bromwich, though the works' main contribution to the air battle was the Spitfire fighter aircraft, around 75 per cent of which emanated from Birmingham.[2] In addition to the Fairey Battle medium bomber, Austin manufactured significant numbers of Lancasters and Stirlings as well as some 300 Hurricane Mk II fighters.[3] Rootes' production of airframes was largely concentrated on Merseyside, though by 1943 work on the Blenheim bomber had been transferred to Stoke, and late in the war the Blythe Bridge works was used to modify American aircraft, the only firm in the region to be engaged upon this type of work.[4] In addition, Standard was responsible for over 1,000 De Havilland Mosquito fighter-bombers, which represented almost 14 per cent of the total built, 3,000 Beaufighter fuselages, and a number of Oxford trainers, while in 1940 Rover began to make airframe parts for a variety of different aircraft.

Although the Midlands contributed to most types of aircraft manufactured in Britain during the war, the Spitfire was of special importance because of its combat success and the large number produced in the region. After a slow start, by the end of 1941 over 1,800 Spitfires had been manufactured at the Castle Bromwich works and by October 1945 the figure stood at almost 13,000 aircraft.[5] Boulton Paul's turret-fighter, with a profile similar to that of the Hurricane, had critical blind spots which rendered it highly vulnerable to air attack so that it was quickly relegated to night fighting and then target towing. The region's combined output of bomber aircraft was also a significant contribution to the air war, with the Stirlings and Lancasters being by far the most important in terms of their strategic value. The Short & Harland designed Stirling was the first operational heavy bomber but it was technically inferior to the Lancaster with its relatively low speed, modest payload, and inability to climb above the fire from the more powerful anti-aircraft guns. Moreover, the Commander-in-Chief, Bomber Command, claimed in December 1942 that about half of the Stirlings manufactured by the parent firm and Austin were 'rogue aircraft' which, he argued, jeopardized their crews and served to compromise 'our only method of winning the war'.[6] It was against this background that it was decided to switch production facilities from Stirlings to the Avro Lancaster. By contrast, the Mosquito fighter-bomber proved a highly successful and adaptable aircraft and its manufacture was one of Standard's most distinctive contributions to the war effort.

Table 2.1 Monthly average for new aero engine deliveries (second quarter each year),* 1939–44

	1939	1940	1941	1942	1943	1944
Bristol parent factory	233	372	270	300	288	213
Bristol agency factory†	—	—	33	265	342	405
Shadow groups	348	593	992	1,148	1,133	1,511

Source: Hornby, Factories and Plant, p. 256.
*Except that 1939 is for June and 1944 is for the first quarter.
†The Bristol agency factory was located at Accrington.

The Midlands was relatively more important numerically in the manufacture of aero engines than airframes, its collective output accounting for perhaps 40 per cent of the British total. This represented about 100,000 engines, the bulk of which came from the shadow factories, though with spares, components, and repair work the region's contribution to the air war was actually far greater than this figure implies. The shadow factories were largely concerned with the production of Pegasus, Mercury, and Hercules engines to power bomber aircraft and in total they accounted for more than twice the number produced by the parent company (see Table 2.1). The first engine sets from the No. 1 shadow group emerged in 1937 and were important in helping to strengthen Britain's air power during the rearmament period and the early years of war. By October 1939 Rover's Acocks Green factory averaged a combined output of 60 Pegasus and Mercury engine sets a week, but under government pressure production was increased to 105 during November and by the end of May the figure reached 153 units weekly. In the seven months from November 1939 to the end of May 1940 the works achieved a 51 per cent increase in the weekly total of units manufactured. Even allowing for distortions caused by variations in product mix and the particular characteristics of the weeks chosen for comparison, this was an impressive expansion of output during the early critical months of war when the shortage of aero engines was most acute. By October 1940 the Acocks Green factory had comfortably exceeded the maximum weekly output which the Shadow Engine Committee thought reasonable and by the spring of 1941 had reached a peak of just over 200 units a week, which it largely maintained until the management was instructed to change to the manufacture of Hercules engines a year later.[7] Progress at Standard's first shadow engine factory roughly paralleled that of Rover. Output reached a weekly average of 125 engine sets during 1940 and by mid-summer the cumulative total exceeded 19,000, a little ahead of Rover production.[8] Like Acocks Green, towards the end of 1942 Standard's Canley factory was also switched to the manufacture of Hercules components. Of the remaining members of the first aero engine group, Austin in particular appears to have experienced problems in maintaining a satisfactory production flow, though the scale and nature of the firm's output rendered it a particularly important contributor to the shadow scheme. By the beginning of 1941 the Austin works was responsible for a weekly total of 105 Pegasus engine sets and a similar number of complete Mercury engines. Production accelerated rapidly from the early summer of 1940 so that while 2,717 engine sets and 984 complete engines were manufactured between September 1939 and the end of April 1940, the corresponding figures for the next seven months, when the war reached a crucial stage for Britain, were 4,442 and 2,355 respectively.[9]

Bad weather, which adversely affected building work, and production difficulties delayed the growth of output from the second shadow engine group. For example, Rover's first components for the Hercules engine were machined at the Solihull plant in January 1940 but it was not until more than a year later that deliveries of the completed units began. Thereafter, however, production accelerated quite rapidly and by the middle of 1942 reached sixty engines a week. Aided by purpose built accommodation, and by new machinery, and with the benefit of experience, the group soon acquired a reputation for high levels of output. Standard's Banner Lane works came to be regarded as a particularly outstanding example of efficient production, and its general layout continued to impress visitors for some years after the war. Output targets were consistently surpassed and altogether the factory, working in tandem with Daimler, was responsible for some 20,000 Hercules engines, or almost 60 per cent of the total produced by the shadow industry. With the addition of the No. 1 group's manufacturing resources, shadow production of Hercules engines increased rapidly from 1942 and at its peak reached 824 units a month. These engines were more powerful than the Pegasus and Mercury models and were used in the heavier bombers, including the highly successful Mk II version of the Lancaster which was involved in the continuous night-time bombing of Germany.

In order further to supplement deliveries of Bristol aero engines, additional factory space was allocated to Rover at Drakelow near Kidderminster. This was an underground works constructed in the form of a series of tunnels to give protection against air attack. Although approval for the installation of machine tools costing £3 million was given in January 1942, only a small number were operational by November and output was correspondingly modest. Labour shortages and worker unrest over housing accommodation further impeded the growth of production and at its peak the works was responsible for only forty-two engines a month.[10]

Aero engine manufacture was dominated in the interwar period by Rolls-Royce, the Bristol Aeroplane Company, De Havilland, and Armstrong-Siddeley, though only the first two had a design capability of any real significance. During the First World War the Coventry based Armstrong-Siddeley company extended its operations from high powered motor vehicles to aeronautical engineering but, despite the success of its Puma engine, the firm failed to develop a design department of sufficient status to challenge its major rivals. The company's Tiger engine was used in the first Whitley bombers but was later replaced by a more powerful Merlin unit supplied by Rolls-Royce. Armstrong-Siddeley's principal contribution to the air war was as a supplier of engines for trainer aircraft.[11] The Cheetah engine, which was introduced in 1932, was delivered in large numbers for the Anson and Oxford trainers and continued in service for more than thirty years. Ansons were used primarily for navigational and gunnery instruction, though some served in an anti-submarine reconnaissance role, while the Oxford was the RAF's twin engined trainer. The Rover company was also commissioned to manufacture Cheetah engines and at the period of peak production about one-third of total output came from this source. Some 33,000 Cheetahs were made between June 1939 and December 1945, giving the two Coventry firms involved a key role in aircrew training.

Armstrong-Siddeley and Rover also played a part in developing the Coventry-born Air Commodore Whittle's jet engine. Whittle's own company, Power Jets, lacked the technical and financial resources to transform the concept of a gas turbine aero engine into practical reality so that the government invited a number of other companies to participate in the research and development programme. By 1941 Armstrong-Siddeley's design team had acquired a favourable reputation among officials at the Ministry of Aircraft Production with the result that the firm was invited to switch its research from the high capacity 'Wolfhound' aero engine to jet propulsion in co-operation with Vickers. This relationship was marred by frustrating disputes, particularly over the exchange of technical information.[12] Rover's involvement with Whittle's project was far more substantial and by the end of 1941 the company had assembled and tested its first prototype jet engine at its dispersal factories at Clitheroe and Barnoldswick in Yorkshire. A second version of the Rover engine appeared towards the end of 1942, but the company then transferred its interest in the programme to Rolls-Royce, receiving in return a substantial contract for construction of the Meteor tank engine. Some of Rolls-Royce's wartime production of jet engines was located in the Midlands region at the company's factory at Newcastle-under-Lyme, while the Meteor project became the mainstay of Rover's work in Coventry until its transfer to Acocks Green at the end of the war.

Apart from the manufacture of aero engines, either complete or in parts, Midlands firms also supplied a huge number of spares and undertook a significant proportion of the RAF's servicing work. Rootes, for example, manufactured spares for both Bristol and Rolls-Royce engines. By the end of 1941 the group's No. 1 shadow factory at Aldermoor Lane in Coventry had produced 1,699 sets of Pegasus and Mercury spares, equivalent to about 8 per cent of its total output of engines.[13] Rootes' nearby Humber-Hillman works, which before the war had been used for the assembly of motor vehicles, became heavily involved in repairing and servicing aero engines. This could involve a lengthy rebuilding operation, while engines which had been badly damaged by enemy action were scrapped and cannibalized for spare parts. The initial contract was for Pegasus and Mercury engines but it was later extended to the Hercules, with the first units of this type being dispatched in April 1940. Servicing and repairs expanded quickly in 1940, though with the national emergency following Dunkirk 'reconditioning was done on the basis of a "spit and polish" overhaul'.[14] The November air raids reduced the flow of engines passing through the plant, but the level of activity picked up again in the following January and by the end of 1942, when work on the Hercules became significant, some 3,351 engines had been renovated. A disused factory in Pontefract formerly used for making Liquorice Allsorts was allocated to Rootes at the end of 1940 in order to enable the group to extend its repair and servicing role, and by the close of 1945 the two works had dealt with 12,514 aero engines. Repairs and servicing were also undertaken by a number of other firms in the region, including Rover, Singer, Triumph, and Alvis. Towards the end of the war Alvis began development work for the Ministry of Aircraft Production (MAP) on American aero engines, but the company's main contribution to the war effort was in the renovation of Rolls-Royce Kestrel and Merlin engines, which was done on a large scale at a number of sites around the country.

Apart from its role in the manufacture and assembly of airframes and aero engines, the Midlands was a ubiquitous supplier of components, from fabrication materials to high technology engineering products. The MAP's local controller noted in October 1945 that the region had been concerned in some way with every type of aircraft and aero engine manufactured during the war period.[15] Most operational aircraft built from the mid-1930s onwards used airframes constructed of light alloys, and as one of the country's principal suppliers of sheet and strip metal the Midlands made an important contribution to this aspect of the air war. Perhaps more important, however, because of the degree of engineering expertise involved, was the region's work on forgings and castings. Forgings in particular were often of a technically complex nature, being required for a wide variety of purposes in aircraft construction, from the manufacture of engine components to airscrews and undercarriages. Production was concentrated among a relatively small number of specialist firms, some of which had been active in the armaments industry during the First World War, including

Smiths Stamping of Coventry and Lincoln which from 1939 became one of the largest suppliers of light alloy forgings to the aircraft companies and their associates.

In addition to its small metal workshops, the Midlands housed a broad range of light engineering concerns, many of them geared to satisfying the needs of the motor vehicle industry, but which in wartime quickly adjusted to the large scale manufacture of aircraft components. It was the highly specialized nature of much of this work which helped to give the region its distinctive and strategically important input to the industrial war effort. Carburettor manufacture was one example of this. By the onset of war, production of carburettors was dominated in Britain by Hobsons of Wolverhampton, serving the Bristol Aeroplane Company, and SU of Birmingham who were linked with Rolls-Royce. Indeed, until the Battle of Britain all the aero carburettors used in Hurricane and Spitfire fighters were manufactured at the SU plant.[16] With rearmament, both of these firms expanded capacity at their main works, but following severe bomb damage in 1941 the SU company moved its operational base to Shirley on the southern fringe of Birmingham. SU output was supplemented from the late 1930s by Riley of Coventry, which was part of the Nuffield organization, and two dispersal plants were later acquired in Yorkshire. Nevertheless, the parent factory at Shirley yielded about 75 per cent of total output of this particular component. Hobsons were supported by three agency factories, two of which were managed by the Standard Motor Company. Production began at the first Standard factory in May 1939 and, aided by the management's customary drive, maximum planned output was achieved within two months, and by June 1941 about 8,000 carburettors had left the works.[17] The second Standard factory was opened in 1942 and the two plants came eventually to equal the output of the parent firm.

Magnetos was another example of a sophisticated engineering product where output was largely controlled by two major undertakings. These were Rotax and BTH, the latter with its factories in Rugby, Coventry, and Leicester being the more important in terms of scale of output. The BTH plant in Ford Street, Coventry, was alone responsible for some 500,000 aircraft magnetos.[18] Almost all wartime production of magnetos emanated from the proprietary firms and it was only in the case of carburettors, where the motor companies enjoyed an engineering advantage, that agency factories contributed significantly to the supply of aircraft components.

In the 1930s Automotive Products of Leamington Spa diversified from motor vehicle components into aeronautical engineering and became one of the firms to pioneer the application of hydraulics to retractable undercarriages. Altogether the AP factories made over two million aircraft parts during the war and these found their way into most operational models flown by the RAF.[19] Among the larger firms, the Lucas plants in Birmingham and elsewhere produced a wide range of technical gadgetry, including fuel injection pumps, dynamos, transformers, and generators. In addition, in 1940 the company was approached by Rover to participate in the jet engine project and by the end of 1945 some 2,500 Lucas employees were engaged full-time on the research, design, development, and manufacture of equipment for gas turbine engines.[20] BTH at Rugby was another important Midlands firm which contributed its specialist engineering expertise to the development of jet propulsion. In another area of high technology GEC researched and manufactured the VHF Radio Link at its Copsewood works in Coventry, a communications breakthrough which proved of immense value to the RAF. It is also interesting to note that the region housed the government's Telecommunications Research Branch which was established at Malvern in 1942 and became the co-ordinating centre for British research into radar and radio technology. The employment of Birmingham's watchmakers and jewellers in the manufacture of instruments, radio parts, and other equipment for use in aircraft demonstrates that a use was even found for some of the region's most traditional crafts.

It was mentioned earlier that some of the larger Coventry motor vehicle companies contributed to the expansion of the aircraft industry as sub-contractors, and the same was also true of Austin of Birmingham. The Longbridge works became a centre of intense and varied manufacturing activity, producing over 4,600 Beaufighter and Miles Master wings, 122,000 Bristol engine exhaust rings, and 359 Housa glider fuselages, as well as a vast number of miscellaneous items such as jerrycans and fire pumps.[21] The company also developed a complicated three-way relationship under which it worked on Rolls-Royce engines as sub-contractor to Ford's shadow factory at Trafford Park, Manchester. Again in

Birmingham, Joseph Lucas supplemented the Castle Bromwich output of wing sub-structures for Spitfires and also became the country's largest supplier of Boulton Paul designed electro-hydraulic aircraft gun turrets. Some firms, especially the smaller ones, remained relatively specialized sub-contractors. Alvis, for example, became heavily committed to De Havilland in the production of propeller hubs, while Laystalls of Wednesbury and Wolverhampton were similarly involved with Rotol, the industry's other main manufacturer. Alternatively, Riley had broad manu-facturing interests and

> Ultimately there was hardly a single type of R.A.F. warplane which did not have in it vital bits and pieces made at Riley's – from carburettors for the single seat fighters, to fireproof bulkheads and engine sub-frames for the great four-engined Lancaster bomber.[22]

Although the larger firms made the most conspicuous contribution to industrial output, the multitude of small factories and workshops in the region were also important, often becoming involved in complex multi-tiered sub-contracting arrangements. By the end of 1944 around 470 firms in the Midland region were said to be engaged upon work connected with the aircraft and motor vehicle industries, about half of which employed fewer than fifty workers.[23]

As the car and truck firms broadened their engineering base, the output of vehicles for general and commercial use declined. Private car sales remained at a significant level into 1940 and some production for this market was sustained throughout the war, including over 9,000 of Rootes' Hillman Minx, but output came increasingly to be dominated by specialist vehicles destined for military service and civil defence. Yet in order to allow resources to be concentrated upon fighting vehicles and aircraft, manufacturing activity was necessarily constrained in some product areas with the gap being filled by a rapid growth in Canadian and American imports. With the outbreak of war, government orders arrived swiftly, particularly for those vehicles which could be immediately converted for military use. Staff cars were ordered in large numbers and heavier vehicles and chassis were modified for a variety of purposes. The output of armoured vehicles took longer to arrive because of the development work involved, so that, for example, it was not until August 1941 that the first Humber light reconnaissance vehicles appeared, some twenty months after the project was first discussed. The Rootes group as a whole was responsible for about 11 per cent of all wheeled vehicles produced in Britain during the war, though not all of these were manufactured in the Midlands.[24] The Hillman-Humber works in Coventry turned out over 64,000 vehicles of different types, including staff and armoured cars, trucks and a large number of four wheel drive models adapted for use as ambulances, personnel carriers, and wireless vans. (See Table 2.2.)

Table 2.2 Selected wartime output of the Humber-Hillman works, Coventry. Vehicles delivered September 1939–June 1945

FWD ambulances	1,153
FWD utility trucks	5,360
FWD pick-up trucks	1,045
Super Snipe staff saloon cars	3,193
Humber scout cars	4,298
Hillman utility trucks	19,776
Civilian Minx	4,585
Export Minx	4,489
Minx De Luxe saloons	5,987
Civilian Commer vans	947

Source: Museum of British Road Transport, Coventry. Calculated from Rootes at War MSS, Hillman-Humber Works.

Production at Austin's Longbridge works, mostly trucks and cars, was substantially above that of the Humber Road plants, but it was heavily concentrated in the first two years of war before the switch to aeronautical engineering was complete. One of the region's main contributions to military transport was in the form of light reconnaissance vehicles, with Humber and Daimler being the country's dominant suppliers, though Standard also developed its own armoured car, the Beaverette which had a distinctive pill-box shape and came to be issued mainly to the Home Guard. Although most of the armoured work on these vehicles was handled by other firms, the motor companies supplied the chassis, engine, and other specialist components and were also responsible for final assembly. The Rootes group contributed around 60 per cent of all armoured cars and 35 per cent of all scout cars manufactured during the war.[25] Yet perhaps Daimler came to enjoy the greatest distinction when Rommel used one of the firm's scout cars to escape after El Alamein.

Daimler already had a scout car in production during 1939. By contrast, the Rootes group was not only late to enter this market but also experienced a number of serious technical difficulties in developing its own light reconnaissance vehicles. The Ministry of Supply ordered 500 Humber armoured cars in June 1940, but less than half this number were delivered before the Mk I version was declared an engineering failure and the first of several design changes were introduced. Even with these modifications, the Humber vehicle found it difficult to cope with the demands of the desert campaign and the firm's designers were clearly stretched in their attempts to create an acceptable product. This was partly the result of Rootes' lack of experience in the development and manufacture of military vehicles, but it also reflected a surprising lack of technical flexibility.

The Midlands also became an important centre for production of the heavier types of armoured vehicles and their components. Gear boxes, clutches, and tank engines were made in large numbers and reference has already been made to the important deal between Rover and Rolls-Royce in respect of the Meteor project. The Birmingham Railway Carriage and Wagon Company was one of the locomotive firms selected by government for the manufacture of tanks, while some 3,000 Bedford troop carriers emanated from Austin's Longbridge works. But perhaps the most interesting developments in this field involved the various branches of the Nuffield organization. Wolseley Motors, for example, became one of the key firms associated with the assembly of armoured carriers, fully tracked vehicles similar to light tanks but without the gun turret and enclosed body. Until the outbreak of war, Nuffield Mechanisation and Aero, a Morris subsidiary formed in 1937 for the specific purpose of armaments manufacture, was the only company with close motor industry links to become involved in tank construction. The firm was concerned initially with design and development work, but in an attempt to apply mass production methods to the industry it was awarded a contract in 1938 for the manufacture of cruiser tanks, forty of which were delivered by the outbreak of war representing about 27 per cent of the national total. Following Dunkirk and an increase in the demand for armoured equipment, additional firms were brought into tank production, including three other members of the Nuffield organization. However, the Nuffield developed Crusader tank proved notoriously unreliable when it was applied in the Western Desert in 1941, impeding military strategy and the effective use of scarce resources.[26] Finally, in addition to its very substantial output of engines, the Morris works at Courthouse Green in Coventry acquired a favourable reputation for its work in pioneering the application of the conveyor belt system to the manufacture of track links, and for its contribution to research on tank metallurgy.

The principal supplier of weapons in the Midlands was the Birmingham Small Arms Company. Gun manufacture at the Small Heath plant declined after the First World War as government contracts were curtailed, making the firm dependent upon its private trade and other manufacturing activities. Rearmament promoted expansion beginning with a contract from the Air Ministry in 1936 for Browning machine guns and continuing two years later with an order from the War Office for the newly developed Besa model, the manufacture of which necessitated the acquisition of additional premises a short distance from the main works. Rifle production was also stepped up, as Table 2.3 indicates. Apart from rifles, machine guns, sub-machine guns, and 20 mm weapons, BSA also became a major supplier of barrels and ammunition from its factories in Birmingham and elsewhere. The government's failure to maintain its level of orders with BSA in the interwar period was potentially most damaging in respect of Browning machine guns which were used to arm Hurricanes and Spitfires. Donovan Ward noted in 1946 that during the Battle of Britain 'R.A.F. lorries and tenders had been lined up day and night outside the Browning shops waiting to rush small batches of finished guns direct to the fighter airfields'.[27] He also claimed that in the later stages of the battle some Hurricanes and Spitfires flew with only half their full complement of Brownings. Several plants in the region manufactured weapons and ammunition but one which justifies particular mention was that at Gosford Street in Coventry for under Nuffield management it accounted for over half the country's wartime output of Bofors anti-aircraft guns. More generally, some 70 per cent of Browning 0.303 guns and 22 per cent of 20 mm Hispano 'cannon' guns used in British aircraft were produced in the Midlands, together with similarly high figures for incendiary and blast bombs.[28]

The spread of machine tool manufacture to the West Midlands

Table 2.3 BSA short pattern rifle output, 1936–40

1936	10,900
1937	9,600
1938	18,400
1939	41,900
1940	68,200

Source: University of Warwick, Modern Records Centre, MSS 19A/3/3/30, Company Statement on Production of the Short Pattern Rifle, December 1943.

in the late nineteenth century was critical in promoting the region's industrial growth during the interwar period, and by 1939 several of Britain's leading firms were located there, the best known being Herberts who had played a particularly important role in serving the needs of the munitions industry in the First World War. In common with other machine tool manufacturers, demand for Herbert products remained buoyant, especially during the early years of war, and between September 1939 and November 1944 the firm supplied over 65,000 machine tools. These ranged from small mass produced items such as dies and chucks to heavier and more specialized equipment, including lathes and drilling machines which were used for a variety of purposes, from the manufacture of ball bearings to oerlikon shells. In addition, Herberts ran a repair service, manufactured spares, and operated as agents for imported American machines.

Although Herberts enjoyed an international reputation, the firm experienced considerable difficulty in meeting its wartime commitments and the problems which confronted its management throw interesting light upon the region's machine tool industry in general. Founded in 1887, by the First World War Herberts was one of the industry's market leaders and largest employers. During the interwar period the company came to depend upon the motor trade for the bulk of its domestic sales, though it also developed an important export business with Russia and Japan, and in 1936 was one of the firms selected for government contracts in connection with the shadow factory scheme. The financial losses of the depression period and the full order books which accompanied recovery appear to have induced a sense of both caution and complacency so that during the 1930s the company lost some of its competitive edge and by the outbreak of war suffered from restricted capacity and a relatively narrow product base. An inability to match supply with demand in the frenetic early years of war caused frustration to mount among Herbert's customers and by August 1941 hundreds of letters arrived in Coventry each week complaining of late deliveries.[29] This problem appears to have affected most of the firm's products, but to give dies as one example, weekly output during the first six months of 1941 was 30 per cent below orders and this shortfall was not remedied until the following year. Market pressure also rendered it difficult to introduce new models, further exacerbating a research and development weakness which was already apparent before 1939, so that in the latter part of the war the firm still manufactured equipment which had been designed thirty years earlier and was recognized to be out of date. Manufacturing capacity was expanded by increasing the company's range of sub-contractors and the introduction of dispersal units, but product innovation remained largely dormant during the war years.

Another Coventry firm, Wickmans, increased its production of machine tools tenfold between 1935 and 1940, which formed the basis for further substantial development during the remainder of the war period. Axel Wickman, a Swede, trained at the Krupps works in Germany before establishing his business in Coventry in 1926. He became famous for the introduction of tungsten carbide tipped cutting machines and multi-spindle automatic lathes, the latter being widely applied in the motor vehicle industry during the 1930s. One of the firm's most significant contributions to the war economy was its milling machines used in the manufacture of spar booms for bomber aircraft. In 1942 the MAP encouraged Wickmans to research and produce an improved version of this machine and, although output was delayed by a number of technical problems and the dismissal of the chief designer, the new model, incorporating hydraulically operated jigs, proved highly successful when it emerged towards the end of the year. Indeed, Wickman spar milling machines were said to have been responsible for some 60 per cent of all wartime output of spar booms.[30] Other Wickman products included optical grinding machines and equipment used in the mass production of guns, shells, and components for aircraft and tank engines. The firm also installed and serviced some 10,000 American machine tools, including a stretching press, the largest of its kind in the world at that time, which was used in the manufacture of Spitfire airframes.

Specialist engineering work in the Midlands involving aircraft, wheeled and tracked vehicles, armaments, and machine tools was supplemented by production of a miscellaneous and huge range of related products, from the 250,000 steel helmets which left Longbridge to a similar number of bomb release clips manufactured by Standard at Canley. Some of this general work was for civil defence, including 25,000 trailer pumps delivered by Climax to the National Fire Service and barrage balloons constructed by Dunlop Rim and Wheel. Although most of the region's output was destined ultimately for use by the RAF and the army, some industrial effort went into the war at sea. Underwater swimming suits were made by Dunlop, Automotive Products were responsible for the hydraulic activation equipment used in the steering of almost all motor torpedo boats launched during the war, while Riley created some of the components used in the midget submarines which attacked the *Tirpitz*. Rubery Owen at Darleston made, among other things, steel lifeboats, some of which were probably equipped with the marine engines assembled at the nearby Austin works.

The growth of war production in the Midlands was accomplished by adjusting the balance of existing resources and by additional inputs of capital and labour. This was accompanied by attempts to improve efficiency and these are discussed in the next chapter. Some firms in non-essential industries were run down or even forced out of business by raw material and other shortages before the policy of industrial concentration was applied early in 1941. The region's manufacturing profile limited the number of actual closures while the main thrust of government policy was to direct orders towards existing firms rather than to create new ones. Important changes were made in the use of plant and personnel, with the confectionery and jewellery trades being among those most affected. Some of Cadbury's resources, for example, were reallocated from the manufacture of chocolate to that of aircraft components.

The slow pace of rearmament in Britain meant that by 1939 investment in buildings designed to service the war economy was relatively modest. The shadow scheme was the most important initiative in this respect, though the factories in the No. 1 Bristol group were allocated only limited floor space, necessitating extensions later which were costly and disruptive to production schedules. By the end of 1941 Rootes' engine plant at Aldermoor Lane had been extended three times in four years, more than doubling its floor area in the process. Structural alterations to the Cofton Hackett works in 1939 appear to have been the result of poor initial planning. The factory was always intended for the manufacture of heavy bomber aircraft but it only became apparent that this required major changes to the fabric of the building when the switch from Fairey Battles to Stirlings was imminent. In order to accommodate higher levels of output, the No. 2 shadow factories were built on a relatively grand scale, with that at Castle Bromwich being particularly large, so that construction costs at each one averaged £2 million, more than six times those of their earlier counterparts. Yet the size and purpose-built nature of the shadow factories helped to generate improvements in the scale and quality of production. Large open areas facilitated the movement of airframes, while factory layout designed to maximize the return on new machinery was more easily accommodated within specialist buildings.

The interwar expansion of the Midlands engineering industry had stimulated factory building, much of which came to be directly employed in the war effort. In anticipation of government orders, Alvis built a modern, well equipped aero engine plant in the mid-1930s which was later used to support the firm's servicing contract with Rolls-Royce. In 1938 Nuffield Mechanisation took possession of purpose-built accommodation adjacent to the Wolseley works in Birmingham, while in the following year Wickmans moved into a spacious new factory at Tile Hill. The Rover plant at Tyseley was built on land acquired by the company after its managing director, Spencer Wilks, convinced the board that the onset of war was imminent and that government contracts would soon materialize. However, a substantial proportion of the stock of buildings in 1939 was relatively old and limited in size, particularly in Birmingham and the Black Country with their long industrial roots and workshop traditions. The physical constraints of this kind, which could seriously impede the growth of output, were partly overcome by extending or adapting existing premises. The floor area of Wickmans' Tile Hill works was doubled between 1939 and 1944, while Armstrong-Siddeley also achieved a major increase in manufacturing capacity with relatively modest structural alterations. Moreover, as inessential production was run down, additional factory space became available for the war industries so that, for example, Lucas acquired part of the Cadbury plant to house its sub-contract work on Spitfires. Despite these initiatives, it also became necessary to build entirely new works so that in Birmingham a total of over 5 million square feet of factory space was constructed between 1938 and the end of 1944, equivalent to almost four units the size of the Castle Bromwich plant.[31]

In many cases the high density of industrial activity in the central areas rendered expansion difficult and promoted a search for additional space in other, less crowded, locations. But the high level of sub-contracting which characterized much of the engineering industry in the Midlands, and the flexibility which this gave, helped to limit what might otherwise have been a serious accommodation crisis. Wickmans, for example, employed thirty sub-contractors who in turn passed on some of this work to around a thousand other firms. The reverse arrangement also applied so that by July 1940 the large Standard complex at Canley carried out work for twenty-four other firms, and it has been estimated that at the peak of wartime production some 14,000 engineering works were employed on contracts for the MAP alone.

The rearmament period and the early years of war saw a marked expansion in the capacity of the British machine tool industry with output increasing more than threefold between 1935 and 1943. Machine tools were an essential prerequisite for the rapid growth of the war industries, including those located in the Midlands. Apart from increases in output achieved by additions to the existing stock of machine tools, new equipment incorporating technological advances held the potential for large gains in productivity. The application of more powerful motors to Wickmans' spar milling machines brought almost a 90 per cent saving in time, which was improved further by the use of hydraulic jigs. It was therefore not surprising that in January 1940 the Ministry of Supply claimed that the success of the British war effort depended upon the speed at which the machine tool industry could expand its production. With the outbreak of war, imported machine tools became more difficult to obtain while demand from the engineering sector quickly escalated so that a supply crisis soon developed. At one time deliveries from the United States had to be booked eighteen months in advance.[32] Shortages were most acute in 1940 and 1941 but thereafter conditions eased as output increased and more effective use was made of the available equipment.

The high priority attached to the expansion of the RAF enabled the shadow factories to obtain their quota of machine tools in relatively quick time, including special imports from the United States. Despite the scale of investment reflected by Table 2.4, inadequate supplies of machine tools was the principal factor delaying the start of production at the shadow engine factories. Output could be retarded for two or three months, which was critically important at a time when the finished product was urgently required. The level of demand for machine tools increased rapidly from September 1939 so that supply delays became increasingly common. The impact of this was felt at Rootes' aero engine repair plant where late deliveries of key tools meant that 'Instead of getting into production as had been hoped by December 1939, it was not until March 1940 that progress began to be made.'[33] This was not an isolated problem, as the minutes of the regional board reveal, for in the summer of 1940 numerous engineering firms in the Midlands were chronically short of essential equipment. This restricted output but also meant that existing machinery became over-used with the inevitable break-downs and less efficient production generally.

The merger of the two shadow factory management committees in May 1940 introduced some flexibility into aero engine production since it facilitated the movement of machinery between different plants according to need. This model was taken up by other engineering firms in the region when in July 1941 a mutual aid scheme was adopted which less than a year later had resulted in some 40,000 exchanges or loans of machine tools.[34] The scheme proved so successful that similar arrangements were introduced into other parts of the country and reflected the fact that the problem was partly a question of maldistribution of machine tools rather than just an absolute shortage. Machinery was also modified to suit new purposes. Thus in 1941 Herberts were asked to adapt fourteen turret lathes intended for the manufacture of shells in order that they could be applied to the manufacture of tank parts. These were exceptional devices which, while they reflected serious supply deficiencies, did promote an improvement in the level of resource utilization.

The relative prosperity of the Midlands during the 1930s brought an increasingly tight labour market to some industrial

Table 2.4 Machine tools on site at Rootes' No. 1 shadow engine factory, December 1937–December 1941

December 1937	344
June 1938	395
December 1938	459
June 1939	501
December 1939	606
June 1940	718
December 1940	898
June 1941	1,135
December 1941	1,305

Source: MBRTC. Calculated from Rootes at War MSS, No. 1 shadow engine factory.

sectors, particularly in Coventry where competition between firms forced up wage rates so that by 1937 the city was said to have had the highest paid engineering workers in the country.[35] By the outbreak of war Coventry's labour market was a virtual free for all, with the engineering employers' association powerless to prevent the rampant poaching of labour. The transition to a war economy created employment problems in areas less fully committed to rearmament, forcing up unemployment until government contracts spread beyond the aircraft industry and consumed the surplus manpower. From the autumn of 1940, however, labour shortages became widespread in the Midlands, rather in advance of other areas, and rendering it the problem region in this respect. It even became difficult to attract unskilled male labour, most notably for heavy work in the drop forging industry. By the second half of 1942, and despite the recruitment of women to the shop floor, the region had also developed a critical shortage of light unskilled labour. It was only in 1944 that the acute deficiencies of the early war period began to recede, while during the following year the problem became one of adjusting to the stresses of industrial demobilization.

Although the air raid threat prompted some people to leave the industrial Midlands, the labour force was maintained by substantial inward migration and by an increase in female participation rates. The detailed characteristics of migration are difficult to assess, though Shenfield and Florence's work on Coventry's labour exchange registration books yields some interesting insights. The high level of inward migration apparent in the twelve months before the outbreak of war was followed in 1940–1 by a decline in the number of young male arrivals. However, this was partly offset by a marked increase in the flow of women and juvenile immigrants, many of whom were drawn from the surrounding towns and villages in Warwickshire, Leicestershire, and Northamptonshire. Overall, most immigrants continued to emanate from Lancashire, Clydeside, and South Wales, but the first two years of the war also saw an increase in the relative importance of the East Midlands, East Anglia, and Greater London as the expansion of the traditional heavy industries of the North of England and Scotland absorbed a growing proportion of the labour force in those areas.[36] The other major industrial centres in the Midlands also attracted migrants from the immediate hinterland and from more distant locations, including Eire. Birmingham in particular housed large numbers of Irish workers, many of whom were employed in the drop forging industry, while some were recruited direct by individual firms, such as Austin and ICI. Italian prisoners of war were a further supplement to the indigenous workforce, with around 1,500 still employed in the region as late as November 1945.[37]

The persistent labour shortage in the Midlands was exacerbated by the difficulty which was experienced in retaining immigrants, between a quarter and one-third of whom returned home after failing to establish a settled lifestyle. The main reason for this haemorrhage was insufficient or inadequate housing, coupled with poor reception arrangements which led easily to feelings of rejection and alienation. Of all the regions, the reception problem appears to have been most acute in the Midlands, stimulating direct intervention by the Ministry of Labour. By March 1941 reception offices staffed by Ministry personnel were operating from 8 a.m. until midnight at the two main railway stations in Birmingham, a model which was later applied to other parts of the country.[38] Although housing was of a relatively high standard, overcrowding in the region was more severe than in the North of England. The problem varied geographically but seems to have been particularly serious in those districts where the air raids of 1940–1 damaged or destroyed a significant proportion of the stock of residential dwellings. Hostels, providing both temporary and permanent accommodation, helped to ease the housing crisis, while many people chose to commute to work from the less heavily populated areas.

Some employers in the Midlands were at first reluctant to engage females, but during 1941 the demand for women workers began to outstrip the supply and by the middle of the following year 20 per cent of the national demand for labour of this type was found in the region, reflecting both the expansion of employment opportunities and the substantial scope for dilution within the light engineering industries. There is evidence, however, that the Midlands' reputation as a target area for enemy attacks deterred many newly qualified women school teachers from seeking employment in the larger towns and it may be that these feelings were shared by other potential immigrants.[39] The transfer of female workers created particular difficulties. By May 1941 the authorities in some regions were transferring women to the Midlands under the security of escorted convoys, while in the reception areas an attempt was made to avoid the social welfare problems which had emerged during the First World War. There were also significant problems of readjustment within the workplace. Smith's Stamping in Coventry, for example, took in a large draft of girls from Brighton, most of whom had been employed as waitresses in hotels and 'had never in their lives seen a place like drop-forging works; nor had they ever heard any noise quite like the thunder of the great hammers'.[40] Although many firms attempted to minimize the disruptive impact of employment relocation, Ernest Bevin pointed out in October 1941 that others in the region were less sensitive to the personal needs of their young female recruits. Like their male counterparts, many women immigrants remained permanently in the Midlands but others found it difficult to settle and eventually drifted back to their home districts.

There was also some difficulty in persuading local women to accept employment in manufacturing industry and, although this was a national problem, resistance in Birmingham and Coventry does appear to have been particularly well entrenched. A special recruitment drive organized by the Ministry of Labour in Birmingham in October 1940 proved relatively ineffective, while another major effort in August and September of the following year also failed to attract women in numbers sufficient to satisfy the labour requirements of the city's principal manufacturing firms. Thereafter the situation seems to have improved, though Birmingham's insatiable appetite for labour sparked a campaign in June

1943 designed to attract older women into industry. The mixed views of Coventry's women towards employment in the munitions sector was well illustrated during the War Work Week held in the city in November 1941. In common with similar events in other areas, this was intended to encourage women to enter industrial employment but, despite patriotic speeches and an impressive procession through the city of tanks, military vehicles, and trucks loaded with aero engines and other practical examples of Coventry's war effort, the response was far below what had been expected. Although some women enthusiastically espoused the virtues of factory work, others pointed to its incompatibility with the normal range of domestic responsibilities and bitterly resented the implication that they were 'shirking'.[41]

Household chores in Coventry were no doubt similar to those undertaken by women in other parts of the country, but the circumstances of family life were in some respects unique. The decline in the number of retail outlets caused by the air raids, together with limited opening hours, often made shopping a lengthy and frustrating activity, while the city's demographic profile meant that a high proportion of women had young children to care for. In addition, many of the larger factories were on the city's periphery, often necessitating a long and sometimes hazardous journey to and from work. There is also no doubt that the air raid threat deterred many women from working a late shift and, following the blitz of November 1941, the same was also true of some men. A number of middle-class and upper working-class women in both Birmingham and Coventry were said to have rejected factory employment because of its low social status. Where this perception existed, it was probably related to the relative absence of a tradition of female factory labour in the region and to the efforts of the trade unions and employers to limit the job opportunities and rewards of women workers.

The various government initiatives, coupled with improved working conditions, increased the flow of women into manufacturing industry so that by September 1942 the number of females employed on munitions work in the Midlands was 150 per cent higher than in 1939 while the labour force as a whole had grown by less than half this amount. The bulk of this additional labour, including those women who were already at work when the war began, was new to the engineering industry. The growth of part-time job opportunities enabled many women to enter employment whose domestic circumstances precluded them from working full-time. At Humber, where this arrangement was introduced at the end of 1941, the number of part-time female employees increased from 100 in August 1942 to 173 by the end of November, allowing the works' aero engine section to be almost 50 per cent staffed by women.

Table 2.5 Regional distribution of employment in the munitions industries, December 1941*

| Region | Total | % of total employment | | |
		Admiralty	Ministry of Supply	MAP
Midlands	19.9	15.5	21.6	23.4
London and SE	19.9	17.2	16.6	22.7
North West	17.7	15.2	19.0	17.0
Scotland	8.2	17.0	9.2	4.5
North East	8.2	6.8	8.5	5.8
North Midlands	5.9	4.7	5.5	6.0
Northern	4.5	12.0	4.1	1.2
South West	4.1	2.4	2.6	6.9
Southern	4.0	3.8	2.1	7.1
Wales	3.9	1.5	6.9	2.4
Eastern	3.7	3.9	3.9	3.0
Great Britain	100.0	100.0	100.0	100.0

Source: Inman, *Labour in the Munitions Industries*, p. 216.
*Includes the engineering and allied, explosives, and chemical industries, including non-ferrous metals but not shipbuilding.

Labour recruitment problems retarded production, though to some extent this was balanced by greater mechanization and more effective works organization. The rapid turnover of labour which plagued some firms at the beginning of the war is also likely to have disrupted output. The BTH magneto factory provided one of the worst examples of this phenomenon for in some weeks during the summer of 1940 the company lost almost as many employees as it recruited. One of the most notable results of the tight labour market was to characterize the Midlands as a region of exceptionally high wage costs, a reputation which in a number of sectors it fully deserved. There was also evidence that disaffected immigrants could be relatively inefficient workers and this was one of the reasons why some firms preferred to expand in other parts of the country, taking on local people. Despite these qualifications, the

Midlands employed a large labour force which was heavily concentrated on munitions work. The general significance of this, particularly for the army and the Royal Air Force, is illustrated by Table 2.5. Moreover, participation rates in some parts of the region were exceptionally high. Towards the end of the war, for example, 47 per cent of Birmingham's rationed population was at work, which, as Sutcliffe and Smith point out, was greater than in any other British city of similar size.[42] These labour and other resource inputs enabled the Midlands to play a key role in the British war economy, but whether they were managed to maximum effect is another important and controversial issue which is examined in the next chapter.

3

The management of resources

The pressures and constraints of the wartime economy placed a premium upon the effective management of resources. Initially, both the market economy and industrial enterprise were left relatively free from outside control, but even when the government became more interventionist the management of production remained largely the responsibility of individual firms. The strengthening of union organization, together with the establishment of Joint Production Committees and similar consultative machinery, helped to modify the decision-making environment, though the structure of authority within most plants remained much the same. Despite a more concerted effort by some firms to monitor output and apply scientific principles to works organization, the apparatus of management, at least in the Midlands, largely retained its pre-war characteristics. Yet there were important initiatives designed to expand output through greater productivity rather than simply the injection of further inputs of capital and labour. However, allegations of inefficiency were rampant. Walter Citrine claimed in 1942, for example, that there 'were continual complaints from all over the country regarding bottle-necks, hold-ups and lack of co-ordination',[1] while more recent criticism has cast doubt upon the conduct of almost every sector of the wartime industrial economy.[2] The debate which has been generated is important because it concerns Britain's economic performance after 1945 as well as during the war itself.

Apart from normal sub-contracting agreements, manufacturing was sometimes shared between a number of firms acting co-operatively and in varying degrees of formality to create the final product. In common with the dispersal scheme, this allowed for the replication of capacity but it also facilitated specialization and the interchange of design and production skills. The aircraft shadow factories were the model for and principal exponents of this type of liaison but other arrangements enabled relatively small firms to cope with large scale government generated orders. By the close of 1940, for example, virtually all the engineering concerns in the Burton area, some of which were relatively modest operations, had combined in one of two groups for the manufacture of munitions.[3] More specifically, in the autumn of 1941 Daimler and Rootes pooled their resources in the design and construction of a new armoured car. This project became dogged by technical problems, some of which may have been related to its co-operative status, reflecting the fact that in common with the shadow scheme other forms of product sharing had their pitfalls as well as advantages.[4]

External relations was an aspect of management which was given particular significance by the special nature of the war economy. Although normal commercial activity was largely suspended, new business links had to be forged and relationships established with departmental officials. The connections between government and industry are examined in more detail later but it is important to note here that because of official controls managers experienced highly unusual conditions in negotiating contracts and obtaining adequate supplies of labour and materials. In addition to the scale and urgency of government orders, changing military requirements and on-going research and development work meant that design specifications were frequently modified, often necessitating a reappraisal of production methods. The monopsony position of government departments also rendered firms highly vulnerable as contracts neared completion or when changes of policy threatened existing or future orders. Perhaps the major source of uncertainty, however, involved other firms since their own dependence upon official largesse rendered them a less rewarding target for persuasive managers than the government supply departments. One illustration concerned the Rover works in Coventry which was largely idle during the early months of 1941 because work on the Albemarle aircraft was at a standstill 'due to the changes in specification that were constantly being made, and the non-supply of the essential material for the prodn. from the Gloster Coy'.[5]

The aircraft industry raised special problems of external co-ordination. This became particularly apparent in the operation of the shadow factory scheme where frequent design changes quickly soured relationships between the parent and their associated companies. In connection with the Fairey Battle contract, Herbert Austin complained to the Air Ministry in June 1937 that although 'we were informed that there would be about 4,000 drawings, we have actually received to the present date nearly 7,000, and the total modifications amount to approximately 6,700'.[6] This was a common problem which the Ministry was largely powerless to rectify and one which continued to frustrate management throughout the war as new aircraft were introduced and existing models improved or adapted to meet changing circumstances. Lord Nuffield attributed delays in the start of production at the Castle Bromwich works to modifications in the design of the Spitfire, but these were modest compared with subsequent changes and by 1945 redevelopment was so advanced that the aircraft was hardly recognizable from its original specifications.

As the shadow scheme developed it also became obvious that production was restricted by variations in output between the constituent firms. This was sometimes the fault of the parent company and in the early stages of the war, for example, Bristols found it difficult to meet the demand for blower clutches, which adversely affected work schedules at the Austin and Rootes plants in particular. More often, however, delays were caused by the inability of the shadow firms to maintain a consistent level of output. As one Air Ministry official noted in 1939, some factories were significantly behind in their programmes and 'no useful purpose would be served by the other shadow companies producing their individual component parts as engines could not be completed until the prodn. was balanced'.[7] This problem diminished as the war progressed and the industry's own coordinating machinery and that of government improved, though it remained a serious irritant in the less formal sub-contracting arrangements which characterized aircraft manufacture as a whole.

The smooth functioning of the shadow factory programme was also impeded by late deliveries of parts and equipment. For example, construction of the Pegasus engine at Rover's Acocks Green plant was seriously delayed by a shortage of forgings from the parent company and it was only with great reluctance that Bristols allowed supplies of these to be obtained from other firms.[8]

The onset of war created additional problems of this type so that it became necessary for Bristols to establish a materials co-ordinating committee. This appears to have been relatively successful, though it never fully guaranteed uninterrupted deliveries of key components.

Supply constraints of this kind were not limited to the shadow industry but applied generally to aircraft and other forms of manufacturing. Shortages of raw materials, especially steel, were particularly acute in the early period of the war, leading to production delays and the inefficient use of machinery and labour. It was reported in 1940 that failure to obtain steel alloys for Rootes' Hillman plant had become 'a frequent source of hold-ups in production',[9] while at the same time a similar problem restricted output at the West Bromwich works of George Salter Limited, one of the country's leading manufacturers of springs. By September Salters were said to be 'seriously behind in their deliveries' which, it was anticipated, would take almost a year to rectify.[10] The industry's strategic significance and the company's role within it were given formal recognition when a few months later a government committee was established to co-ordinate the supply of springs. Deficiencies of other items were said to have halved Lucas's potential output of aircraft gun turrets during the spring of 1940,[11] and later in the same year caused more than one hundred men to be laid off at the Humber engine works in Coventry.[12] In January 1941 Austin was forced to cancel sub-contract work on aircraft components, including wings, fins, tails, and rudders, 'owing to the shortage of machinable items'.[13] Although complaints of this type gradually receded, one senior MAP official noted at the end of 1942 that output from a number of the region's largest factories was determined as much by supplies of materials as labour.[14]

But management was not totally impotent in meeting this problem. Herberts, for example, developed a progress chasing system which extended to their suppliers and even involved advisory staff being seconded to sub-contractors. Although government allocation arrangements helped to direct materials to priority areas, lobbying by persistent individuals, such as Spencer Wilks, Rover's managing director, remained important in securing official support.[15] This company also appears to have benefited from a skilful purchasing operation which helped to minimize supply problems at its Birmingham factories. Duplicate sources of supply were maintained and whenever possible stocks were deliberately kept at a high level as cover against interruptions to deliveries. The company's buyer devoted much of his time to establishing and fostering contact with distributors, identifying alternative materials, and serving as a first line of quality control.[16] The highly competitive nature of this aspect of management was emphasized by Alick Dick, the buyer and materials controller for Standard, who recalled that every time he secured a promising new contact Bristols 'pinched them and we were left with the worst suppliers'.[17]

Works' efficiency was crucially influenced by the organization of production and even relatively modest adjustments in factory layout and manufacturing processes could yield significant productivity gains. By the close of the interwar period the Midlands contained a number of large, professionally managed business concerns, some of which formed part of more complex organizations with ultimate control located in London or elsewhere. The scale and professionalism of these enterprises promoted the application of modern techniques of management and production, though the region also housed many smaller concerns which were run on more traditional lines. By the end of the war there were some 4,559 firms in the region employing less than 50 people, the overwhelming majority of which were located in the Birmingham area, accounting for almost 10 per cent of the region's labour force. A further 1,554 firms employed between 50 and 500 workers, representing another 30 per cent of the labour force.[18] According to one senior government official, some of the smaller firms were

> not slow to adopt improved types of machinery and new methods, but they place their faith in practical application and experience and are generally suspicious of theory and the more intellectual approach to problems. For this reason they are rather behind hand in factory organization and modern methods of management.[19]

Yet even the industrial giants were often frustrated by the ambiguities and practical constraints of an industrial economy pressed to secure a speedy acceleration of output in areas where this was not always possible, or where it was achieved only at relatively high cost.

Perhaps the most notable development in workshop practice during the 1930s was the growing popularity of flow systems of production, a technique which was extended to new product areas during the war years. In Coventry, for example, Morris Engines pioneered the application of conveyor belt methods to the manufacture of steel tank track links, while car production lines at the nearby Humber works were adapted for the assembly of light armoured vehicles. Success in achieving high levels of output was one of the principal reasons why the leading British volume car manufacturers were invited to participate in the shadow aircraft scheme. However, it soon became apparent that Air Ministry hopes were unduly optimistic. Ernest Lemon, one of the Air Ministry's industrial advisors, pointed out in June 1939 that although the manpower and administrative skills located within the motor vehicle industry rendered it a vitally important resource for the aircraft expansion programme, 'detailed investigation has confirmed that the car engine plants are far less appropriate to aero-engine manufacture and will require far greater supplementation with new equipment than was at first appreciated'.[20] With the benefit of hindsight, Sir Charles Craven of Vickers informed Kingsley Wood in March 1940 that aircraft manufacture was 'more of a quantity production type than a mass production problem' and that a serious mistake had been made in placing too much reliance upon the particular organizational skills of the motor vehicle companies.[21] Craven's remarks were made in the context of the Castle Bromwich take-over, but even so they contained the essential truth that production methods were not necessarily transferable from one sector of the engineering industry to another.

The complex nature of aero engine technology rendered it difficult to achieve dramatic increases in the speed of assembly, while the need to accommodate frequent design modifications exerted a similar influence. Construction methods, including the use of particular jigs and other specialized equipment, were laid down by the parent company, leaving little scope for innovation by the subsidiary firms. Standard's Banner Lane plant acquired a reputation for efficiency but this did not emanate from the transfer of the firm's car tracks to aero engine work for these were dismantled in 1940 and put into store for the duration of the war. As Alick Dick pointed out, production methods were dictated by Bristols and 'we had to copy what they were doing'.[22] Similar constraints affected all members of the engine shadow groups. Joe Walton, works manager first at Rover's Acocks Green and then

Solihull plants, observed that 'you had specific items of plant to do a specific item of work'.[23] Similarly, although the machine shop at Rootes' Aldermoor Lane works ran 'in parallel lines the full length of the factory' and the whole plant was arranged to facilitate 'the "straight flow" machining sequence',[24] final assembly took place on benches in the traditional manner. Yet this example does indicate that, with large new purpose-built factories and accumulated experience of volume production methods, the potential for efficiency gains existed; indeed, as the war progressed, productivity within the Bristol shadow engine groups does appear to have increased. Standard's shadow factories provided perhaps the best example of good practice, due in large measure to the skill and experience of its management team led by R. B. Cole. He joined the firm in 1936 having previously worked for Triumph as chief rate fixer and Daimler as chief planning engineer. Cole's unique background in labour and production management enabled him to improve upon Bristol's own manufacturing techniques, introducing conveyors where appropriate and devoting particular attention to the planning and timing of jobs.[25]

There were also problems in applying volume production techniques to airframe construction. One of the Air Ministry's earliest disappointments in this respect concerned the Fairey Battle, output of which was delayed because working conditions in the centre section were so cramped that it was necessary to limit the amount of work in progress at any one time. It was noted, 'If for any reason the work gets behind, it is quite impossible to catch up supply by putting more men on the job for the simple reason that they cannot get near it to work.'[26]

A relative absence of standardization at the design stage was a further impediment to the achievement of high levels of output. As early as June 1937 Colonel Disney drew Lord Weir's attention to the sixteen sets of fuselage jigs and twenty-four wing sets at Armstrong-Whitworth's Baginton works, and queried whether 'it would not be advisable in future policy, to insist on aircraft being designed from a production point of view'.[27] This proved a particularly obdurate problem since design specifications were frequently upgraded, while the Air Staff's requirements were modified according to changes in military strategy. Moreover, with capacity at full stretch the introduction of new aircraft or model changes inevitably caused a fall in output as fresh jigs and tools were installed in the workshop area. Nevertheless, standardization and interchangeability did improve and it became common for airframes to be manufactured and assembled in separate locations. The dispersal policy encouraged this so that after 1940, for example, erection of Armstrong-Whitworth aircraft took place at a number of sites away from Coventry. There was also an attempt to apply some aspects of mass production techniques of manufacture to airframe construction. The large Spitfire factory at Castle Bromwich was designed with this in mind, but there were significant developments elsewhere, including in 1941 the complete reorganization of Austin's Longbridge works to facilitate 'the nearest possible approach to line production on aircraft'.[28] The problem remained, however, that while the output of aircraft components was substantially increased, the assembly of aero engines and airframes continued to be relatively labour-intensive and time-consuming.

By accelerating the processing of materials and reducing operatives' waiting time even fairly modest changes in shop floor organization could yield significant productivity gains. Perhaps a typical example was the introduction of a network of gangways designed to promote easier movement of metal carrying trolleys around the armaments factory of Tube Investments at Aston in Birmingham.[29] But the reverse was also true. Towards the end of the war an internal investigation revealed that productivity at Herbert's Coventry plant had declined consistently since 1939. One of the explanations for this appears to have been poor organization in the machine shop leading to 'a very slow cycle of manufacture and an excessive amount of work in progress'.[30] According to one senior manager, the arrangement under which drilling, turning, and grinding were perceived as entirely separate operations inhibited output and should have been replaced by the introduction of sections, working to a specific timetable, and responsible for a complete unit of work.[31]

Inefficient factory organization was caused by management inertia and a variety of practical difficulties. Despite considerable investment in new machinery and changes in working practice, Mass Observation found several weaknesses in the management of Tube Investments' Aston works. Apart from specifically labour problems, production was said to have suffered from inadequate co-ordination of throughput. Although the factory's progress department was reorganized in the summer of 1942, the production manager was reported to be unsympathetic to this initiative so that, according to one company director, 'we have to go very carefully, a step at a time'.[32] Conservatism was also a problem at Herberts. It was not until 1941, for example, that a systematic attempt was made to identify the causes of production blockages by collecting data on orders, output, and deliveries. Some innovations designed to speed up manufacturing processes followed, most notably in the inspection department, but major change appears to have been retarded by the belief that labour shortages, particularly in the foundry, placed the problem beyond management control. Although there was some justification for this claim, the impression remains that there was scope for greater management flexibility in works organization and that additional resources were too easily seen as the principal route to higher levels of output.

The application of time and motion study to production issues was extremely limited throughout the Midlands' engineering industry, partly because of the strength of trade union opposition, but also in some cases because of management reluctance to depart from traditional operating practices. Stopwatches were used but principally to fix prices for a job rather than to change its character. Early in the 1930s a proposal to introduce the Bedaux time and action system at Rover's Coventry plant aroused considerable labour opposition and it may be that this helped to deter other firms in the region from experimenting with the more formal principles of scientific management.[33] As late as 1943 Rover's management was in dispute with the Amalgamated Engineering Union (AEU) concerning the application of stop-watches to the production of parts for Lancaster aircraft.[34]

Another important practical obstacle to the reorganization of factory layout and other aspects of shop floor organization which affected most firms concerned the ensuing disruption to output. This was the reason why in 1941 Alfred Herbert personally vetoed a proposal to replan component manufacture at the company's Coventry works.[35] This was a genuine problem which became more intractable as the war progressed and the need for higher levels of production forced management to consider ways of increasing efficiency but deterred them from enforcing a stoppage of work. Much depended upon the co-operation of labour and the adaptability of plant as well as the skill and determination of management. At Standard's Canley works John Black was able to introduce a policy of re-grouping long-term contracts into self-contained workshop units without any loss of output even though this involved the maintenance department in moving 840 machine tools in fourteen days.[36]

The effective organization of production enhanced worker efficiency during a period when labour was extremely scarce, but the wartime management of human resources introduced new and complex issues which were approached in different ways and with varying degrees of success. One of the most critical problems concerned the shortage of skilled labour, while it was also frequently alleged that output was impeded by the poor overall quality of the workforce. This was one of the chief reasons given by Vickers' management for their failure to raise production quickly during the initial period following their take-over of the Castle Bromwich plant. Alexander Dunbar, the company's director with responsibility for aviation affairs, claimed, 'The inefficiency of labour at Castle Bromwich is such that there is a very excessive amount of scrapped work, particularly in the Machine Shops, and the existing shortage of materials is to some extent due to this cause.'[37] Some wastage of this type was to be expected with labour which had little or no experience of employment in the engineering industry, though it was also explained by the frantic drive for output during the early stages of the war, as well as by inadequate management of the shop floor and a failure to develop satisfactory training methods. As one critic observed, 'The urgent need for aircraft and the gearing of energies of the industry to fulfilling this need in the shortest possible time led to a concentration on maximising output with little regard for the productivity of the labour engaged.'[38]

Deficiencies in the supply and quality of the workforce were tackled in several ways. As controls were gradually introduced on the movement of labour, the distribution of skilled workers was determined by the priority allocated to firms by government officials rather than by the normal recruitment practices. Some companies managed to establish their claims more successfully than others. The output of aircraft from the Castle Bromwich plant benefited from the secondment in 1941 of a team of engineers from the Royal Air Force.[39] By contrast, in the following year the Alfred Herbert works in Coventry suffered an employment crisis because of its persistent inability to escape from a low priority status for labour. These examples almost certainly reflected differences in the ability of management to influence government departments, as well as the prevailing national priorities. Attempts were also made to maximize output from key areas of production by relocating workers within and between plants, a strategy most easily adopted by the larger concerns with their greater flexibility. In May 1940 Herberts increased the number of people working the night shift in their Coventry tool room by transferring apprentices from other parts of the shop.[40] There were occasions, too, when labour was made redundant or sacked in order to improve efficiency or to facilitate re-employment on other tasks within the same factory. One of Dunbar's first management initiatives at Castle Bromwich was to fire 184 staff employees, including 120 from the technical department, of whom 49 were re-engaged on what was considered to be more useful work.[41]

Technical training schemes were introduced to combat an increasingly inelastic labour market and to help quell trade union fears over the contentious issue of dilution. During the interwar period large sections of the engineering industry in the West Midlands developed graduated schemes of technical training based on part-time day attendance at a local authority college and by 1939 these arrangements had made a significant contribution to the region's pool of skilled labour.[42] With the onset of war, however, many firms preferred to utilize fully the existing skills of their young workers rather than to invest in training for the future, while in some cases boys were expected to work such long hours that they were even precluded from attending evening classes. Crash technical college courses were set up to facilitate retraining or upgrading, but these were often rejected by employers for their alleged bias towards theory and relative neglect of the more practical aspects of employment. A number of firms, particularly the larger ones, developed programmes of in-house training. Standard was one example where this facility was expanded significantly to cope with the training needs of the large numbers of workers recruited for the shadow aero engine factories at Canley. A large proportion of these were female, and by the end of June 1941 some seventy-five women were being trained by the company each week.[43] Training arrangements developed surprisingly slowly and were apparently fairly rudimentary at Vickers' Castle Bromwich plant. To begin with, instruction was provided by foremen and selected skilled workmen on what seems to have been a rather ad hoc basis and it was not until the end of 1940 that arrangements became more organized when a specialist teacher was appointed to train machine operators.[44] There is, however, no way of assessing the quality of these schemes, their effectiveness, or the size of the clientele. The Midland Area Board adopted a pessimistic view, arguing that the numbers attending officially sponsored courses were low because the workers were themselves extremely apathetic.[45] What can be said is that at a minimum level any form of relevant training was likely to have been of some benefit, and that in the majority of cases basic instruction was all that was required.

Increasing the number of hours worked was a strategy which was widely adopted to help compensate for labour shortages. Within months of the outbreak of war additions to the working week of 20 per cent or more were recorded in the region, pushing well beyond the established norms for the engineering industry as a whole. Although the financial incentives often proved attractive and helped to blunt trade union opposition, employees were sometimes forced unwillingly into working excessive overtime with the threat of reprisals if they refused. The Ministry of Labour's local officer claimed in December 1940, 'The principal single issue now affecting industrial relations in the Midlands is the question of working hours.'[46] The First World War demonstrated that very long hours of labour undermined efficiency as workers became fatigued and demotivated. In order to avoid a repetition of this, government attempts were made from 1940 to regulate working hours and conditions, though the drive for output often meant that these enjoyed only partial success. Perhaps the main pressure to limit the working week emanated from the employers' own recognition of the diseconomies associated with high levels of overtime. This was certainly the case at Castle Bromwich where working hours were cut at the beginning of 1943 in an attempt to curb the rising incidence of mental illness, which was particularly prevalent among male employees.[47]

It was commonly assumed that very long working hours were one of the principal causes of absenteeism, a problem which appears to have been widespread in the industrial West Midlands. It was also believed that absenteeism could seriously weaken productive efficiency through both its immediate and its more general effects. According to Daimler's works manager, much of the waiting time in the factory 'was caused directly by the absenteeism and slackness of a number of the operatives who, by wasting machine hours, were not giving the output that was required to keep the Fitting Sections going'.[48] Despite a number of initiatives, absenteeism was an aspect of labour management which remained a problem throughout the war, largely because its causes were improperly understood or not easily resolved. The management response spanned a continuum from threats of prosecution to improvements in working conditions. Some employers obliged their workers to state on their clock cards the reasons for absence, a practice designed to expose and deter the persistent offender. Standard's management, while often sympathetic to the problems experienced by its labour force, sometimes adopted a particularly uncompromising position on absenteeism, introducing financial penalties when these were thought appropriate. In practice, however, absenteeism was a complex phenomenon generated by a range of economic and social variables as well as occupational stress, the relative importance of which varied between different parts of the region. For example, Shenfield and Florence argued that in Coventry, where the problem was particularly acute, high wages served as a disincentive to effort, while poor transport and social conditions helped to breed an anti-work culture. In addition, most of Coventry's industrial employers had a poor reputation for accommodating the domestic responsibilities of their female workers, which may help to explain why rates of absenteeism among this particular group were sometimes double the national average.[49] In general, the introduction of a shorter working week appears to have proved the most effective way of attacking absenteeism.

Poor time keeping, and lack of commitment and effort were problems closely related to absenteeism which could have had a similarly damaging effect upon production. The war emergency did not prevent employees from arriving late, leaving early, or taking excessively long breaks during working hours. The spread of the clocking out system in Coventry was partly related to the growing habit among workers of leaving early in order to catch a particular bus home.[50] Mass Observation's report on Tube Investments' Aston factory contained some interesting impressions of the nature of these problems. It was claimed that female employees in the 'dogging-up' room, where steel tubes were placed on benches and forced through gauges to be made narrower or longer, commonly arrived ten minutes late for work, took more time for breaks than was strictly permitted, and spent up to a quarter of an hour chatting and smoking in the cloakroom after meals. Rather inconsistently, MO's reporters condemned these practices but because of the arduous nature of employment in that section of the factory welcomed the frequent informal breaks caused by normal interruptions to the flow of work. It was also suggested that some workers, particularly the older ones, were 'unambitious and casual' and had calculated 'how much work should be expected from them in any given time'.[51] Conversely, migrants to the area were said to be more highly motivated than the locals and 'critical of their easy-going ways', while Irish girls were often given the more responsible jobs in the factory because of their superior education.[52]

It is understandable that the exceptional conditions of war alienated many workers, bringing absenteeism and other mani-festations of poor commitment. Moreover, these forms of limited withdrawal served as a physical or emotional release from the rigours of the shop floor, or as a symbol of dissent at a time when other types of industrial action were difficult or unavailable. Part of the problem was that labour was usually viewed from a narrow instrumental perspective, with coercion and financial incentives as the principal tools of change management. A wider approach to personnel issues was often difficult in the smaller industrial units which proliferated in the West Midlands, but even at the larger plants, such as Vickers' works at Castle Bromwich, where social and welfare amenities were said to be good, high rates of labour turnover and absenteeism suggest that productivity growth may have been handicapped by a failure to understand and respond fully to the myriad of problems associated with changes in the nature and environment of work. Table 3.1 provides an indication of the main reasons for labour turnover at Castle Bromwich which, although representing only 4.3 per cent of the total workforce for the quarter ending 31 March 1944, was still fairly large in absolute terms, particularly in a period when the official restrictions on movement remained in operation. Ill health was the most important overall reason for labour turnover, though this was a category which was probably applied in a very general way. Domestic factors represented the largest single cause of movement among women and again this was an area where a more sophisticated approach to welfarism might have yielded a high return.

Table 3.1 Main reasons for labour wastage at Vickers' Castle Bromwich works for the quarter ending 31 March 1944

	Works		Staff		Total
	M	F	M	F	
Leaving of own accord					
Health	82	82	11	13	188
Pregnancy	—	42	—	11	53
Domestic	5	98	1	37	141
HMF	44	1	4	—	49
Travelling	3	1	—	2	6
Change of residence	—	1	—	2	3
Better position	—	—	1	—	1
Dissatisfied	11	2	3	—	16
MOL withdrawals	12	4	6	2	24
Miscellaneous	2	1	4	1	8
Discharges					
Conduct	20	13	7	—	40
Redundant	11	5	1	—	17
Prolonged absence	3	40	1	1	45
Unsuitable	21	1	4	—	26

Source: University of Cambridge Library, Vickers-Armstrong Ltd, Quarterly Reports on the Castle Bromwich Works, 212, 31 March 1944.

Company welfarism did improve but sometimes with apparently limited results. At Tube Investments, for example, a welfare office was established to help cope with the accommodation and other personal needs of the firm's employees who had migrated to Birmingham from other parts of the country. It was reported, however, that the system failed to function smoothly because of a lack of co-operation between the welfare office and the labour and first aid department, which continued to work as separate units. In addition, welfare services may have suffered because the chief officer was unpopular with her staff and also deliberately distanced herself from shop floor workers.[53]

Dilution was one of the principal responses to the national shortage of trained engineering labour. This practice, which also created greater shop floor flexibility, was widely adopted during the First World War and involved the de-skilling of work processes or the up-grading of semi-skilled labour to skilled status. Dilution was adopted as government policy during the rearmament period, though a formal agreement with the Amalgamated Engineering Union was delayed until August 1939 and it was not until some time later that the new arrangements began to be implemented throughout the engineering industry. De-skilling provoked some local trade union opposition, particularly in Coventry where in February 1940 the official scheme was reported to be 'practically at a dead end'.[54] However, this was mainly the result of a determined stand taken by a limited number of skilled workers and does not appear to have been either very prolonged or of wider significance. Indeed, in general, dilution among males appears to have occurred fairly quickly in Coventry, aided by the local definition of skill which was based on the nature of the job rather than length or degree of training.[55] Disputes involving dilution were normally localized and specific in character, though one of the most common problems focused upon the distinction between job changes which were the result of the normal process of industrial evolution and those which were forced by the emergency conditions of wartime and therefore eligible for registration under the national agreement. Organized labour was naturally anxious to protect its members' interests but the general unions in particular had much to gain from a well negotiated settlement. Jack Jones, district secretary of the Transport and General Workers' Union (TGWU), recalled that some people rejected any diminution of skill and 'were inclined to treat anybody who was not apprentice served as somebody who was inferior', but added that 'we had to fight this'.[56] Very often the main impediment to dilution was not trade union intransigence but the limited vision of employers who failed to appreciate the urgency of the labour position. It was not until late in 1940, for example, that the Area Board was able to report that 'managements throughout the Midlands have now come somewhat belatedly to recognise that for future needs fully trained personnel will not be forthcoming'.[57]

Perhaps the most contentious issue involving dilution sur-rounded the employment of women in jobs which were formerly the preserve of skilled males. Although a number of national and local agreements sought to discriminate against female dilutees, some trade union leaders and their members remained unwilling to depart from traditional practices. W. H. Stokes, the AEU divisional organizer, was particularly incensed when Herberts began employing women in the tool room, an area which, he claimed, 'lends itself to men of high skill and should be reserved for male labour'.[58] Stokes was pursuing a lost cause, partly because the labour market in Coventry rendered change inevitable but also because employers were influenced by the more flexible arrangements which were to be found in Birmingham and elsewhere. Nevertheless, the AEU continued to be particularly watchful to ensure that employers in Coventry did not breach agreed procedures and so may well have constrained the pace and scope of dilution with respect to female employment. The absorption of women into routine engineering work encountered less strident trade union opposition, the main concern being to ensure that male labour was not displaced and that wage rates were maintained. Some employers attempted to devalue work carried out by women, but until the later stages of the war, the tightness of the market often forced a change of policy as female recruitment suffered.

Although some firms successfully resisted trade union incursion, labour relations in the Midlands followed the national pattern in being transformed by the circumstances of war so that collective bargaining increasingly became a key area of management responsibility. In 1939 some sectors of the engineering industry were hardly touched by trade union organization, while in others, including the Black Country tube and metal trades, membership had peaked and then fallen quite sharply. The tradition of unskilled trade unionism in the region, which had its roots in the activities of the Workers' Union earlier in the century, had also been severely undermined by the unemployment of the Depression years. The war brought dramatic change as local officials, 'anxious to show results', took advantage of the new employment situation to begin a major recruitment drive.[59] The growing demand for labour increased the power of union negotiators, while inward migration inflated the number of potential recruits. Some of these migrants were already committed trade unionists who used their experience to promote the movement in their new workplace, the influx of Welsh tinplate workers to the Morris Engine foundry in Coventry being one notable example.[60] From the workers' perspective, the trade union umbrella helped them to exploit the tight labour market through the achievement of favourable wage rates, while the demands of wartime employment rendered some form of collective security highly desirable. In addition, the air raids strengthened the social role of trade unions for they often became a rallying point in the chaos which followed a major attack.[61]

The Essential Works Order of 1941 limited management's powers of dismissal and therefore provided a useful measure of employment protection, particularly for unskilled workers who did not always benefit from market scarcity. Trade union activists, sometimes planted by sympathetic staff at labour exchange offices, were less likely to be victimized by hard line employers, and indeed the proliferation of the shop stewards' movement is one of the outstanding features of labour organization during this period. The number of shop stewards in Coventry's engineering firms rose quickly during the war years, reaching a peak of 441 in 1943, and in the process became so well organized that on occasions they represented a serious threat to the authority of the official trade union bureaucracy.[62] The Birmingham stewards also became extremely influential, sometimes taking the initiative in raising issues with employers and politicians on a city-wide basis.[63]

Yet the spread of collective bargaining was not the result of union pressure alone for it also offered several potential benefits to employers in simplifying and producing a more orderly framework for the conduct of industrial relations. The Ministry of Labour's local conciliation officer argued early in the war that stable trade unions helped to promote industrial peace, and it is evident that official influence was a factor in the growth of union recognition among the region's engineering employers during this period. Some workers remained apathetic or hostile towards the trade unions and a strike among unorganized Black Country forge workers in 1944 was condemned by the regional conciliation officer who noted in exasperation that 'not even the fact that their previous demonstrations have proved unprofitable has convinced them that they have anything to gain from an orderly approach towards a solution of their problems under guidance from a Trade Union'.[64] By contrast, at Stewart & Lloyd's Halesowen plant, where, with Ministry encouragement, union density was almost 100 per cent, labour relations were said to be exceptionally good.

It is also important to recognize that many trade union leaders were strongly anti-fascist and keen to support rather than undermine the industrial war effort, one aspect of which was the containment of militant shop floor interests. In the unusual conditions of wartime, these interests would probably have surfaced anyway so that the trade union presence helped to steer industrial unrest into a highly structured and relatively conservative negotiating machinery. Workshop conferences frequently ended in a 'failure to agree', but at least they gave an opportunity for grievances to be aired and views exchanged, while the process itself provided a cooling off period for mature reflection on the relevant issues. In many situations, therefore, it was to management's advantage to grant formal recognition to trade union negotiators. Moreover, although the shop stewards helped to legitimize and provide a channel of expression for shop floor dissidents, they too appear to have supported the drive for production, sometimes from a very patriotic position. In April 1944, for example, the stewards at Austin's Longbridge plant called for a 'complete victory over Fascism', arguing in very frank terms that

> above the searching for holes in agreements, above the dodging, the jiggery-pokery, the slick manoeuvring and the sharp practice, lies the dominant fact of our obligations to those of ours who have pumped their life blood on to the beaches of Dunkirk, Salerno and Anzio.[65]

Unions with a base in the motor vehicle and aircraft industries were the principal beneficiaries of the wartime growth of organized labour. Before the war the leading motor car firms successfully resisted the trade unions but from 1941 this changed dramatically, especially in the Midlands where union density sometimes exceeded 50 per cent of the workforce. This was approximately double the figure for Ford and Vauxhall,[66] the difference being explained by variations in regional labour markets as well as local trade union traditions. The relative conservatism of the craft unions allowed the TGWU in particular to achieve major recruitment gains in the engineering industry, including female workers who were excluded from the AEU until 1943. Jack Jones and other officials of the TGWU used to meet newcomers at Coventry railway station, issuing them with leaflets detailing the location of the union's office and urging immediate membership. Although strikes were made illegal in July 1940, they continued on an unofficial basis throughout the war with only a small number of workers being subjected to prosecution. Until 1944 go-slows were not a particularly common form of industrial action in the Midlands, mainly perhaps because of the financial implications for workers on piece rates. Indeed the high earnings prevalent in the region's engineering industry probably constituted a far more effective deterrent to the withdrawal of labour than the formal legal constraints. Strikes and go-slows were usually the product of disagreements over the pricing of jobs and their suitability for different grades of labour, though redundancy and other issues concerned with the run-down of armaments production became the major source of friction during the latter part of the war. Piece rates were widely used to encourage greater effort but the workplace situation was complicated by the frequent need to revise prices as modifications were made to the product and its method of manufacture. This was exacerbated by employers' attempts to economize by redefining and squeezing the prices paid for jobs as government contracts became less generous. This was a particular problem in the Midlands where labour earnings in the aircraft and motor vehicle industries were said to be exceptionally high. The setting and revising of piece rates made the rate fixer's job very important but also very difficult. The rising level of activity within the engineering industry meant that many new rate fixers were appointed, many of whom were relatively inexperienced, with the result that jobs were sometimes over-priced or allocated unduly long periods for completion.

A variety of other influences helped to sour labour relations and strikes were often the product of several different grievances, some of which were personal and of long standing. It is noticeable, too, that certain types of disputes tended to be concentrated in limited periods. Claims of victimization appear to have been especially marked during the first two years of the war when the unions were attempting to establish and consolidate their positions, sometimes against determined employer opposition. Because of its broader implications, one particularly significant example concerns the AEU's battle with Standard in September 1940 over the company's attempt to sack a convenor for holding a meeting outside the prescribed hours. Prompted by a walk-out of 250 men, the union's District Committee adopted a firm stance on the rights of stewards and convenors and soon managed to achieve a management climbdown. The Standard workers were supported by men from Armstrong-Whitworth's Coventry plant and it may well be that the threat of a more general disruption to production in the city explains why the affair was so speedily resolved.[67] Events at Standard were paralleled by similar, though less serious, disputes at Alvis, Gauge and Tool, Jaguar, and other Coventry firms so that much of the AEU's time during 1940 was taken up with investigating claims of unfair dismissal. Victimization again became an issue in Coventry in 1943 when local officials of the National Union of Sheet Metal Workers and Braziers alleged that a number of the smaller firms in the city were notorious for discriminating against trade union activists, including shop stewards, even refusing to reinstate sacked workers when ordered to do so by the national service officer. On this occasion, however, the workers' claims were resisted and, after a Ministry of Labour investigation, Ernest Bevin reported that there is 'No evidence to show any tendency on the part of employers in Coventry to disregard their obligations under the Essential Work Order'.[68]

Some companies became the subject of industrial action with unusual regularity. The regional conciliation officer claimed in May 1944 that over several years the British Thompson Houston electrical engineering works at Rugby had been the most consistent source of trouble, a phenomenon which he attributed to 'the unauthorised activities of three local Trade Union office-bearers who appear to be entirely undisciplined, but possess a great deal of influence over the work people'.[69] Yet the Rootes group experienced industrial action which in terms of its scale and ramifications was probably more serious than that at BTH. The trouble was concentrated at the Humber works in Coventry and the No. 2 aero engine shadow factory at Ryton and usually centred upon wage rates. It is also clear, however, that the group's shop floor management sometimes adopted a rather confrontational style of labour relations which generated mistrust and uncertainty among the workforce. A 'large number of men' at the Ryton factory went on strike in October 1941 in protest at the imposition of what they considered to be unfair piece rates.[70] Although the Regional Board's recommendation that a Joint Production Enquiry be set up to consider the issues was rejected by the company, it does suggest the existence of a genuine problem. The dispute provided an opportunity for other grievances to be ventilated and at a subsequent works conference some 150 complaints were itemized and signed by 1,000 individuals. The AEU minutes recorded that

71

the 'whole of this Conference was devoted to a discussion on the general attitude of the management towards our Members'.[71] The Humber works was the focus of a number of disputes during the war period, but perhaps the most damaging of them occurred in January 1945 when almost 5,000 workers took unofficial action for nine days. Again the reasons were complex, but included the behaviour of the works manager whose unfair practices were said to range from a refusal to grant subsistence allowances for transferred workers to padlocking the tea urns. The factory was again severely disrupted by industrial action in the following year, this time over proposed reductions in piece rates as Rootes attempted to increase competitiveness by lowering unit labour costs.[72]

Despite these examples, the Midlands was not an unduly strike-prone region. For example, between January 1943 and December 1944 the aircraft industry in Britain experienced fifty-two serious strikes each involving a loss of more than 10,000 man-hours, of which only four were on the Coventry-Birmingham axis. The most damaging of these was among Rootes' workers in Coventry where 56,000 man-hours were lost in April 1944. However, this was a relatively modest toll compared with that at Rolls-Royce's shadow factory at Hillingdon where in the previous November industrial action cost over 700,000 man-hours.[73] Strikes and go-slows were only part of a whole complex of variables which influenced output, rendering it difficult to isolate and quantify, except in very specific cases, the relative importance of these and other forms of industrial action. One example where this may be possible concerns Vickers' Castle Bromwich works where aircraft production was said to have suffered at the end of 1942 because 'the tendency to direct action has increased'.[74] The output of Spitfires for that December was 6.5 per cent below the planned target, while the following month saw another fall of just over 3.5 per cent. However, for the thirteen months from December 1942 to December 1943 output was only just over 2.0 per cent below target and, though this did represent a potential loss of sixty-eight aircraft, it does suggest that some production could be redeemed when circumstances became more favourable. In practice, the throughput of aircraft fluctuated according to the frequency and extent of design changes, the level and quality of resource inputs in general, as well as temporary phenomena such as air raids and influenza, so that in relative terms industrial action was probably a fairly modest impediment to production. When in 1943 the MAP began to take more interest in manufacturing efficiency it soon became apparent that changes of aircraft type were mainly responsible for the leakage of man-hours within the industry as a whole.[75]

Some strikes and go-slows inevitably had a serious effect upon war production but the military significance of this is not always easy to discern. Any loss of Spitfire production was likely to have had serious consequences, but even so, much depended upon the timing of the dispute. In the critical period after Dunkirk, for example, the Ministry of Labour's conciliation officer reported that the region was not only strike-free but that every effort was being made to maintain the flow of armaments production. This industrial calm continued into the following year and in June 1941 it was noted that 'there has been no major stoppage of work or serious clash of interests in the Midlands for some months'.[76] Moreover, the labour action which occurred in the last two years of war, while important, was less critical than it would have been in 1940. Strikes were also of relatively short duration, representing an immediate response to particular pressures and frustrations rather than a strategy deliberately designed to inflict maximum industrial damage. By providing an outlet for emotional tensions it was even possible that strikes helped to maintain worker morale. This was certainly the view of the regional conciliation officer who reported in September 1942 that the

> mere fact of making a demonstration seems to do the workpeople good. The fiery first few hours of a strike seem to bring considerable relief and it generally becomes a question of how to secure a resumption of work without making the stoppage look foolish.[77]

One area where local trade unionists enjoyed a special influence was in the creation of joint consultative machinery. Supported by the Ministry of Labour, a formal agreement for the engineering industry was concluded in March 1942 which allowed for discussion on ways of maximizing output within the framework of plant based Joint Production Committees (JPCs). Much of the impetus behind this initiative came from the Midlands where in September 1941 the Regional Board unanimously agreed to support the establishment of joint consultative machinery. Billy

Stokes, the AEU district organizer in Coventry and the board's vice-chairman, was largely responsible for this success. Although an ex-Communist Party member, Stokes was by this time fervently anti-communist and it may be that his support for the JPCs was in part an attempt to curb the growing influence of left-wing extremists whose allegations of management slackness were beginning to attract national attention.[78] Yet Coventry employers in particular remained staunchly opposed to trade union intervention in issues which they considered to be the prerogative of management, and by the beginning of 1942 many of the city's largest firms would not even tolerate the presence of informal consultative machinery. The appearance of JPCs in the spring of 1942 appears to have been largely the result of very public criticisms of management voiced by the shop stewards rather than deliberate pressure exerted by the Regional Board. The Birmingham and District Shop Stewards Council claimed in September 1941 that the munitions factories were badly mismanaged and that because of the uneven flow of work the men at one factory 'played darts throughout the whole of a nightshift'.[79] The attack came from an unexpected quarter at the beginning of the following year when the general manager of an engineering firm in Coventry claimed that machines 'which should be helping to turn out weapons of war, are standing idle and that dozens of precious precision tools in the district work only a few hours a day or not at all'.[80] The issue came to a head in February when it was angrily asserted at a meeting of Coventry shop stewards that war production in the city was in chaos due to gross management inefficiency. This claim received considerable media attention and probably contained sufficient truth to fuel public concern and force some employers into making conciliatory gestures.

It is difficult to assess the truth of these allegations since it is certain that there was often a very fine distinction between rhetoric and reality. Furthermore, once they were established, the contribution of the JPCs to war production is equally uncertain. Lewchuk implies that the JPC set up at Austin's Longbridge plant in June 1942 was a significant advance in the search for improved efficiency based upon co-operation with organized labour.[81] There is no evidence to suggest that this was in fact the case and the firm's authoritarian management style was one of the prime reasons for the serious strike which occurred at Longbridge in

September 1944.[82] A similar blend of optimism and disappointment characterized the history of the more informal Works Consultative Committee introduced at Castle Bromwich towards the end of 1941. To begin with, it was hoped that the committee would provide a 'medium whereby information can be passed to the workers and through which their complaints and constructive suggestions can be considered'.[83] However, it was claimed at the end of June 1943 that the committee 'provided scarcely any examples of suggestions to improve actual production directly and have centred mainly on working conditions'.[84] A more constructive atmosphere may have prevailed at some other factories. For example, the first meeting of the JPC at the Humber-Hillman works in Coventry saw the creation of a system of mobile gangs which could 'be switched from one section to another to meet varying requirements of production'.[85] By the end of 1942 production methods were a major item on the agenda of most JPCs in the aircraft industry, though many of the issues were probably of a minor kind which had formerly been dealt with on the shop floor. Significantly, too, action appears to have been taken most often on welfare issues, though this could have had an important, if unquantifiable, impact upon labour efficiency.[86] Allegations of mismanagement became less common in the Midlands from the summer of 1942 but this may simply mean that union representatives were less inclined to attack an industrial structure of which they had become a part. In this respect the JPCs had become an important, if unintended, feature of the employers' labour relations strategy.

The manipulation of wage rates was the key instrument of labour management used by the Midlands' principal employers during the war period, especially in the aircraft industry. This was, too, the area where organized labour was most effective in gaining benefits for its members. The trade union leadership was pushed hard by the rank and file to obtain immediate financial gains. The regional conciliation officer commented in March 1941 that it

would be true to say that responsible Trade Union Officials offer no support to the initiation of claims for unreasonable wage levels, but they are frequently placed in an embarrassing position by pressure from elements operating from within the workshop, and have no alternative other than to pursue the claims of their members in the best possible interests of the organisations.[87]

The situation was much the same at the beginning of the following year when it was reported that 'the new recruits want speedy results from their union membership'.[88] In addition, however, wage rates in the Midlands were influenced by the tradition of high earnings associated with the pre-war motor industry, while some of the initiatives designed to alleviate the labour supply problem exerted further upward pressure upon wage levels. One particularly important example of this was the Coventry Tool Room Agreement of 1941 which was designed to prevent the drift of skilled labour to production work in search of higher incomes but which had the effect of exerting a ratchet-like effect upon engineering wages in general. Wages varied between different sectors of the engineering industry and from one factory to another but overall the Midlands eventually acquired particular notoriety for its exceptionally high income levels, including bonus payments. An investigation by the Ministry of Aircraft Production in 1942 found that at one Coventry motor factory the bonus on some jobs was as high as 581 per cent, with a works average of 324 per cent.[89]

From the employers' position, a flexible wages policy was more than simply a recipe for industrial peace for it facilitated dilution and the adoption of new working practices and, it was believed, promoted endeavour at a time when the monopsony demands of government were difficult to resist and labour hard to acquire. Ironically, though, by encouraging absenteeism and indifferent attitudes towards work, high wages eventually undermined efficiency, generating in effect a backward sloping supply curve of labour. This problem was recognized and attacked by Vickers' management in 1941 when prices in the wing assembly section at Castle Bromwich were significantly reduced, as a result of which output was said to have 'appreciably increased' while average earnings were maintained, suggesting that there was a simultaneous rise in worker effort.[90] However, despite government support, initiatives of this type appear to have enjoyed relatively little success, certainly in the aircraft industry, so that as late as 1944 Horace Pryor, the works manager at Humber, lamented that the repair of aero engines consumed more man-hours in Coventry than in any other part of the country. According to Pryor, the only way to achieve higher levels of output was through a contraction in piece rates.[91]

Resource management assumed new importance in wartime Britain. Raw materials, equipment, and labour were all in short supply, while the demand for high levels of output became increasingly intense. The example of the Midlands' engineering industry reveals that physical resources were often mobilized surprisingly quickly and with a fair degree of efficiency and imagination, though as one would expect a number of firms were clearly unprepared for war and found it difficult to adjust to the new circumstances. Large inputs of labour, much of it unused to manufacturing employment, were soon absorbed into a variety of jobs with relatively little friction. Yet in general labour continued to be regarded as an inanimate factor of production, motivated largely by financial reward, and it was this which often posed the greatest threat to the efficient conduct of what was a particularly important segment of the wartime economy. The quality of business leadership was variable. However, it is important to recognize that the general expansion and adjustment of manufacturing activity placed a premium on management skills, a commodity which was already scarce at the outbreak of war. The absorption of a number of leading industrialists into government service exacerbated this problem, although in many cases the deficiencies were most pronounced on the shop floor where works managers, foremen, inspectors, rate fixers, and progress chasers assumed new importance, partly because of the production imperative but also because the environment of labour relations was changing dramatically.

4

Government and industry: the problems of monopsony

The war forced government and industry into a relationship of mutual dependence which raised a number of contentious political and economic issues. Although rearmament assumed a high priority in the late 1930s, there was little inclination to disturb the industrial routine; even when war was declared and state bureaucracy expanded, the regulation of economic activity remained a hybrid of direct controls and secondary manipulation of the free enterprise system. Management was allowed to manage but within the context of a regulated allocation of resources and under conditions of near monopsony, with government as the sole or principal purchaser. The recruitment to Whitehall of senior businessmen as advisors and administrators helped to forge a greater understanding and a more sympathetic atmosphere between government and industry, but it was an initiative rendered necessary by a shortage of competent civil servants rather than any ideological commitment to corporatism. Despite a high degree of central direction, Britain's industrial war effort was expected to occur within some, at least, of the normal rules of the market economy. While this inevitably produced points of tension, it accommodated the British political tradition and also met the need for the state to be distanced from the autocracy of the Axis powers.

The expansion of the RAF ensured that the Midlands was one of the first industrial regions to be touched by rearmament, and indeed the shadow factory scheme became something of a test case in the developing relationship between business and government. In addition, however, the region's manufacturing profile guaranteed a lasting and pervasive interaction between industry and the apparatus of the state which raised problems common to other

78

parts of the country but which were also in some respects unique. The central issue was one of accountability, the nature of which was distorted by the changing character of the market. Central government was responsible for ensuring that the armed forces were effectively provisioned, but it was also accountable to Parliament for the overall level of expenditure, its distribution and rate of return. Profiteering by management or workforce was unacceptable and yet a positive response to government orders seemed essential, even at the expense of cost efficiency as the need to sustain high levels of output began to assume paramount importance. But the war also involved problems of industrial contraction as well as expansion and the evidence for the Midlands suggests that in some ways government was better equipped to deal with the former than the latter. The prospect of a return to peacetime conditions posed enormous problems for manufacturing industry which attracted ministerial interest but which resulted in relatively little positive action. The purpose of this chapter is not to examine the rationale or machinery of control, but rather to analyse some of the key issues generated by the monopsony position of government.

Rearmament provided the opportunity for firms with ambitious managements to seek large government contracts which could form the basis for substantial expansion of both output and capacity. In many cases these bids were part of a continuing relationship, while in others they represented an attempt to cultivate a new market and source of income. BSA was one of the most notable examples of a Midlands contractor whose production became largely directed towards government consumption and which in the 1930s was particularly anxious to benefit from rearmament. The firm extended its Birmingham works considerably during the First World War and by 1918 was manufacturing some 20,000 rifles a week, together with large quantities of Lewis guns. With the Armistice, however, government orders declined sharply and by the mid-1930s BSA's weapons department was largely sustained by its private gun trade. As the company's former secretary noted at the end of 1935, there had been no government orders for the past seventeen years 'beyond a few oddments in the nature of spares'.[1] BSA was paying the price for over-dependence upon War Office largesse and a government policy directed towards sustaining a minimum level of activity at the Royal Ordnance factories at

Woolwich, Waltham, and Enfield. Significantly, too, the company was also experiencing financial problems with Daimler, the motor vehicle branch of its operations, and this helps to explain the enthusiasm with which it courted involvement in the aero engine shadow factory project. By the late 1930s the firm's survival depended upon its ability to attract large scale British government contracts.

Alvis did not have the same military traditions as BSA but by 1935 the company's managing director, T. G. John, was also concerned about the size of the market for its products. The company was founded by John in 1919 and soon acquired a sound reputation for its stylish, high-powered sports and touring cars. Demand remained buoyant in the 1920s, and though the world slump caused a temporary dip in the company's fortunes, it was less severe than for many other firms, and by the end of 1931 recovery appears to have been well advanced. However, when sales, particularly in the London area, dropped sharply during the first half of 1935 the board decided that 'the changing conditions in the Motor Car Industry' justified diversification into other areas of production, including aeronautical engineering, and with this in mind an agreement was concluded in August to manufacture under licence the French designed Gnome Rhône engine.[2] A purpose-built factory was erected in Coventry and equipped under the supervision of Alvis's chief engineer, Smith-Clarke, who made sure that his new plant should be the best money could buy'.[3]

The move into aero engine production was not precipitated solely by flagging car sales in 1935 since the matter was already being considered by John during the previous summer when the business was enjoying a period of considerable success. John was an ambitious man and it seems likely that he was influenced by his previous experience as works manager at Siddeley-Deasy, a firm which prospered during the First World War as a result of its entry into the market for aero engines. Rearmament was becoming a reality by the mid-1930s and John was sufficiently percipient to recognize that government demand for raw materials was likely to grow rapidly and prove lucrative, as his attempt concurrently to establish a subsidiary for the manufacture of armoured vehicles indicates. The authority which was necessary to put his ideas into practice arrived fortuitously in March 1935 when, following the death of the previous incumbent, John assumed the additional role of company chairman.

By circumventing the normal costs of research and development, the Gnome Rhône licence was a speedy and relatively inexpensive way into the aero engine business. The Alvis works was furnished with modern machine tools, many of them of recent American construction, and with a total area of 100,000 square feet was only slightly below the size of the first shadow factories. Yet government orders were slow to arrive and by July 1936 the factory employed only some seventy operatives, mostly on sub-contract work for Rolls-Royce. As John informed Colonel Disney at the Air Ministry, much of the firm's 'very valuable plant is lying idle in anticipation of your telling us what you would like us to do'.[4] The Ministry, however, remained obdurate, refusing to sanction orders for Alvis's French-designed aero engines and adopting a similarly negative attitude towards the company's request for inclusion in the first shadow scheme. This was a cause of particular irritation to John since the participant firms had spent some time in studying the layout of the Alvis aero engine works, its equipment and testing arrangements. As early as May 1936 Swinton and his officials agreed that Alvis's most appropriate role was as a sub-contractor to the existing aircraft companies and their shadow partners, a policy which was largely retained during the rearmament period and beyond, though the firm's own Leonides engine was eventually developed for use in helicopters.

By 1935 a number of other companies had already attempted, unsuccessfully, to enter the aircraft industry on a similar basis to Alvis. The construction of a purpose-built and equipped factory made Alvis a special case but in addition T. G. John sought to strengthen political and media support for his company in a deliberate attempt to pressurize the Air Ministry. One official warned Swinton in May 1936 that Alvis 'might prove troublesome, since they had a certain amount of influence behind them', and there was particular concern that the company might succeed in recruiting to the board Sir John Salmond, formerly Chief of the Air Staff.[5] Relations between Alvis and the Air Ministry gradually deteriorated and by the autumn of 1938 the dispute was being used by outside interests to attack the government for the slow pace of rearmament. Publicity in the national press was accompanied by an internal investigation conducted by Sir Amos Ayre and S. R. Beale, both of whom were members of the Air Ministry's Industrial Panel. Their report was broadly supportive of the status quo, noting that before the Ministry could be justified in departing from the policy of non-multiplicity of types to which it is working a new engine would have to show a very great advance technically beyond existing attainment, and, at the same time, meet some definite requirement in the aircraft programme of the Ministry, which the Leonides engine does not.[6]

The report confirmed that Alvis's most appropriate role was as a sub-contractor, though its authors accepted that the firm possessed great technical knowledge and skill, adding, 'In almost any other circumstances than those so fundamentally governed by the policy as to engine types, the Alvis project would probably have been rewarded by success.'[7]

Alvis was never a serious contender for inclusion within the first aero engine shadow project because the board's primary aim was for the company to become an independent manufacturer. This was reflected by the way in which the factory was initially equipped so that by the summer of 1936 only about half of its machine tools were suitable for the assembly of Bristol or Mercury engines. A further complication was that these tools were said to be appropriate only for the manufacture of the larger components, which would have unbalanced output from the group as a whole.[8] With a substantial volume of aero engine manufacture already planned for Coventry, an additional major development would have raised serious manpower and strategic issues. Even had Alvis been fully committed to the shadow scheme in 1936, there seems little doubt that its inclusion would have been resisted by the Bristol Aeroplane Company, which was anxious not to promote the development of any potential future rivals. As the Air Ministry came under criticism for not fully utilizing Alvis's capacity, pressure was placed upon Bristols and Lord Austin to allow the company to join the shadow scheme. An agreement was eventually negotiated in the summer of 1938, though severe restrictions were placed upon the parameters of Alvis's involvement in the aero engine business. In practice, however, the general expansion of the aircraft industry in 1939 ensured that the firm's Coventry plant would be fully employed in the sub-contracting role which the Air Ministry had originally intended for it.

Alvis's original agreement with the Gnome Rhône company involved the manufacture of aero engines which by the mid-1930s were of rather outdated design and certainly technically inferior to the new generation British models. During 1935, however, Alvis's designers began a major programme of engine redevelopment so that towards the end of the following year John felt able to inform Lord Swinton that 'No foreign control of the slightest sort exists in this direction', adding that 'We are completely independent and self-contained.'[9] It was also claimed that the Alvis-developed Pelides was both more powerful and more reliable than the Bristol Pegasus engine. This was received with some scepticism within the Ministry, while Swinton's senior officials also denied John's assertion that several firms had been in touch with him over the possibility of fitting Alvis engines to their airframes. In reality, Alvis entered the market for aero engines too late to be a serious competitor to Bristols, for by the end of 1936 even those models which were at the most advanced stage of development had not yet been subjected to proper technical trials. The view which came to be accepted within the Air Ministry was that 'the firm have seriously under-estimated both the difficulties and the time element in the development of aero-engines'.[10] However, the official who voiced this opinion also believed that 'experience and time should expose false estimates, and they may then be more amenable to making use of their works in ways which would be really useful to us'.[11] Apart from the technical considerations, Alvis lacked the capacity to produce aero engines in quantities large enough to meet the Air Ministry's projected requirements. When Colonel Disney visited Coventry in December 1936 he was impressed by the modernity of the Alvis works and was prepared to recommend adoption of the company's engines providing that they satisfied the necessary technical specifications, but only for aircraft which were likely to be ordered in very limited numbers.[12]

Although the Air Ministry's policy towards Alvis was perfectly consistent with established practice, it is probable that attitudes were hardened by the company's attempt to manipulate Swinton and his successor, Kingsley Wood, and their departmental officials. John purchased the Gnome Rhône licence against the Ministry's 'strong advice not to proceed', believing perhaps that in a period of rearmament it would be politically difficult for government to reject the overtures of a company possessing an impressive aero engine manufacturing facility. When Swinton proved intransigent, John attempted to exert pressure by enlisting the support of Sir

Thomas Inskip who, as Minister for the Co-ordination of Defence, already enjoyed an ambivalent relationship with the Air Ministry.[13] This strategy must have been particularly unwelcome at a time when Lord Nuffield was already seeking to undermine the Ministry's credibility. By the autumn of 1938 relations between Alvis and the Air Ministry had reached a particularly low ebb and following the Ayre–Beale inquiry John claimed that his letters 'have suddenly ceased to be either acknowledged or replies received from them'.[14] A further spate of newspaper articles at the very end of 1938 and the beginning of 1939 sparked another furious row and on 2 January Harold Balfour, the Under Secretary of State, telephoned John, with two witnesses present, to inform him that unless the press leaks ceased the Air Ministry would make public the full story of the Alvis débâcle.[15]

Once it became clear that Alvis's diversification into the manufacture of aero engines was not to receive Air Ministry support, John had little alternative but to lobby as widely and as vigorously as possible on his firm's behalf. By 1938 this began to assume an air of desperation, partly because the Ministry was proving such a difficult opponent but also because John was facing criticism from his own board and the company's shareholders. His letter to Kingsley Wood on 21 November pointed out that he would soon have to explain to shareholders why Alvis had incurred such heavy losses since the construction of its aero engine factory three years earlier.[16] By that time rumours were already circulating in the city that the firm's development policy was about to be reviewed. In the following April an internal enquiry into the management of the firm was set in motion and after a particularly uncomfortable AGM the board introduced a number of changes to the decision making structure.[17] The effect of these was to strengthen the board's control over financial, technical, and marketing issues with all decisions on management staffing, manufacturing programmes, and capital and research and development expenditure requiring collective approval. Yet the outbreak of war and the arrival of substantial Air Ministry contracts failed to solve John's problems for the company's wholly owned subsidiary, Alvis Mechanisation, had proved unable to secure War Office contracts of any size for its armoured vehicles and by 1941 was suffering heavy losses. Once again John was left to lament that Alvis's 'treatment had been very unfair'.[18] By 1944 John had finally lost the board's confidence and, with post-war reconstruction demanding new initiatives, he was asked to resign from the company. Ironically, this was at the very time that orders for the Leonides engine began to mount.

If in 1939 Alvis's directors had reason to feel let down by government, the reverse must have been true at Singer Motors Limited where Air Ministry support ensured the survival of an ailing company. The firm's financial reconstruction in 1936 failed to solve the problems associated with poor management and, in a highly competitive market for motor vehicles, Singers ended the decade heavily in debt. Rearmament orders began to accumulate in 1938 and in November a major deal was negotiated with Vickers-Armstrong for the manufacture of 375 sets of geodetic panels for the Wellington bomber. Production of these was concentrated at the firm's Birmingham factory, while the Coventry plant was simultaneously occupied on a sub-contract basis with machining and similar general engineering work for a number of aircraft and other firms. With the outbreak of war, orders began to expand so that the company could claim, with some justification, that it was a potentially important element in the country's industrial war economy.

Charles Latham, the company's chairman, claimed that the onset of war exacerbated Singer Motors' delicate financial position since the swift run-down of car production left the firm with a number of creditors on this side of the business but without the funds which sales of the finished product would generate.[19] Late payment on some rearmament contracts was a further embarrassment to the company. Design changes retarded work on the Vickers order, though it was also alleged that remittances were delayed because Singers were themselves slow 'to get down to the job'.[20] By the autumn of 1939 the company's survival depended upon the patience of its commercial creditors, some of whom had already taken out writs, and the willingness of Lloyds Bank to continue its overdraft facility. The situation was finally brought to a head in September when Lloyds reduced the company's overdraft limit by half and in the following month demanded immediate compliance with the new conditions. Lloyds were concerned that the company was drifting towards insolvency, taking an overdraft of £74,000 with it. Lloyds' own view, which it made known to the Air Ministry, was that the company's position 'can only get worse, despite the additional orders they may obtain; the profits they may make on these will not enable them to overcome the accumulated difficulties of the past'.[21] Singers needed an injection of outside capital if they were to avoid liquidation and the expectation that this would be provided by the government explains Lloyds' tough policy towards the firm.

Lloyds had placed the Air Ministry in a dilemma. It had no wish to provide public funds in support of an ailing company, yet recognized the political repercussions of allowing a very substantial manufacturing facility to fall into bankruptcy. In addition to its assembly and machine shops, Singers possessed a well equipped sawmill, press shop, and foundry, and employed a total labour force approaching 3,000 people. As Latham was quick to point out, 'The company has the Works, qualified staff and working organisation with skilled and unskilled labour to carry out the requirements of the Government and private contractors.'[22] Apart from having numerous business interests, Latham was highly experienced in local politics and well connected in the Labour Party, all of which he was prepared to exploit in order to rescue Singers. This was reflected in the advice given by Harold Balfour that action should be taken promptly 'as what we must avoid is any accusation at some later date of delay whereby their position has deteriorated'.[23] The Air Ministry was unwilling to meet Latham's request for a government loan to the company of £150,000, though it did apply pressure to Lloyds by pointing out that a larger overdraft limit would enable the company to continue with work 'of vital importance to the defence needs of the country'.[24] The bank remained unmoved, however, and in a final attempt to save the company from insolvency the Air Ministry insisted that money owed to Singers by Vickers-Armstrong for sub-contract work be paid immediately. The Air Ministry was clearly reluctant to press Vickers in this way but explained that Singers was an exceptional case and that 'the action we took was necessary to preserve the firm in being'.[25] Vickers proved extremely co-operative, but in defence of their position pointed out that 'we find Singers very grasping and it is exceedingly difficult to get them to put in their returns in the way the Ministry require'.[26]

These examples, together with that of the first shadow factory programme, demonstrate that during the period of rearmament the relationship between industry and government, as exemplified by the Air Ministry, was one of mutual dependence, but not a coalition of equals. While the Ministry was certainly influenced by business interests, the boundaries of manipulation were narrowed by the growing confidence of the politicians and their officials so that by the onset of war central control over many facets of aircraft production was already well advanced. As Robertson notes, this was achieved partly through the Ministry's dominant position in the market, but also via the direct extension of productive capacity, the purchase and holding of stocks of raw materials, and the promotion of research and development.[27] Alvis's attempt from the mid-1930s to manufacture its own aero engine and its rebuttal by the Air Ministry illustrates the point that government had both a direct and an indirect influence upon the private business sector. It seems unlikely that without the prospect of Ministry contracts John would have been tempted to invest in the Gnome Rhône licence and the construction of a costly aero engine factory. The Alvis case, like many others, demonstrates that the government's influence was by no means transient for the company's post-war development was determined by the decisions taken in 1935. More broadly, the evolution of the shadow factory scheme and the geographical location of its first participants ensured that light engineering would assume an even higher profile in the industrial West Midlands after 1945.

The rescue of Singer Motors in 1939 suggests that the banking sector remained relatively independent of government pressure. With the allocation of government contracts, bank overdrafts became increasingly important in facilitating initial purchases of equipment and materials, and bridging the gap between orders and payments. Moreover, as the manager of the Coventry branch of the Midland Bank recognized, 'there may be times when the remittances from the Air Ministry do not come to hand when expected'.[28] The banks' concern to protect their financial interests became one important factor which helped to shape the wartime relationship between government and industry. Progress payments, for example, became essential supports to bank overdrafts and in November 1940 Lloyds even attempted to arrange for payment of instalments due on Rover's Cheetah aircraft contract to be forwarded direct to the bank, a suggestion which the company firmly rejected. More generally, the banks acted as a buffer between industry and government which ensured that some at least of the normal rules of commerce continued to apply.

The essential task of government in its relationship with industry was to ensure that output was sufficient to meet the agreed requirements of the armed forces, but with the relaxation of normal market constraints, one of the problems which confronted the Treasury and supply departments was to determine how this could be achieved economically and efficiently. It was within this context that the debate over suppliers' prices and profits was conducted during the late 1930s and into the war period. The issue was brought to prominence in 1936 during the negotiations with Herbert Austin over the financial settlement to be agreed in respect of the shadow factory scheme. Although each of the participants was free to negotiate individually, Austin was the first to begin the process and it was anticipated that the settlement arrived at with him would set the pattern for the programme as a whole. The bargaining, which, to begin with, involved simply the contract for 900 Fairey Battle airframes, proved much more difficult than Air Ministry officials appear to have expected. Agreement was reached on the broad structure of the contract which involved the payment of a management fee, a fixed sum for each airframe, and bonuses related to productivity gains, but Austin rejected the detailed terms offered by the Ministry, while his own proposals were described by Swinton as 'fantastic'.[29] Negotiations proceeded but eventually reached an impasse in early May with Austin demanding a total of £275,000, excluding bonuses, for the contract and the Ministry refusing to exceed £185,000. After receiving authority from the Defence Policy and Requirements Committee, Lord Swinton finally agreed a compromise with Austin at the end of the month which involved the Ministry extending its offer to £230,000.[30]

This episode is important for a number of reasons, but particularly because the distinctive features of the shadow scheme, especially the management by outside firms of government owned factories and plant, drew official attention to the financial complexities of rearmament and helped to set in motion debate on the contractual relationship between the supply departments and private industry. Despite the productivity clauses built into the agreement with Austin, there is little evidence that in 1936 the government was fundamentally concerned with the promotion of manufacturing efficiency. Its main objective was to achieve a rapid expansion of airframe and aero engine capacity consistent with political propriety, an imperative reflected in the willingness of the Treasury to delegate to the Air Ministry responsibility for the financial settlement. With Austin apparently so intransigent, the Ministry considered direct control through the creation of government owned factories as a way of expanding capacity but this was soon rejected as impractical so that Swinton was forced to admit that there was no alternative but to settle with Austin. The problem for the Air Ministry was that there appeared to be no way of estimating the cost to Austin of their involvement in the shadow scheme and therefore no logical method of calculating a suitable rate of return. Swinton argued, however, that the firm's input to the programme ought to be measured in terms of opportunity costs since the transfer of resources would inevitably disadvantage its main business interests. By employing this relatively fluid concept the Air Ministry was able to avoid embarrassing productivity issues since, as Swinton pointed out, 'Approximately the same amount of time and trouble and risk will be incurred by Austin's whether the expenditure is on the higher or lower scale.'[31]

As rearmament progressed the methods used to remunerate government contractors were modified, sometimes becoming more flexible but also more complex. In the case of the shadow factories an arrangement was introduced in 1941 under which the managing firms were rewarded on a sliding scale according to the amount of capital involved, and with no bonus payments. However, the degree of direct ministerial control varied according to the nature of the activity so that, for example, sub-contractors enjoyed relatively more freedom than the government's principal suppliers and were sometimes able to make substantial gains from the rapid growth of competition for their products. In general, the controlling mechanisms were said to have worked quite well, but mainly within the context of avoiding profiteering rather than the promotion of industrial efficiency. Attempts were made to reduce suppliers' profit margins and to reward those firms which risked their own capital and displayed enterprise, but, as Ashworth notes, the overriding objective was to ensure that no contractor benefited unreasonably from the war economy.[32] It may be that in the longer term the constraints on profit margins, including the imposition of relatively high levels of taxation, limited capital accumulation to such an extent that it retarded the process of readjustment to peacetime conditions. This was an issue which troubled Austin's

89

board in 1941 when financial negotiations with the Ministry of Supply appeared seriously to disadvantage the company. More generally, it was noted that with 'taxation at its present level there was little, if any, chance of creating Reserves for post-war business out of the limited profits allowed by the Government Departments'.[33] Ironically, Austin was paying the penalty for greater efficiency since as improvements to production methods raised rates of return so government departments attempted to squeeze the company's profit even further.

In practice, it proved extremely difficult to calculate levels of profit which were thought to satisfy the public interest as well as the commercial needs of industrialists. Assessment of profit on the basis of capital employed was made easier by the war since firms' output was usually destined entirely for government consumption so that confusion over the application of plant to different purposes was largely removed. However, businessmen were often very unhappy with this arrangement since assets were written down at Inland Revenue rates which were less generous than those commonly employed within industry itself, excluding, for example, goodwill. It remained possible, however, to secure additional profit on the basis of turnover so that the system was more flexible than might at first appear.[34] Even so, this involved calculations of efficiency according to departmental criteria which, as the minutes of Rover's Shadow Factory Management Committee reveal, sometimes led to protracted bargaining. This was in itself an important opportunity cost for it consumed the limited time of both senior management and high level government officials, and, in at least one case, was said to have seriously retarded the establishment of an important dispersal factory.[35] Variations between government departments in the use of fixed or costed contracts could also lead to confusion and excessive bureaucracy, while each had its own particular implications for both profits and efficiency. Fixed price contracts, for example, enabled manufacturers to benefit from continuous improvements in production methods, a phenomenon which was said to have contributed to inflated profits among the aircraft manufacturers. Output levels became so high that the ratio of turnover to capital employed in the aircraft industry increased rapidly, leading eventually to an additional annual income about 1·5 per cent higher than would have been possible under the original calculations.[36] Costed contracts, where profit levels were determined after the work was completed, enabled government departments to maintain much greater control over firms' rate of return. This form of contract was favoured by the Ministry of Supply, which seems to have gained a reputation for its sound financial practices.

By contrast, the Ministry of Aircraft Production came to be regarded as lax, even profligate, in its relations with the aero industry, where labour costs in particular were said to be unreasonably high. The shadow aircraft factories in the Midlands attracted particular criticism and were a special embarrassment because of their unique financial relationship with the Ministry. The issue involved the effective utilization of labour rather than simply firms' cost structures since high wages came to be perceived as detrimental to worker effort in a period of acute manpower shortages. An investigation by the Ministry's Production Efficiency Board at the beginning of 1943 suggested that slackness and indiscipline were rampant among workers in some Coventry factories. The root of the problem, it was argued, 'appeared to be the fixing of times and prices which resulted in high earnings without a corresponding high effort'.[37] Experience demonstrated, however, that it was easier to identify the cause and implications of high wage costs than to cure the malady. Without a formal mechanism for the control of wages, the Ministries of Labour and Aircraft Production could only attempt to persuade employers and trade union leaders that moderation in wage bargaining was an integral part of the nation's war effort. The Coventry and District Engineering Employers' Association attempted to encourage local trade union officials, as well as its own members, to limit wage claims, but with relatively little success. Only one firm, Standard, responded positively, with a one-third drop in piece rates for workers engaged on the Bristol aero engine contract. This reduction was achieved in the face of strong trade union opposition, mainly, perhaps, because of the exceptionally high level of worker–management co-operation which characterized industrial relations at the firm's shadow factories.

Direct intervention by government in works' efficiency increased as the immediate threat of defeat subsided and resources, especially labour, became more difficult to obtain. The degree of intervention appears to have varied between departments, with the Ministry of Aircraft Production once again acquiring a reputation for relative inactivity. According to J. B. Jeffreys, 'The peacetime relations between employers and employed were left undisturbed, and in contrast to other aspects of production the Ministry remained on the side lines offering advice in some instances but in no case interfering directly.'[38] Some initiatives were taken, but of a rather general kind. For example, in 1940 Boulton Paul were advised to seek outside assistance on the reorganization of works management to help facilitate more effective production of the Defiant turret-fighter.[39] A change of policy from 1942 coincided with Stafford Cripps' appointment in November as Minister. Members of the Production Efficiency Board toured aircraft factories and made recommendations on ways of improving the productivity of both capital and labour. No indication appears to remain of the board's influence among aircraft manufacturers in the Midland region, though it seems likely that its members' technical expertise gave it considerable professional authority. As the war progressed and its powers increased, the Ministry of Labour also became more interventionist. A report by the Ministry on Rover's No. 2 shadow factory at Solihull in April 1942 claimed that 'considerable slackness and loss of time occurred in the Works'.[40] The company's senior management rebutted these allegations and, though it was recognized that the Ministry might make it difficult for Rovers to recruit additional labour, there appears to have been no immediate sense of alarm, merely a feeling of irritation. In practice, Rover's management fully appreciated that the Ministry of Labour, or any other government department, could ill afford to take punitive action against one of the key partners in the shadow factory project.

Government control over the size and employment distribution of the workforce gradually increased following Ernest Bevin's appointment as Minister of Labour in May 1940. Although the effectiveness of the Ministry's initiatives varied over time and between different firms and sectors of industry, its influence in the Midlands was potentially very significant because of the region's heavy concentration of engineering employment and tight labour market. Surprisingly, the machine tool industry in general seems to have been relatively disadvantaged in terms of labour allocation. This was reflected locally in the problems experienced by Herberts in Coventry where, it was claimed, production was consistently held back by labour shortages. As early as November 1939 it was noted that the firm's main 'bottle neck is the shortage of labour and that dilution, which would be of great help to us is very much hampered by the government and our agreements with the unions'.[41] These comments were principally concerned with the employment of females but, although the firm soon began to recruit more women, it remained plagued by labour shortages and by May of the following year was forced to resort to sandwich board advertising in neighbouring towns as a way of attracting additional workers. Despite promises of labour priority, Herberts do not appear to have received particularly favourable treatment from the Ministry of Labour. This probably reflected official views on the adequacy of the overall stock of machine tools, though it may also have been an indication of the Ministry's assessment of the firm's relative importance within the industry as a whole.

When Humber's aero engine repair division experienced a fall in the volume of its work in October 1940, the firm's management did not attempt to hoard surplus operatives but immediately contacted the Ministry of Labour and arranged for the transfer of some workers to employment elsewhere.[42] Such a magnanimous gesture was perhaps unusual and no doubt became even more so as the market for experienced engineering labour tightened. In practice, however, the aircraft industry in the Midlands appears to have been generously served by the Ministry of Labour, perhaps too generously, as the controversy on overmanning, which erupted in 1942/3, suggests. Even so, during the first two years of the war Vickers' works at Castle Bromwich appears to have been handicapped by serious labour shortages, with the management complaining in March 1941 that the Ministry 'have so far not been able to supply us with the types that have been requisitioned'.[43] During the preceding three months shop floor labour had, in fact, increased by 12 per cent, or over 700 workers. By the end of 1941, however, manufacturing labour totalled 7,577 workers, representing a gain over the March figure of only 608 employees. Much of this increase was accounted for by unskilled female labour, though the company continued to complain of the difficulty of attracting women to the shop floor. The situation eased during 1942, though most of the new female recruits were from outside the Birmingham area and were not, it was claimed, particularly well suited to employment in the engineering industry. Indeed, according to Vickers' management, many of these women 'are of a poor type; a

93

percentage of them are really bad and give a good deal of difficulty to our women overseers'.[44] The indifferent quality of some sections of the labour force was not the responsibility of the Ministry of Labour alone, but this reference does illustrate one of the major long-term shortcomings of government in its relations with industry, namely the relative failure to develop really effective programmes of technical training. This issue had been debated within government as early as 1936, but Baldwin had taken the view that the supply of skilled labour was a matter for industry itself.[45]

Despite its relatively wide powers, the Ministry of Labour's ability to influence the local pattern of employment was in reality limited by a range of practical constraints. The high concentration of engineering employment in the Midlands inevitably placed pressure upon the local labour market. This was exacerbated by the creation of the shadow factories and the expansion of other firms in the region following the outbreak of war. In October 1940 the Area Board expressed dismay at the proposed take-over by ICI of Singer's machining shed, mainly because of its implications for the labour market in Birmingham. At the end of the month a letter was sent to the Production Council's Industrial Capacity Committee urging consultations with the board 'before taking such action as was likely to cause outside firms or departments to move into this Area'.[46] Following representations from the Ministry of Labour and the Labour Supply Division of the Ministry of Supply, an attempt was made in the following March to discourage production branches from sanctioning additional plant requiring significantly more labour in areas where employment was already tight, including most of the industrial West Midlands. Control over the siting of new or expanded works was gradually strengthened, but it remained possible for technical factors, or even the whim of influential contractors, to overcome established policy.

The industrial character of the Midland region, with its many thousands of small workshops as well as large manufacturing units, rendered it difficult to exercise effective control over labour recruitment. The Regional Board noted at the beginning of 1942 that it was far from easy to withdraw workers from firms engaged on the manufacture of munitions even though they might have a very low labour priority since inspection of each employer would be necessary and this was simply impractical.[47] The same problem may have worked in reverse when, in the autumn of 1940, a chronic shortage of labour forced Salters, the Wolverhampton-based spring makers, to fall seriously behind on their orders, a situation which took several weeks to resolve.[48] Part of the problem, too, was that in some cases management did not inform the appropriate regional authorities of their particular labour requirements and so failed to receive the assistance to which they were entitled. Technical reasons also explain why it was often impossible for the Ministry of Labour to prevent poaching, or even the casual movement of workers between firms, both of which could disrupt production. Claims of ill health appear to have been commonly used as a device to circumvent the Ministry's regulations on labour movement. In June 1943, for example, Vickers' management explained:

> The standard of male and female labour has steadily deteriorated over the last six months as many of the individuals find movement from firm to firm comparatively easy because their health gives them an ever ready reason for release whenever they are discontented.[49]

From May 1940 the government gradually adopted a more prescriptive policy towards the employment of women in war work and by 1943 the Ministry of Labour possessed considerable powers of compulsion in this respect. However, as we have seen, many women resisted employment in the munitions industries, and Ernest Bevin was not particularly anxious to invoke the full weight of the powers at his Ministry's disposal. In practice, much reliance was placed upon persuasion, particularly War Work Week exhibitions and parades, and similar forms of propaganda designed to strike a patriotic chord among women and generate commitment to the war effort. There were, however, many reasons why women were reluctant to seek employment in the munitions factories, some of which were beyond the influence of the Ministry of Labour. For instance, family commitments were often time consuming and tiring, and militated against employment outside the home. As one female employee at Tube Investments' Aston factory explained:

> I'm going home to do an evening's scrubbing. First, I've got to do my bit of shopping on my way home. I have to queue for it, because they make no allowance for me being in the factory all

day. My two little boys are in school all day. They have their dinners there, and the teacher keeps them till 6 o'clock when I call for them. But I have to get them home and wash them and put them to bed. Then I have to get a meal ready, and there's always some washing and mending to be done every night. I never get to bed before 12.[50]

There was often little alternative to this kind of exhausting routine for low income families, particularly as the policy of industrial concentration took effect, but for those with a greater degree of financial independence and similar domestic responsibilities, work in the munitions factories was something to be avoided. According to one of the Ministry of Labour's welfare officers, different considerations influenced attitudes towards war work among many of Birmingham's middle-class women. In this instance, women were prepared to occupy their free time in a variety of ways provided that they 'did not impinge upon a husband's responsibility to support his family'.[51] In either case, however, it was not easy for the Ministry of Labour to attract women into the war industries without exercising its coercive powers.

Although labour supply remained tight in the Midlands until late in the war, the Ministry of Labour succeeded in restricting the problem to manageable proportions. Market intervention, however, brought costs as well as benefits, with friction between employers and employees being potentially one of the most important of these. By the summer of 1941 the government's limitations on the movement of labour were becoming increasingly effective in the Midlands, generating widespread complaints from the trade unions that 'unfair advantage was being taken of the restriction on the workpeople's right to leave employment'.[52] Conversely, there were allegations that labour was forced into alternative employment, sometimes in other parts of the country. In particular, the suspicion developed in 1942 that workers were being transferred to relatively low wage areas in order to economize on production costs. The resentment caused by Direction Notices was occasionally translated into strike action, and the threat of labour unrest may have been instrumental in limiting the number which were actually issued. More generally, there were complaints that the Ministry of Labour's local representatives were not always able to make accurate assessments of firms' manpower requirements. This was alluded to by the Coventry District Production Committee when it noted in September 1944 that the Ministry 'has made decisions with regard to the direction of certain workers which have not always been in the best interests of production'.[53]

Efficient production demanded optimal utilization of resources other than labour. Responsibility for this rested ultimately with management, though there were a number of important areas of interface between the government and its suppliers. One critical task was to ensure that the existence of spare capacity was made known to the supply departments and to the government's main contractors. This problem was particularly acute in the Midlands because of the region's vast number of firms engaged on sub-contract work where much of the responsibility for placing orders rested with the private sector. The evidence suggests, however, that plant was sometimes under-employed, especially in the early period of the war, because the machinery for linking main and sub-contractors did not always function effectively. This was one of the tasks of the Area and, later, the Regional Boards, but according to the minutes of these bodies they were often not informed of government priorities and did not possess the necessary powers to ensure that resources were fully utilized. As Sir John Nixon, the chairman of the Midland Area Board explained in November 1940, 'he did not know when a particular component was out of manufacture, whether there were adequate stocks of a particular component, or which if any component was more urgently required than others'.[54] This reference also points to a failure to prioritize government orders, an example of poor purchasing procedure which was equally confusing to the regional authorities and the suppliers. Perhaps one of the most important ways in which the Regional Board in particular promoted the employment of resources was through its trade union representatives who in effect acted as a source of information and public watch dog. The effectiveness of the Regional Boards appears to have improved over time as government departments became more willing 'to repose greater confidence in and to pass fuller information to their Regional officers; in brief to extend their delegation'.[55]

The situation in the case of main contractors was rather different since they had a direct relationship with the supply departments. Here, one of the chief potential dangers to the effective utilization of resources derived from uncertainty over the flow of government orders. The problem was not new but assumed fresh importance as rearmament proceeded and more firms became suppliers to the government. Completion of an order was commonly preceded by a lengthy period of intense bargaining between management and the relevant supply department over the nature of follow-up contracts. For example, discussions between the Ministry of Aircraft Production and members of the No. 1 shadow factory aero engine group on a replacement for the Pegasus and Mercury contracts began more than a year before the sanction was due to expire. When the Ministry proposed transferring the group's resources to the manufacture of Sabre engines, its chairman, William Rootes, pointed out that since the jigs and tools had not yet been ordered this would mean a gap in production of several months.[56] In this instance, the Ministry recognized that the loss of perhaps 5,000 engine sets was unacceptable and decided instead to apply these resources to the assembly of Hercules engines. The shadow factory aero engine committee was sufficiently influential to play a major role in shaping government supply policy. The same could be said of some firms and their senior managers. For example, in July 1943 John Black, Standard's managing director, was able to report that 'as a result of pressure on our part' the Ministry of Aircraft Production had modified its position on the firm's assembly of Mosquito aircraft with the result that 'there will be no breaks in production flow'.[57] Where government orders were cancelled or substantially modified it was likely to have been the smaller firms which suffered most as the larger organizations reneged on sub-contracts to help maintain their own works in full production.

Until late in the war, changing military needs and technical factors were usually responsible for alterations to the supply policy of individual departments. Although rearmament brought a rush of orders to the aircraft industry, the Air Ministry anticipated that a number of these would not progress beyond the development stage. As one senior civil servant admitted in April 1940, 'I think it is true to say that we expected at least one of the big bombers to be so seriously wrong that it could never be taken into service, and it was for this reason that they were triplicated.'[58] On a similar note, but much smaller scale, Herberts found their contract for oerlikon shell drilling machines cancelled because of deficiencies in the design of the equipment. Changes in the theatre of war often necessitated technical modifications which could take months to achieve, consuming precious labour and material resources. Like a number of other firms Humbers, for example, invested heavily in modifying the specifications of their armoured vehicles for use in both sand and water, and also to enable them to carry weaponry appropriate to different military conditions.

Readjustment to peacetime conditions was another important area of interaction between government and industry. Although some firms began to consider post-war product development as early as 1941, the need to push resources into the war effort meant that few of these initiatives achieved significant progress. During 1944, however, it became increasingly clear that the industrial war economy would soon experience a sharp contraction as Germany's defeat by the Allies appeared inevitable. This raised a number of financial and commercial issues, but primary concern centred upon the timing of the transition process. In March 1944 the regional commissioner for the Midlands noted that since several companies were beginning to plan for the post-war economy 'some clear direction should be given to firms as to what they could and could not do'.[59] Stronger views were expressed six months later by the chairman of Fisher & Ludlow, who argued that 'we are about to be caught with our pants down; we cannot continue as a race with this "too little, too late" type of planning, which nearly cost us the war'.[60]

The heavy concentration upon munitions production made readjustment a particularly sensitive issue in the Midlands. This was due in part to the need for equity in terms of firms' release for non-war work, but it also reflected the scale of change as radical alterations were made to manufacturing programmes, including product structure. Transition from the assembly of airframes and aero engines to cars, trucks, and other commercial vehicles was a major undertaking. At Austin's Longbridge works 'almost every machine in the factory had to be uprooted; painting equipment, ovens and tracks had to be reinstated, assembly tracks and finishing tracks with miles of conveyors, had to be laid down'.[61] Similar problems confronted the industry's components sector so that, for example, Lucas's chairman reported in December 1945 that readjustment 'has resulted in major upheavals which include structural alterations to buildings, complete changes in layout, extensive re-tooling, and training of operatives'.[62] The region's numerous small sub-contractors appear to have been particularly disadvantaged by being kept 'completely in the dark' over the nature of the transition arrangements as Board of Trade officials focused their discussions upon the government's principal suppliers.[63] This had a ripple effect for, according to Stafford Cripps, one of the reasons for the slow pace of reconstruction among Coventry's motor vehicle firms was the 'difficulty in getting sub-contractors reconverted at the same rate as the main manufacturers'.[64]

The government's cautious approach to the release of firms from war work is partly explained by the problem of predicting when hostilities would end. One senior local Ministry of Production official was said to have admitted in September 1944 that 'military events have moved so rapidly that the authorities have been taken by surprise'.[65] By the beginning of 1945 many firms in the region were still fully occupied with munitions contracts and even the conclusion of the European war did not end the government's ambivalence towards a resumption of normal industrial activity since there was no indication that the Japanese surrender was imminent. It is clear, however, that strong differences of opinion existed between government departments over the timing of the readjustment process. The Board of Trade was particularly anxious to support management in preparing for a return to peacetime conditions. As Sir Percival Liesching, the board's second secretary, noted in July 1944, 'I think we must rally ourselves and other interested Departments to give some sort of lead.'[66] This was not entirely a product of Liesching's prescience for it reflected pressure applied to the board by William Rootes who had apparently become impatient with the 'defeatist post-war outlook and lack of cohesion' of the Society of Motor Manufacturers and Traders (SMMT) and had decided to take the initiative in raising with the Board of Trade the question of when it would be practicable to move towards a resumption of normal trading conditions.[67] Rootes' reputation as one of Britain's most energetic and influential industrialists seems to have unsettled the board's officials for, as Liesching noted, 'I feel that Sir William Rootes is capable of making undue trouble about this.'[68]

During the course of 1944 the SMMT itself became increasingly critical of the government's industrial policy, noting in particular that while Britain's resources were still fully absorbed in the war effort American companies were capturing world export markets for motor vehicles. Yet even when the Board of Trade allowed some resources to be transferred to post-war product planning, many companies remained reluctant to take advantage of this concession. As one board official explained in July 1944, it was known that if the Ministry of Labour's inspectors

> find any skilled labour engaged on post-war work, they will immediately conclude that the employer has got more skilled labour than he wants for his war production, and will remove some workers, as redundant, in order that they may take part in somebody else's war production.[69]

It was therefore argued that the board needed to give more explicit assurances on the resource issue to firms engaged on experimental work and that this required Ministers 'to agree to the principle of a slight derogation from the *overall* war effort'. This suggestion received some support from Sir William Palmer at the Ministry of Production, though he insisted that the board should proceed with extreme caution in order not to prejudice American attitudes towards Britain or to elicit a negative response from the supply departments, which would further retard the readjustment programme.[70]

The provision of raw materials, plant, and labour became a key aspect of the post-war industrial economy which further extended the relationship between government and the business community. Some firms were better prepared than others to manage the transition from war to peace. Financed by earlier investments, Austin was able to allocate £850,000 to reconstruction, while John Black's special relationship with Hugh Dalton at the Board of Trade enabled Standard to secure assurances concerning supplies of steel and light alloy forgings. However, even these firms found their progress inhibited by shortages of raw materials, especially steel. In reviewing progress during the previous year, Austin's chairman, Leonard Lord, referred in March 1946 to the 'long series of disappointments and hold-ups, of struggling for delivery of materials. Week after week our programme was not achieved, and more and more employees had to be declared redundant.'[71] Thereafter, the situation appears to have deteriorated further for in December Lord informed shareholders, 'During the year we encountered every supply difficulty we could imagine, and many of which were completely beyond our conception.'[72] Austin's management, like that of other motor vehicle companies, became increasingly frustrated by its inability to meet growing home and overseas demand for its products. The national shortage of raw materials and plant rendered this inevitable, though there is a hint that political forces may have operated to limit allocations to the motor vehicle industry and retard the overall speed of its readjustment to the post-war business environment. In April 1945 the SMMT informed the Board of Trade that Ministry of Supply officials with responsibility for fighting vehicles wished to prolong their own jobs by deliberately restricting the growth of private car production. Moreover, it was claimed that Vauxhalls appeared to be at the root of the problem since 'they have lent several of their officials to the Ministry of Supply and that, as Vauxhalls are employed on Fighting Vehicles for a long time ahead, the firm is peeved that other manufacturers can go ahead if they are allowed the necessary materials'.[73] There is little evidence to support or deny these allegations, though if they were true they contained critically important implications for the post-war development of Britain's motor vehicle industry.

The gradual contraction of government orders during 1944 brought important changes in the character of labour relations. Working hours, dismissals, and demarcation disputes replaced piece rates as the major cause of dissension between employers and the trade unions. However, anticipating the post-war expansion of consumer demand, many firms were extremely reluctant to release skilled workers. It was also politically expedient for government to assist in the reabsorption of labour into peacetime employment. Official assistance was provided through the manipulation of government orders which enabled selected firms to retain a nucleus of key workers. More importantly, government used its control over the release of raw materials and plant to promote industrial recovery in areas where labour was felt to be a problem. For example, the allocation of production targets to the motor industry in the twelve months after the war was partly conditioned by 'the concentration of the industry in the Coventry area with the consequent danger of unemployment if the industry is not fully occupied'.[74] In practice, the rehabilitation of the post-war economy meant that by the end of 1945 Coventry, like some other parts of the region, was again short of engineering labour. Recruitment, wages, and the maximization of output once more became the focus of labour management, though this time without direct ministerial intervention.

The relationship between government and industry changed dramatically as the war drew to a close. The market economy was restored, though controls of various kinds continued as a reminder of the precedents which had been established during the previous five years. Government intervention had increased the importance of the Midlands as a centre of the engineering industry, reflected by the presence of additional factory space, plant, and labour. Some firms, such as Singer Motors, were saved by wartime contracts, while others were removed by the policy of industrial concentration. New products and systems of manufacture were developed, some of which permanently changed the character of individual firms. For some companies, however, the war was also a time of lost opportunities, as the example of Rover and the jet engine illustrates. Government orders allowed profits to be accumulated, perhaps too easily in some cases, creating a complacency which was ill-suited to the demands of the post-war period. Yet perhaps labour was the main beneficiary of the interface between government and industry for an environment was created which helped to promote a remarkable rise in both real incomes and trade union membership.

5

The economic impact of the air raids

The Midlands experienced its first air raids during the summer of 1940, but from October these increased in both frequency and severity as the Luftwaffe redirected its efforts from London to the industrial provinces. The intensity of the Coventry blitz, which occurred during the night of 14 November, and the resulting heavy casualties and widespread physical destruction, signalled a new phase in Germany's air offensive. It was followed five days later by the Luftwaffe's heaviest raid on Birmingham, involving a force of some 350 bomber aircraft, though the most sustained air attack on the city was reserved for 11 December. As Christmas approached, however, the German bombers extended their operations to Merseyside, Manchester, Sheffield, Portsmouth, and other centres of strategic importance before returning again to the Midlands to inflict serious damage upon both Coventry and Birmingham in night attacks from 8 to 10 April 1941. The last heavy raid on the Midlands in that year was directed at Birmingham on 16 May, after which enemy air activity in general was sharply reduced as defence measures improved and the German war effort turned to the Soviet Union. Thereafter the Luftwaffe returned only sporadically to the Midlands, most notably on 27 July 1942 when Birmingham was the target for the heaviest raid on Britain for many months, so that the main thrust of the German air raids in the region was sandwiched in a period of some five months between November 1940 and April 1941.

The German air attack on Coventry began on 18 August 1940 but this was a relatively modest skirmish and the first raids involving serious casualties did not materialize until later in the month when some thirteen bombs were dropped on Hillfields, which had been the nineteenth-century hub of the city's silk industry.[1] However, the Luftwaffe's real interest in the Midlands dates from October when Coventry was attacked six times and Birmingham eleven, including a raid during the night of the 25th when casualties were exceptionally heavy. Yet it was the 14 November blitz on Coventry which captured public interest and has since been identified as a watershed in the history of modern warfare. Although the raid was principally directed at the city's manufacturing districts, it was also seen by Hitler as retaliation for an attack by the RAF on Munich earlier in the month. The raid inevitably had a profound effect upon civilian life and, according to O'Brien, 'was used as an occasion by the Germans for the coining of a new word, intended to strike terror into their opponents, *Coventrieren* or to "Coventrate" '.[2] The casualty rate was high and environmental damage extensive in what was still a relatively compact city bearing many of the spatial characteristics of its medieval antecedents. The Coventry blitz has also assumed importance because of its technical aspects and the controversy surrounding the British government's degree of prior knowledge of the raid and the extent to which adequate warning was passed on to the civil defence authorities. In the longer term, the raid came to influence allied bombing strategy and, ironically perhaps, elevate Coventry and its new cathedral as a symbol of international friendship and reconciliation. Coventry suddenly became a focus of national and international attention. On 16 November the King, accompanied by politicians and journalists, inspected the wreckage and proffered support in a symbolic gesture of national condolence. As one senior government official later recalled, 'Coventry came into the news as the supreme example of the Huns' barbarity. The city was held up as the example and proof of the proud claim that "Britain can take it".'[3]

The new method of attack employed by the German air force on 14 November involved the dropping of flares and incendiary bombs designed to create fire beacons which would guide the main force to the target zone. At this stage of the war, night flying still created problems for the Luftwaffe so that in addition to the incendiaries a new navigational tool, the Knickebein, was used for the Coventry raid.[4] This was introduced earlier in 1940 and involved the transmission of intersecting radio beams which could be followed by the German pilots. In operational terms, and from the German perspective, the raid was a considerable success. With a clear night and a particularly bright moon, the first aircraft located Coventry with relative ease, their bombs seriously disrupting the city's water supplies, and allowing the incendiaries to illuminate the skyline for the main attack. Altogether some 400 aircraft raided the city for eleven hours, releasing around 500 tons of high explosive bombs and land mines and between 30,000 and 35,000 incendiaries.[5]

The role of the British government, and Churchill in particular, remains the most controversial feature of the literature on the Coventry blitz. It has been asserted that the decrypters at Bletchley Park in Buckinghamshire may have given the Prime Minister as much as forty-eight hours' advance warning of the raid but that Churchill chose to sacrifice Coventry in order to prevent the Germans from learning that their Enigma encoding machine had been broken. In fact, recently released Air Ministry documents indicate that it was not until just after 13:00 on 14 November that Coventry was positively identified as the Luftwaffe's target and even then this was the result of the interception of the German radio beams rather than the skill of the code breakers. It is also clear that Churchill was not seriously troubled by the agonizing decision of whether or not to alert the civil defence authorities in Coventry since a plan already existed, code-named Cold Water, to jam the enemy's transmissions and to attack Luftwaffe airfields on the Continent and the radio station at Cherbourg. Although operation Cold Water was activated, human error rendered it largely unsuccessful since the RAF jammers were given the wrong frequency and so failed to disturb the German radio beams.[6]

The Coventry blitz remains the most highly publicized aspect of German air activity in the Midlands during 1940 and 1941 but other raids were of comparable ferocity and had similarly important social and economic consequences. Like Coventry, Birmingham experienced a series of relatively modest incursions from August 1940, but during the night of 19 November a force of some 350 aircraft dropped large quantities of incendiary and high explosive bombs which affected most parts of the city and inflicted the heaviest casualties of the war with some 400 deaths.[7] Other raids followed, and during the blitz period of September 1940 to May 1941 Birmingham, together with Plymouth and Liverpool, experienced more major attacks than any other provincial city. However, bomb damage varied according to local circumstances and when the Luftwaffe next returned to Birmingham in strength during the night of 22 November some 200 aircraft were said to have caused more disruption than the larger force three days before. Further small scale attacks followed in late November and early December, but on the night of 11 December some 200 German bombers raided the city for over thirteen hours, the most sustained foray of the war, but, although fire damage was well contained, casualties were high with 263 deaths and 245 seriously wounded.[8]

The most concentrated onslaught against the industrial West Midlands occurred during the nights of 8 to 10 April 1941. Coventry was the target on 8 April followed the next evening by Birmingham. The Luftwaffe's opening attack on 10 April was directed at Birmingham, but from around midnight attention switched to Coventry and by the time the bombers left the city had experienced its most intensive raid since the previous November. Thousands of high explosive and incendiary bombs once again rained down upon the two cities bringing extensive casualties, and physical damage to historic and public buildings, and to commercial and residential property. The Coventry and Warwickshire Hospital suffered ten direct hits, killing two doctors, seven nurses, and twenty-one patients, leaving only the out-patients department to function normally.[9] In Birmingham the city centre suffered some of the worst effects of the raids when on the night of 9/10 April a fire at the corner of New Street and High Street spread quickly, engulfing many of the neighbouring buildings. The heat became so intense that 'the very road was on fire and a molten stream of tar pushed its way downhill towards New Street station'.[10] Further destruction was avoided when collapsing buildings created a natural fire break.

Although the air raids were a challenge to the nation's social fabric, of perhaps greater immediate concern to government was their impact upon industrial output, particularly at a time when American aid was still meagre. Coventry was especially vulnerable to air attack for, as the city's Reconstruction Co-ordinating Committee reported in December 1940, 'it would be difficult to find in all England a town at once so compact and to such a degree engaged in vital armaments production'.[11] Soon after the November blitz a government report calculated that one-third of Coventry's factories had been destroyed or very seriously damaged by fire or explosion, though a later estimate for the 180 largest units put the total figure at more than 70 per cent. All major areas of industrial activity were affected. Most of the aircraft plants were hit, though two of the shadow factories on the outskirts of the city escaped altogether and damage to Alvis's aero engine machine shop was negligible. Daimler's No. 2 shadow factory in Brown's Lane was less fortunate, suffering direct hits from two parachute mines which temporarily crippled the erecting and machine shops. Apart from a number of incendiaries, twenty-six high explosive and three delayed action bombs landed on the Hillman-Humber works, demolishing the service department. Rover, Armstrong-Siddeley, Morris Engines, Lea Francis, and Daimler's Radford plant were other important contributors to aircraft production which suffered significant damage during the 14 November raid. Other components of the local economy which experienced serious disruption included Herberts, Renold Chains, the Coventry Machine Tool Company, GEC, and BTH. The raids of the following April again interfered with output at several of Coventry's major factories, including Armstrong-Siddeley, Courtaulds, and the GEC works at Copsewood where work was proceeding on the VHF radio link. Daimler suffered further attacks with a total of fifteen acres of buildings at the Radford works and the No. 1 shadow factory being destroyed. Altogether, some twenty firms engaged in munitions work reported serious damage, though the general impact on production was said not to have been as great as during the November blitz. Experience gained in preparing for and dealing with the after-effects of air raids helped, but in addition many firms had dispersed their activities to other, less vulnerable, parts of the country.

Many of the Luftwaffe's raids on Birmingham were designed to cripple the city's industrial war effort, but the relatively dispersed nature of factory production made this a more difficult task than in Coventry. A number of works in the central areas, most notably BSA at Small Heath and Morris Commercial Cars at Adderley Park, suffered serious bomb damage, but in the outer fringes many of the most important factories, including Austin at Longbridge and Coften Hackett, and Nuffield/Vickers at Castle Bromwich escaped major attack. Around 200 bombs were dropped on the Castle Bromwich site killing at least eleven people, but the damage to machinery and buildings and the consequent production losses were containable. This works was fortunate to have avoided the Luftwaffe's particular attention for, in addition to its strategic importance, the size and layout of the buildings in regular sections bounded by the road network made it easily recognizable from the air. Ironically, the works suffered some of its worst damage from natural forces when in May 1943 freak winds tore away some 200 square yards of the flight shed roof. Fisher & Ludlow, making metal pressings, were less fortunate, losing about 40 per cent of the floor space of their several factories during the raids of 1940. Fort Dunlop was another major target but despite several attacks disruption to output appears to have been minimal.

Table 5.1 Claim by Alvis Ltd for losses to buildings, machinery, and equipment as a result of air raid damage, 14 November 1940

Item	Claim (£s)
Car building	155,768
Repairs to aero buildings	40,000
Plant and machinery	62,520
Furniture, fixtures, and fittings	23,046
Loose tools	20,362
Jigs, patterns, and drawings	11,727

Source: CRO, Alvis Board Minutes, 23 April 1941.

Apart from any destructive impact upon the building stock, the air raids caused valuable drawings and equipment to be damaged or destroyed. In some respects, this had particularly harmful consequences. When the Humber-Hillman works was bombed in November 1940 the accumulated data of years kept by the planning engineer's department were destroyed and it was reported that 'the effect of this will be felt for a long time to come'.[12] Table 5.1 provides an example of the physical damage which typically was sustained by firms throughout the region. Given the acute shortages of the period, the loss of machine tools was a particularly serious impediment to manufacturing output, though the overall significance of this is difficult to assess. This is partly because of the relative lack of information on the extent of the problem, but also because of variations in the degree of loss sustained by different firms. The BSA plant at Redditch, which made barrels for Browning machine guns, was particularly unfortunate when in

August 1940 enemy action caused the destruction of machines valued at £283,000.[13] In addition, the firm's main works at Small Heath was very badly damaged during the night of 19 November 1940 bringing further losses of equipment. Conversely, although the Morris Engines factory was hit during the Coventry blitz, only seven machines were destroyed and a further twenty-nine damaged and, while losses were greater during the raids of April 1941, they were still fairly low so that normal production was achieved within three weeks.[14] Altogether, the 14 November raid immobilized between 500 and 600 machine tools in Coventry factories, the majority of which bore the Herbert marque.[15] These losses and the resulting impact would have been greater but for the transfer of equipment between plants in Coventry and elsewhere, and an active salvage campaign. However, repairs and installation could take many months to complete so that, for example, by the middle of March 1941 Herberts had managed to return only 17 per cent of their own machines sent to them for repair after the Coventry blitz four months earlier.[16] Lessons were learned during the 1940 attacks which probably helped to reduce the impact of subsequent raids. Attempts were made to relocate machinery performing similar functions to different parts of the same factory, while gauges, precision instruments, and plans were increasingly kept in steel lockers or strong rooms. Blast walls and roofs were also installed to protect vital equipment, though these sometimes inadvertently acted as ovens generating heat which damaged the plant. One of the main threats to machinery came after a raid, for if a roof had been blown away the damp night air and rain could quickly lead to rusting. The use of tarpaulin covers and application of bitumastic compounds helped to alleviate this problem, though it was reported in May 1941 that 'Almost as much damage has been caused by leaving machine tools unprotected in the open after damage as by actual blast.'[17]

The level of damage sustained by factories which were hit by explosive or incendiary bombs was influenced by several factors, including chance. In October 1940 five delayed action bombs struck the Riley works in Coventry, two of the bombs nestling in the shop where the layout for Beaufighter undercarriages had just been completed after many months' work. Under conditions of extreme danger, the general manager and a number of shop floor workers spent the night hauling away the valuable jigs and tools until the army arrived to render the bombs harmless.[18] Similarly, during the November blitz a giant armour-piercing 'Hermann'-type bomb, one of the largest explosive devices dropped by the Luftwaffe up to that time, landed in the area of the Hillman-Humber works reserved for servicing Bristol aero engines, but luckily failed to detonate.[19] Rover, a short distance across the city, was less fortunate when the first direct hit on 14 November 1940 demolished the works' fire station. Incapacitated by the loss of three fire engines and other equipment, the company's staff were unable to prevent the plant's largest buildings, which before the war had been used for car assembly, being burnt out. This was ironic since, unlike most other local firms on that night, Rovers, with the Coventry Canal on their doorstep, were not short of water. The raid halted the construction of Albemarle airframes and also disrupted the manufacture of Cheetah aero engines.[20]

A factory's structural characteristics were also critically important in determining its ability to withstand bomb damage. Newer installations, particularly the shadow factories, were built in anticipation of air attack so that fire resistant materials and reinforced walls were normally incorporated into their design. Adequate fire fighting arrangements were also essential in the shadow factories, partly because of the threat posed by the Luftwaffe, but also because of the normal risks involved in aircraft manufacture. Rootes' Ryton works was particularly well served by its architects. Apart from special design features incorporated into the fabric of the building, each machine was surrounded by blast walls fourteen inches thick and constructed to different heights according to the configuration of the equipment being protected. Fire precautions were also extensive and apparently well organized. In addition to a purpose-built fire station manned by twenty-three full-time officers, each principal block of buildings was surrounded by a ring main connected to the works' own underground high pressure water supply and pumping mechanism, which made it quite independent of outside supplies.[21] Similar precautions were adopted at Vickers' Castle Bromwich plant, including high, splinter proof walls and non-flammable roofing materials. These particular measures raised building costs and generated some government criticism, but they eventually came to be regarded as essential by the Air Ministry, for as one official remarked, the works is 'probably one of the best marked down targets for enemy action'.[22]

Ironically, however, the shadow factories largely escaped direct attack by the Luftwaffe so that the efficiency of these and similar defensive measures was never fully tested. In general, older buildings constructed from traditional materials were most vulnerable to blast and fire damage and this was sometimes compounded by a reluctance on the part of management to invest in precautionary measures. Initiatives in this direction sometimes arrived too late. For example, the timber and felting used in some of the Daimler buildings at Radford were replaced by less combustible materials, but only after the works had been seriously damaged by fire during both the November and April raids.[23] Similarly, it was not until after the Coventry blitz that blast walls were placed around the jig borers at Herberts, while the removal of wooden partitions and the final dispersal of machinery around the factory was only completed after the air raids had virtually ceased. Fire was a particular hazard with older buildings but this was sometimes exacerbated by poor management of inflammable substances such as swarf, timber, paper, oil, and magnesium. One of the reasons for the rapid spread of the fire at the Daimler works, for example, was the use of wooden storage bins which burned easily and were liberally distributed throughout the workshops. The dispersal of oil stocks around the plant was not even discussed by Herberts' senior management until July 1941.[24]

The destruction of much of BSA's Small Heath works during the night of 18 November 1940 brought perhaps the most damaging loss of production and personnel from air attack sustained in the Midlands throughout the war period. Most of the casualties were suffered in the main factory which was struck by several heavy bombs. These brought down the rear block, which was six storeys high, the rubble and machinery falling to the basement where a large proportion of the 1,500 work people in the building at the time of the incident had gathered. Apart from the loss of output from one of the country's most significant armaments works, the BSA catastrophe was important because of its impact upon the morale of the company's employees and the Birmingham public in general. According to the City Engineer, 'it was kept very secret by the factory and the Ministries concerned and they attended to the matter themselves'.[25] The news, however, could not be contained and, as one government official noted, the impact on 'the other work people was depressing in the extreme, and rumour as to the extent of the disaster and casualties had a disturbing effect on local and public opinion'.[26] Rescue work continued for two weeks but it was suspected that some of the bodies were never recovered. The older parts of the building dated from the 1860s and the wooden roofs and floors, some of them heavily impregnated with oil, were easily ignited, creating a conflagration which lasted for some twelve hours. The Ministry of Home Security's report on fire damage at the works was highly critical of BSA's management. It was noted that, despite the nature of the firm's manufacturing activities, none of the buildings was installed with a sprinkler system, while the works' fire brigade was undermanned and badly equipped. As one inspector reported, 'It was apparent during my interview that the Management were entirely unprepared for raiding.'[27] It was also pointed out, however, that pressure in the town water main was very low.

The Coventry blitz provides an important example of the ways in which damage to public utilities could influence industrial production. The most serious problem involved interruptions to the supply of gas, which was required for hardening and heat treatment processes. Among the most important firms to be handicapped in this way were Alvis, Riley, Herberts, Daimler, and the British Piston Ring Company. Despite its highly vulnerable location at Foleshill, the city's gas works escaped damage but the distribution network was less fortunate with the mains suffering some 374 fractures.[28] With the help of the Board of Trade, emergency piping was supplied and a number of fitters were drafted in to help restore services; a temporary main was laid in the gutter. However, the work proceeded fairly slowly and it was not until January 1941 that the service was fully restored. Priority consumers, including key manufacturing firms engaged in the war effort, were afforded special treatment, but even by the end of November the daily output of gas was only 8 per cent of its normal figure. Although this was a serious constraint upon industrial production, its impact was alleviated somewhat by the application of alternative sources of energy. The shadow factories, for example, used electric furnaces and also experimented with oil burning equivalents, while within a fortnight of the raid there were some 30 to 40 gas producer plants employed in Coventry factories, including six at Brett's Stamping works alone.[29] In several cases, work which required heat treatment was sent outside the city, sometimes to newly acquired dispersal units, but also to other manufacturers.

Electricity was also crucially important to industry and in this respect Coventry was fortunate since, although damage was widespread, much of it was superficial involving meters and other equipment which was easily replaced. For example, one of the switchboards at Sandy Lane Power House was demolished by a bomb but within days a new one was in place and fully operational. Power supplies to Alvis and Daimler's No. 1 shadow factory were interrupted when a sub-station was destroyed, but again the installation of fresh equipment was achieved fairly quickly. Within four days the city's supply of electricity was back to about half its pre-raid level and by mid-December had largely returned to normal. In the meantime, some firms were obtaining power by improvised means. The aero engine repair section at Humber was able to start work within three days of the raid because electric cables were run to Rootes' No. 1 shadow factory where power was still available.[30] Some jobs requiring electricity were sent outside the city for completion, while once again a priority system was introduced for the restoration of supplies.

Although the reservoirs serving Coventry were largely unaffected by the raid, the main and subsidiary pipes suffered a number of fractures which disrupted water supplies to industry as well as domestic and other users, including the fire brigade. In addition, several hydrants were demolished by blast bombs rendering it impossible to turn off supplies so that hundreds of thousands of gallons of water simply flowed to waste. Like gas and electricity, water was indispensable for many of the engineering industries located in Coventry so that when supplies were terminated or reduced the impact on production was severe. Some firms maintained their own storage tanks which could be topped up from natural or other sources when the normal service was disrupted. At the Humber works, for example, non-drinking water was pumped into the company's reserve tanks from the river Sherbourne, some three-quarters of a mile away.[31] Most firms, however, were highly dependent on the public supply and although this was restored to some consumers within a few days of the attack, it was only at low pressure. Full restoration of supplies to industry took some weeks and was only made possible within that time by the combined efforts of the water department and a team from the Royal

Engineers who together laid six miles of temporary water main.

Transport and communication facilities were dislocated by bomb damage although, with the exception of the telephone network, limited services were restored relatively quickly. Many roads were made temporarily impassable by building debris and bomb craters but clearing up and maintenance operations began immediately and 'by early evening it was possible to drive nearly everywhere in the town'.[32] Yet the tramway was so badly damaged that the system was eventually abandoned altogether and although bus services soon began to be restored there was criticism of the slow pace at which this occurred. The buses were supplemented by a large fleet of RAF coaches and lorries brought in from Cambridge and based at Rootes' No. 2 shadow factory at Ryton. These were important in facilitating an early return to work, but absenteeism remained relatively high for some time, due in large measure to poor public road transport. Many railway lines together with the main station and its sidings were heavily bombed, though it was still possible to travel north and south by using the facilities at Tile Hill and Brandon. This undoubtedly had an important impact on industry for it restricted the movement of both materials and work people. Moreover, the employment of stations in other towns, which could have been easily served by road vehicles, seems to have been poorly organized. The telephone exchange escaped serious damage, though around 75 per cent of lines were put out of action and faults to the system were said to represent the equivalent of three years' normal maintenance programme. Coventry's Reconstruction Committee believed that the telephone service was restored too slowly, noting at the end of December, 'The absence of telephone facilities is an appalling handicap to industry.'[33] Being in the centre of the demolition area, the main post office was unable to function for a week after the raid, though the survival of the sorting office did help to restore postal services more quickly than might have been expected. Mail deliveries were also made possible by the development of in-house company messenger schemes.

The raids on Coventry during April 1941 did not have the same disruptive effect on public services as the November blitz. Fractures to gas and water mains were again widespread but within two weeks both services were virtually back to normal. This was made possible by the rapid mobilization of technical and manpower resources from other parts of the region and beyond. In the case of gas, for example, workmen converged on Coventry from London, Leicester, Nottingham, Hinckley, and Loughborough. In addition, since the previous November more firms had installed their own gas producer plants and oil fired burners and these were said to have proved capable of providing a satisfactory alternative to town gas. Electricity supplies also escaped lightly. According to one report, 'some mains were damaged but were quickly repaired and supplies to factories were restored with very little intervening disturbance'.[34] Road and rail links were also relatively unscathed. A direct hit on a bus garage wrecked 12 and damaged 36 vehicles but replacements were quickly brought in from other authorities. Public transport, however, remained a problem for several weeks because of an exceptionally high rate of absenteeism among drivers, conductors, and maintenance staff. Telephone services were again badly dislocated due to damage to trunk junctions and other equipment which, in the immediate aftermath of the raid, cut off the lines of some 80 per cent of subscribers.

Absenteeism was often quite marked after a raid. The fear generated by the Luftwaffe's attacks encouraged many people to leave both their home and place of employment, sometimes permanently. In addition, when bomb damage caused production to be suspended, unemployment increased and many workers were forced to register for benefit and accept what was often a substantial reduction in income. After the November blitz the number of unemployed in Coventry rose by some 3,000 and at one time over 15,000 were in receipt of emergency benefit. Some employers used production workers to remove damaged machinery and building debris but this was only a temporary and limited expedient and was no real solution to the unemployment problem. These twin threats brought a sharp fall in the city's resident population, though the decline in the labour force was less marked, as female employment increased and more people commuted to work from the surrounding towns and villages.

Reluctance to engage in night work was an aspect of absenteeism which presented special difficulties. The Coventry Reconstruction Committee noted in December 1940 that following a major raid there was a tendency 'to assume that night work is out of the question'.[35] The committee blamed both management and labour for this and argued that the problem could be solved by improved blackout arrangements and a more flexible transport system. The figures for absenteeism at this period are unreliable, though the Ministry of Home Security argued that following the November blitz the level in Coventry was more 'than the post-raid situation really warranted'.[36] However, conditions for night shift workers were especially difficult since the threat of further attack was always present. This appears to have had a severe impact upon production at Vickers' Castle Bromwich works for it was reported in August 1940 that 'the nightshift are in a very nervy state and are not working to more than 50%–60% of dayshift efficiency'.[37] In addition, damage to the fabric of a building could expose workers to the elements and also destroy the factory's heating system. For these reasons, workers were often instructed to report as usual, but in extra warm clothing, and to take frequent breaks for hot refreshments. The Humber-Hillman works was a typical example where, following the November raid, 'Many operators, in the Machine Shops particularly, were working with no roof and no heat except for coke braziers here and there.'[38] A group of about forty night shift workers at the Herbert factory appears to have been exceptionally intransigent, claiming that the firm's air raid precautions were inadequate and demanding bonus payments for time spent in the shelters. This problem was eventually resolved with the help of local union officials, though as late as mid-June 1941, when the weather was better and the air raid threat had subsided, only 55 per cent of the possible night shift complement in the firm's drilling and boring department were at work compared with 80 per cent before the November raid.[39] This and other evidence suggests that absenteeism was more significant and complex than was often assumed and from 1942 it was an issue which the government began to take more seriously.

As the Herbert example illustrates, absenteeism was partly a question of morale linked to employee perceptions of works' security during air attack. Air raid precautions varied considerably between firms, though deaths at work during a raid appear, with the exception of the BSA tragedy, to have been relatively light. The first purpose-built shadow factories were particularly well served by air raid precautions, some of them having deep shelters with direct access from inside the works. As the war approached and resources became scarce, the Treasury attempted to impose economy in this area. At Castle Bromwich, for example, there was strong Air Ministry resistance to the provision of an expensive bomb proof shelter capable of housing the entire workforce, officials arguing that a number of cheaper splinter and blast proof alternatives would suffice. Ease of access and discipline in the use of shelters were also important in promoting safety for they enabled the works to be cleared quickly once the alarm was given. By the time of the Coventry blitz well over 2,000 people employed at Rootes' No. 1 shadow factory could be evacuated to the works' deep shelters in just three and a half minutes. The same degree of efficiency did not apply at BSA's Small Heath plant and indirectly this was one of the main reasons for the large number of casualties in November 1940. As the secretary of the Birmingham Trades' Council later explained:

> The BSA shelters were sited, where, after a warning for dispersal was given, a lag of not less than 10 minutes would elapse before complete dispersal to refuge could be effected. These shelters had been constructed away from the shops on a sloping canal bank and access to the shelters was only possible by crossing narrow emergency bridges. Night shift workers dreaded the crossing and, it is believed, preferred to take a 'chance' in the basement of their workshops, with fatal consequences to them in the raid of 19th November.[40]

In April 1941 eight night shift workers at Alvis were killed when their shelter received a direct hit. In general, however, works' shelters provided a reasonable degree of personal security, though some employees remained reluctant to use them. The general manager of the Standard shadow factories recalled that it was his practice to walk along one of the principal gangways when the siren went in order to give the workers confidence and to encourage them to retreat to the safety of the shelters. He also made a practice during the period of the raids of standing by the main gate when the night shift went on to demonstrate his own commitment to the war effort and confidence in the works' own air raid precautions. There were other ways, too, in which management could attempt to raise morale.[41] In August 1940, for instance, the Rootes' Group introduced an aid programme which was available to all its employees following an air raid. This scheme was fairly comprehensive and included housing and clothing as well as financial assistance.

The relentless danger associated with the air raids appears sometimes to have affected morale in extreme ways. There is evidence that some workers became particularly agitated by the sound of distant gunfire and that on at least one occasion this developed into an attempt to rush the factory gates. Industrial morale was probably at its lowest in Birmingham following the BSA disaster. At one stage the firm's employees took over and controlled the entrance to the factory with the authorities 'powerless to control the temper of the several thousand workers'.[42] The crowd eventually dispersed when an air raid alert was sounded, though a large number of the firm's employees continued to demonstrate their disapproval of the management by refusing to return to work for several days, despite a plea by the company chairman to do so. This incident resulted in an obvious loss to production but it remains unclear how far the labour effort was influenced by this and other less serious examples of worker unease. Any final assessment also needs to include the compensating effect of the camaraderie which the German attacks undoubtedly stimulated in a number of factories.

Morale was also unsettled by the air raid siren warnings for these signalled a threat to both the workers and their families. Much of the impact upon production, however, emanated from factory evacuation which brought work to a halt as the labour force sought refuge in whatever shelter accommodation was available. This was a widespread problem which by the summer of 1940 was seriously disrupting output. Much of this dislocation was in fact unnecessary since the alarm was frequently sounded accidentally or merely indicated the approach of reconnaissance aircraft which offered no immediate danger. Even the Luftwaffe's bombers did not necessarily pose a threat to individual factories since their target range was often very broad. The government therefore made it clear in July that labour engaged in the war effort should remain at work until an attack in the immediate vicinity seemed likely, even though the public warning system may have sounded.

This was a significant shift of policy which changed the balance of interest between production and personal security and was indicative of the gravity with which the issue was perceived at that time. To help protect factory and other workers a roof-watching scheme was introduced with look-outs trained to raise the alarm when danger appeared to be imminent. The new arrangement was of immediate benefit in the Midlands where daylight alerts in particular usually proved of little consequence. After the watcher scheme was introduced the maximum weekly loss of man-hours at the Humber-Hillman works due to air raid warnings was reduced from 30,000 to 2,780, representing a saving of approximately 5 hours a week for each of the 5,000 employees.[43] Rootes' management adopted a progressive attitude towards air raid precautions and it seems likely that at the less well organized firms the look-outs were neither so well trained nor so successful in achieving such large labour economies. It was against this background of growing concern at the general efficiency of the watcher scheme that a supplementary industrial alarm system was developed, beginning first in Coventry.

The new arrangements involved the creation of a bell and, less usually, speech telephone link between the Royal Observer Corps' group centres and industrial and other establishments. This mechanism facilitated the relay of a short, two minute warning of the approach of enemy aircraft, together with a release message when the area was considered to be free from the danger of attack. The scheme was designed to employ the personnel and skills of the Royal Observer Corps (ROC) in strengthening the existing look-out facility and reducing the warning period to the absolute minimum consistent with safety. Coventry was selected to initiate the experiment with a young observer, C. J. Forsyth, appointed as the first regional alarm officer. Forsyth's task was to establish a local alarm network and to train the ARP spotters and also those attached to individual factories.[44] Operations began on 14 October 1940 with fourteen factories receiving the alarm and release signals, and by the following January a further twenty-one firms had joined or were about to join the network, including almost all the major armaments producers in the city. The scheme was soon extended to other parts of the region; when a centralized Alarm Centre was opened in Birmingham at the end of March 1941 it was linked with nine local schemes which included 520 bell and speech links. Three years later the total number of recipients had increased to 1,218 covering some 800,000 workers.

It has been estimated that some 11 million man-hours had been saved nationally by the end of the war as a result of the spotter and ROC warning systems. The savings for the Midland region are impossible to calculate, though they were probably very considerable. The difference between the public alert and ROC alarm warnings in Coventry for the period 14 October 1940 to 4 January 1941 amounted to 8 hours 58 minutes. Since the fourteen factories connected to the network during this period were all very large employers it seems likely that the saving in man-hours was very considerable. However, as Table 5.2 illustrates, there were marked differences in the evacuation times between the participating firms.

Table 5.2 Duration of evacuation, Coventry firms, 17–31 December 1940

	Hours	*Minutes*
Rootes No. 1	16	10
Rootes No. 2	—	—
Daimler, main works	32	15
Standard, main works	1	15
Standard No. 1	1	5
Standard No. 2	—	18
Alvis	—	—
Rover	—	—
BTH	4	1

Source: Forsyth Papers, Alarm Officer's Progress Reports, Midland Region.

It is also clear that many firms in the region did not at first regard the ROC warnings as the signal to take cover, suggesting that in some cases the alarm period was regarded as too conservative. A more sophisticated arrangement providing detailed information on the nature of the alarm would have made it possible to reduce evacuation times even further. The written evidence provided by the scheme's first participants suggests that some firms benefited disproportionately from its availability according to the efficiency of their own air raid precautions and established practices.[45] For firms like Singer and Coventry Radiators without their own night spotters, the scheme appears to have been of very considerable value in maintaining production during the period immediately before and after an air raid. At the very least the ROC presence helped to raise the confidence and morale of both the roof-spotters and the factory workers.

The dispersal of manufacturing activity to less vulnerable parts of the country was promoted by the air raids of 1940 and this was important in adding to productive capacity and also ameliorating the impact of subsequent air attacks in the Midlands, particularly those which occurred in the following spring. It is worth noting, however, that some degree of dispersal was almost inevitable simply because of the region's increasingly inelastic supply of human and physical capital. Most firms were limited to one or two dispersal units, but in the aircraft industry the number could be much higher. Alvis's work came to be spread between twenty or more sites, some of them near to the main factory but others located as far away as Ealing and Maidenhead. BSA operated twelve factories in the region, but this was unusually high for the armaments industry.

Table 5.3 Production of 'Wimet' tipped tools, 1939–44

	Coventry	Total all factories*
1939	156,301	208,635
1940	260,822	323,300
1941	336,007	520,519
1942	446,100	807,500
1943	533,425	936,425
1944	265,713	727,200

Source: Anon., The War Record of A. C. Wickman Limited Organisation, n.d., p. 47.
*The company's first dispersal factory at Ilkley was acquired in 1940.

Dispersal could bring large additions to output, as the Wickman example demonstrates (see Table 5.3), though there were costs as well as benefits, and it is significant that Hornby is rather cautious in his assessment of the overall yield, at least for the aircraft industry. It may be argued that dispersal did not go far enough nor at sufficient speed to achieve a dramatic improvement in the overall level of manufacturing output. Rover's management, for example, became extremely frustrated by the slow pace of development at their underground dispersal factory at Drakelow near Kidderminster which was delayed by labour and building problems. Although negotiations with the Ministry of Aircraft Production began early in 1941, it was not until the winter of 1942/3 that manufacturing began, several months later than anticipated, causing, it was alleged, considerable disruption to the company's planned output of aero engines.[46] Some firms, including Herberts, found entry into new premises delayed by construction problems, but even the conversion of existing buildings could seriously inconvenience the start of production. At the end of 1940 Rootes' management decided to open a dispersal factory at

Pontefract for the repair and servicing of aero engines, but alterations to the building and the installation of new machinery, together with staff training, meant that the first engines were not delivered until September 1941, and it took a further five months for the plant to reach a satisfactory level of throughput.[47] Perhaps it was for these reasons that the Coventry Reconstruction Committee warned against a hastily conceived and executed transfer programme, noting that there is 'no point in moving a single machine which can be worked where it stands until the new premises are in a condition where it can be put to work immediately upon arrival'.[48]

Shop floor labour in the dispersal areas appears generally to have possessed the type of transferable skills which facilitated a positive response to the new working patterns. Similarly, the relocation of workers to a new environment did not generate serious problems, the one notable exception being Alvis in March 1943 when the whole of the firm's aero division was brought to a halt by an instruction from the Ministry of Labour to move some employees to the firm's Mountsorrel plant in Leicestershire. The Direction Notices were withdrawn following negotiations between the Alvis management, officials from the Ministry of Labour, and the trade unions, and work was quickly resumed.[49] The quality of management is another aspect of the labour issue as foremen and more senior personnel were transferred to the new factories or simply allocated additional responsibilities. By 1944 Rover's own payroll numbered less than 4,000 employees, but with dispersal factories and other commitments the firm was responsible for an additional 20,000 workers. The significance of this for management efficiency is impossible to determine but it was certainly an important aspect of the dispersal balance sheet.

It is impossible to calculate the extent to which the Luftwaffe's bombers managed to dislocate industrial activity in the Midlands during 1940 and 1941. This is partly due to the inadequacy of the data but it also relates to the large number of variables which influenced output during the period of transition from peace to war, including problems of labour supply and training, the installation of new machinery and manufacturing systems, and adjustment to the production programmme itself. Air attacks in other parts of the country also created supply problems which disturbed output schedules. Enemy raids on Birmingham, Sheffield, and Manchester, for example, were said to have adversely affected work at Rootes' Humber-Hillman factory for many months after the November and April attacks.[50]

The German raids seriously disrupted production at a number of major engineering works in the Midlands, most notably Fisher & Ludlow, GEC, Daimler, and BSA. Significantly, however, most of the region's aircraft factories escaped the worst of the Luftwaffe's attacks so that the shadow engine and airframe programmes suffered relatively little dislocation and even when bomb damage did occur in this and other industries, work was usually resumed fairly quickly. This is partly explained by the fortitude and ingenuity of management and the labour force, while in Coventry the work of the Reconstruction Committee under the chairmanship of William Rootes appears to have been effective in promoting a positive approach to post-raid organization within both the factories and the public utility services. The air raid precautions adopted by individual companies and the dispersal arrangements, both before and after November 1940, were also instrumental in limiting the physical impact of the German attacks. Yet it remains unclear how far the less obvious features of the raids, especially time lost through alerts and the general impact on worker morale, served to depress industrial output. In addition, Midlands' industry enjoyed a significant element of good fortune since a number of key factories remained largely undamaged during the critical early period of war. These included Serck Radiators of Tyseley who manufactured the radiators and coolers fitted to all the Spitfires and Hurricanes which flew during the Battle of Britain. With better intelligence and more effective navigational aids, the German bombers might have inflicted substantially more damage on the region's industrial war effort. It is also significant that the attempt to undermine civilian morale through the destruction of city centres weakened the effectiveness of the Luftwaffe's assault on industry, particularly in Birmingham where many of the most strategically important firms were located in the peripheral areas. As the City Engineer reported in February 1942, the raids have 'not been concentrated on heavy industrial or business premises'.[51] The geographically concentrated nature of war production, which had been reinforced by government policy, ultimately proved less of a handicap than seemed likely during the latter half of 1940.

6

Civilian morale: did the people panic?

The maintenance of civilian morale was widely regarded as an important prerequisite of a successful war effort, reflected in the survey and propaganda work of the Ministry of Information and other government departments. A variety of methods was employed and agencies were developed to provide for the care and protection of civilians and to influence the trend of public opinion. The physical controls associated with rationing were highly successful in a functional sense and probably also in other ways for they were seen to allocate scarce resources in a manner which was both efficient and equitable. Other forms of control, including those concerned with the media, are more difficult to evaluate, partly because of their less tangible nature but also due to deficiencies in the government's own monitoring procedures. For instance, although some ministries made considerable use of Mass Observation (MO) reports, surprisingly few doubts appear to have been expressed on the validity of the research methods employed or the results obtained. It was recognized, however, that a high level of civilian morale was fundamentally important to the nation's willingness to accept the deprivations which accompanied total war. This was a particularly sensitive issue during the first two years of conflict when Dunkirk and the air raids seemed to leave Britain poised on the edge of disaster. Subsequently, however, attention switched to the problem of maintaining morale during a drawn out period of war. Although six-monthly cycles in public morale were first identified in 1941, two years later officials within the Ministry of Information were still unable to offer a satisfactory explanation for this.[1] Ironically, in the Midlands the run-down of the war economy and doubts over the readjustment process, particularly in respect of employment, came to pose one of the most serious threats to general public confidence. As one Coventry woman commented in September 1944:

> The first signs of unrest on the home front. Coventry aircraft factories are to receive a 25 per cent cut in personnel. There is bickering between the skilled men and the 'dilutees' as to who should be the first to be stopped. They say that married women will be the first. Already one hears rumours that such and such a place have sacked many.[2]

By that time, however, civilian morale no longer commanded the same degree of government attention as it had done during the earlier part of the war.

Government interest in the civilian morale issue was intensified by the Coventry blitz of 14 November 1940. This is partly explained by the city's strategic importance as a centre of armaments production but it also reflected the way in which the attack was used as propaganda to help symbolize Britain's resistance to the Luftwaffe's atrocities. MO's investigations immediately after the raid cast doubt upon this resilience, but these were quietly shelved by Ministry of Home Security officials, mainly because it was expedient to do so. The matter was resurrected some months later but only in the more general context of the long-term social implications of air raids. In 1972, however, MO's report became the basis of a claim that the German assault on Coventry had caused mass panic and a large scale exodus from the city. McLaine appears to accept the broad truth of this argument, noting that there is no reason to believe that similar behaviour did not occur elsewhere, merely that Home Intelligence failed to report it.[3] By contrast, reaction in Coventry among those people who had experienced the raid at first hand was universally hostile. Birmingham and other parts of the region did not attract the same degree of intensive scrutiny, either at the time or since, though there were reports that popular emotions sometimes reached a very low ebb, being 'stretched almost to breaking point'.[4] The purpose of this chapter is to examine the controversy surrounding civilian morale and the Coventry blitz and to suggest that the debate is only meaningful if the issues are examined within their broader historical context.

Public attitudes and emotions were naturally influenced by the confusion which accompanied and followed an air attack. As we shall see in the following chapter, this was exacerbated by deficiencies in the civil defence provision, especially after-care arrangements, and by a general lack of public service information. Each survivor was left with unique memories of the raids, but a number of shared experiences may be identified. Noise was one such phenomenon. The drone of aero engines, together with the accompanying anti-aircraft fire, was usually the prelude to the 'hailstones' of falling bombs and the variety of sounds which followed their impact on buildings, roads, and open spaces. One Birmingham resident recalled that on the evening of 14 November 1940

> The noise of aircraft engines grew louder until the flying squadrons suddenly streamed off towards Coventry. In a matter of minutes numerous flashes from the direction of the city lit up the horizon and the sound of explosions mingled with the scream and rumble of aero engines.[5]

From George Hodgkinson's vantage point within Coventry itself, the bombs pierced 'the air like the rush of a railway train'.[6] The explosive devices brought the crash of falling masonry, and even buildings which were merely shaken by bomb blast suffered smashed windows and torn away roofs. MO believed that one of the biggest tangible effects of the raid on Coventry was the 'astonishing number of houses with no windows'. The crackle of fire was another distinctive sound which became closely associated with the air attacks on Coventry. On the night of the blitz the city centre was turned into a huge bonfire by thousands of incendiary and explosive bombs. The burning of the cathedral came to symbolize Coventry's plight at that time, but many local people were perhaps more affected by their own immediate experiences. For example, the wife of a police motor cyclist described how, during her husband's attempt to return to his station garage, he was forced to mount the pavement outside the Council House because all the buildings on the other side of the street were on fire. She continued:

> As it was he was scorched by the intense heat. He turned down Little Park Street. Bushells was blazing fiercely and he had to ride in the centre of the road and blind through it. The heat was

intense. It was impossible to reach the top of the street as the flames were meeting across the road and the roadway was blocked by piles of bricks and girders. If it hadn't been for Cheylesmore Car Park he would have been trapped, but was able to ride across the car park into Cheylesmore where two more fires at the old Swift Skating Rink were blazing well. From there to Much Park Street to the police garage there were other fires. In fact the whole of this area was a blazing inferno.[7]

The smoke and lingering flames contrasted sharply with the sunshine and frost which appeared the following morning.

The noise of the raid itself was followed on the morning of 15 November by scenes of widespread physical destruction, which added to people's sense of personal and collective disorientation. Around a hundred acres of the city centre was in ruins, including the fourteenth-century cathedral which retained only its tower, spire, and the burnt-out shell of the main structure. Office buildings, hotels, garages, and leisure facilities were devastated, and over 75 per cent of shops in the central area were badly damaged. The familiar landmarks of the Market Hall, Owen Owen's store, the Empire Theatre, and the municipal swimming baths had suddenly been removed from public view. One visitor from Birmingham who travelled through the city two days after the raid recalled that 'the only building of any size standing was the Police Station. Street after street which only a few days earlier had been a busy town centre was now piles of rubble. It was a terrible sight.'[8] The main post office was one of the few public buildings not to have received a direct hit though, according to those inside it at the time, the whole structure was shaken by successive explosions nearby.[9] Over 46,000 houses were damaged, of which more than 2,000 were rendered uninhabitable, many of them in the working-class districts close to the city centre. When Mrs Clara Milburn, who lived near the village of Berkswell, recorded in her diary on 26 November how she still could not bear to face the reality of Coventry's destruction she must have echoed the feelings of many of those who were familiar with the city.[10] Yet the psychological shock of such dramatic spatial change must have been even more disturbing to those people who lived and worked within the city boundaries.

Environmental damage was accompanied by very considerable

human loss, with 568 fatalities and 863 people seriously injured.[11] Moreover, it was widely rumoured at the time that the official death toll had been deliberately deflated in order to disguise the seriousness of the attack, something which was encouraged by the lack of information emanating from the authorities and the media. As one report commented, 'There were many strongly exaggerated rumours about casualties and damage which quickly spread to the surrounding countryside. They are increased by the lack of press and radio news.'[12] This problem was made worse by the city's relatively compact nature which, it was claimed, generated a high level of personal acquaintanceships so that in the aftermath of the raid 'nearly everybody knew somebody who had been killed or was missing'.[13] This spatial consideration and its social implications was one of the principal reasons why MO believed that conversation in Coventry was 'more dominated by talk of disaster and destruction than was observed in Stepney following the blitz on that area of London'.[14] Some members of the general public, as well as the civil defence services, were exposed to particularly horrifying images of death and injury. George Hodgkinson, for example, was deeply moved by the tangled mass of bodies of those women who had taken refuge in the beer cellar of the Motor Hotel, which received a direct hit.[15] The general level of mutilation was high with some 40–50 per cent of bodies being unidentifiable.[16] Private burials, except for those living outside the city, were prohibited, a restriction which caused much public anxiety and criticism. The funeral processions were accompanied by large crowds, which added to the sense of community as well as personal loss, and served to reinforce the psychological impact of the disaster.

Contact with family and friends was made difficult by disruption to postal, telephone, and transport services, adding to the general sense of anomie. MO was particularly critical of the slow pace at which local bus services were reintroduced. It was reported on 25 November, for instance, that public transport remained chaotic and that while the RAF operated a skeleton bus service the vehicles did not follow specific routes and travelled at no fixed times. The same report also referred to the strength of feeling among local residents at the failure fully to restore electricity, gas, and water supplies, which often rendered normally simple activities, like making a pot of tea, complex and laborious tasks.[17]

Sewage disposal was also a problem and one which posed another type of threat to human life. Four days after the raid one Coventrian noted in her diary: 'Still no water. Smells all over town horrid.'[18] Disease remained a serious danger for some time after the raid when, according to the city's Medical Officer of Health, 'we lived on the edge of a volcano'.[19] In the three weeks following the attack some 17,000 people were inoculated against typhoid and the rule that drinking water had to be boiled was not relaxed until the end of the year. More generally, the normal routines of life were overturned by the Coventry blitz. It became much more difficult to fulfil the usual domestic tasks, while work patterns were disrupted and lifelong relationships severed.

The ravages of the Coventry blitz undoubtedly brought extensive emotional and sensory confusion but whether this resulted in a unique response characterized by extreme behavioural abnormalities is another issue. Certainly there were indications of a breakdown in social order. Looting, for example, appears to have become a major concern to the authorities, though some increase in crime was to be expected as partially destroyed shops, factories, and private dwellings increased the opportunity for theft. Much of this was in any case the work of juveniles and amounted to little more than pilfering rather than serious crime, and despite the complaints emanating from some magistrates did not represent a major challenge to the police and judicial authorities. It was, moreover, something which occurred in other bombed cities, including Birmingham.[20] The principal evidence for a collapse of civilian morale is contained in an MO report completed in the two days immediately following the raid. It was claimed that two main behavioural problems were manifest. First, local people were said to be extremely pessimistic in their attitudes towards the city's future. According to MO, ' "Coventry is finished", and "Coventry is dead" were the key phrases of Friday's talk.'[21] Moreover, on Friday, 15 November, the city was said to be in a state of 'unprecedented' depression with the dominant feeling being one of 'utter helplessness'.[22] Second, it was suggested that there were indications of a dramatic decline in personal self-control.

There were more open signs of hysteria, terror, neurosis observed in one evening than during the whole of the past two months, together in all areas. Women were seen to cry, to scream, to tremble all over, to faint in the street, to attack a fireman and so on.[23]

It was also asserted that on Friday evening 'there were several signs of suppressed panic as darkness approached. In two cases people were seen fighting to get on to cars, which they thought would take them out into the country.'[24]

A number of problems arise when assessing the accuracy and significance of MO's claims. There is no indication, for example, of the extent or degree of public hysteria or of the ability of MO's team to recognize its symptoms. Moreover, even the lesser deviations from controlled behaviour, such as panic, may be defined in several different ways which do not easily lend themselves to generalization. Nor was there any attempt to reconcile the fact that in the midst of acute public depression there were 'very few grumbles', no signs of 'anti-war feeling' and 'admiration for the ARP and AFS services'.[25] It is also apparent that a two day investigation allowed only the most impressionistic coverage of social attitudes in Coventry which, although highly compact in its central areas, was characterized by very considerable interwar suburbanization. Similar methodological problems arise when comparing the social impact of the Coventry raid with that in other parts of the country since no attempt was made to form common criteria or standards of measurement.

This study, and a similar one prepared for the Ministry of Information, stimulated extensive debate and criticism within government circles. According to one civil servant, both reports 'are a most extraordinary mixture of fact, fiction and dangerous mischief'.[26] The methodological imperfections of MO's work caused particular vexation, though officials at the Ministry of Home Security were also concerned about overlapping departmental responsibilities since the main report had been prepared for the Admiralty. As Sir George Gater informed Herbert Morrison in January 1941, the vital point is that 'the admiralty has an organisation for reporting upon the work of the Civil Defence Organisation, which works independently of the Ministry of Home Security and of the Regions. Its information is not accurate, and its criticism is often ill founded.'[27] One important implication of this statement is that interests within the Admiralty, critical of some aspects of the performance of the Ministry of Home Security, may have helped to engineer the general tenor of MO's report for one of its chief conclusions was that civilian morale was closely linked with specific aspects of the civil defence after-care provision. Friction of a similar kind also emerged elsewhere for it was alleged that the Admiralty/MO report 'was of the same sort of calibre which caused all the trouble with the Ministry of Information'.[28] MO's activities continued to rankle within the Ministry of Home Security and at the end of 1941 another report, which referred to defeatist attitudes and criticized aspects of civil defence in Coventry, caused further ill feeling among officials. In particular, its research methodology was again questioned, including the failure of its authors to consult with the Ministry of Home Security or regional officials in Coventry and Birmingham.[29]

In his official history of civil defence, Terence O'Brien claimed that while people were stunned by the November blitz their morale remained unbroken. Evidence to support this view came from a variety of sources. The Ministry of Health discovered that the raid brought no change in the number of neurotic out-patients attending Coventry's hospitals,[30] while a report compiled for the Foreign Office in 1941 arrived at a similar conclusion.[31] The conflict of opinion on this issue derives in part from the question of timing. When John Forsyth, the Royal Observer Corps' regional alarm officer, travelled into Coventry on the morning of 15 November he found no evidence of defeatism. On the contrary, many of the surviving shops had quickly opened for business and some displayed notices proclaiming: 'Hitler can't knock us out.'[32] Significantly, too, Forsyth recalled that while some workers were despondent, others were keen to return to their jobs, with the enthusiasm of management often being the decisive influence. William Rootes, for example, mounted a crate in Humber Road from which he urged a renewed commitment to the war effort, an appeal which apparently struck a chord among his workforce. On the following day, Saturday, 16 November, one senior regional official claimed that 'morale is first class',[33] while MO itself admitted that by that time a quiet night and fine weather had 'changed the atmosphere for the better'.[34] The Ministry of Information's intelligence report for the week ending 25 November 1940 noted that in Coventry 'the morale, as disclosed by intercepted telephone conversations, is of the highest order, notwithstanding the town's ordeal'.[35] Attitudes began to change in the following week, however, and it was reported that 'as the shock of the raid wore off grumbling steadily increased. There is a feeling that as soon as things are straightened out another raid will put them back where they were.'[36] The respite from air attack during the early part of 1941 provided an opportunity for relative calm to be restored but the April raids brought 'a definite lowering of morale' and 'much grumbling that the new raids were the result of optimistic press statements after Coventry's first blitz'.[37]

It has also been alleged that many thousands of people fled Coventry after the November raid, some of them never to return, and that this was a further important indication of a collapse in civilian morale. The city's population did fall after the raid, though it is not possible to say by how many. Some outward migration was to be expected following such a major attack, particularly since bomb damage to factories caused a temporary rise in unemployment, while the high number of migrant workers was likely to have given Coventry a potentially mobile population. Clearly, too, some people whose homes had been destroyed, or who were simply alarmed at the prospect of further heavy raids, moved to nearby towns, such as Nuneaton and Bedworth, and continued to work in the city. Others, such as the elderly, who found it difficult to cope with the aftermath of a serious air raid may also have moved for a variety of reasons other than panic. In addition, the raid prompted a sharp increase in the outflow of young children. By December 1940 about 14,000 children of school age had been evacuated privately or under the official scheme and a further 6,000 were no longer in school attendance.[38]

Nightly trekking, rather than permanent departures, has received particular attention as a measure of the emotional stability of Coventry's populaton after the November raid. Some indication of the scale of this phenomenon is provided by a survey conducted among civil defence and other local officials by the Friends' Ambulance Unit.[39] Estimates of the number of people who slept out varied widely; even so the figures suggest that during the blitz period at least one-third of Coventry's population left the city during the two hours which preceded the blackout. By October 1941 the minimum figure had fallen by almost a third but still represented around 25,000 people. Most of these nightly evacuees took refuge within the small towns and villages which proliferate within a twelve mile radius of Coventry. Leamington and

Nuneaton were the most popular locations, each taking around 5,000 migrants during the period of the raids. In addition, the Warwickshire Rest Centres accommodated almost 7,000 people after the November blitz, most of whom were nightly evacuees rather than the victims of homelessness.

Most forms of public and private transport were employed to ferry the evacuees from Coventry. At the time of the raids the Midland Red Bus Company used every available vehicle to duplicate its normal services to the outskirts of the city where military lorries were deployed to allow passengers to complete their journey. Once the necessary track repairs were finished and debris cleared, local train services were also heavily used, and so too were the roads as large numbers motored to safety. Some evacuees cycled or walked from the city. Perhaps not surprisingly they became the first group to end the practice of sleeping out. By October 1941 private cars were the most common form of transport with a variety of arrangements being devised to economize on the use of petrol. The majority of motorist evacuees after the November blitz were said to be sufficiently well off to pay for a night's accommodation and also maintain their homes in the city, an important indication of the differential social impact of the raids. Many of these people also lived in the more affluent suburbs away from the principal target areas.

At first, few evacuees had prearranged accommodation, some sleeping in cars or even the open air. Others found refuge in rest centres, halls, and churches, while many were taken in by sympathetic householders. The more ad hoc arrangements disappeared fairly quickly and as billeting became more organized it also became more commercial. According to the Friends' Ambulance Unit, 'The emotion of pity does not seem to have lasted long. Some quite extortionate prices are now being charged.'[40] The accuracy and general applicability of this assertion are difficult to gauge, though some evacuees were obliged to return to Coventry because they were unable to find suitable billets outside the city. Part of the difficulty was that local people competed for accommodation with evacuees from Birmingham, London, and elsewhere who added to the pressure of demand and forced up prices. Another aspect of the housing problem concerned the discrimination practised by some landlords. For example, the Midlands' evacuation officer later remarked, 'The main difficulty experienced in the billeting of homeless persons in this region was that of disposing of dirty and ill behaved persons into private houses. Problem cases of this kind were normally sent to communal billets or hostels.'[41]

Sleeping out did not necessarily indicate a panic reaction to the Coventry blitz, and indeed may well be interpreted as a perfectly rational response to an external threat of immense proportions. Moreover, there is no indication that trekking occurred in anything other than an orderly manner, or that it was accompanied by outbreaks of anti-social behaviour. Although evacuation from Coventry occurred on a large scale, it was not a unique phenomenon, nor was it new or as great as some contemporaries had expected. During the raids on Merseyside in May 1941 a total of some 50,000 people were said to have trekked each night from Liverpool, Bootle, and Birkenhead.[42] The situation was different in London but perhaps only because tube stations provided relatively convenient and secure protection. Similarly, although nightly evacuation was less pronounced in Birmingham than Coventry, this is partly explained by the contrasting spatial configurations of the two cities. Traffic flows suggest that residents in the central areas of Birmingham sought refuge from air attack in the outlying parts of the county borough, something which was made possible by its large size.[43] Following the Coventry blitz MO reported that local coach firms had for some time transported people to the countryside where they slept rough.[44] This is supported by the Ministry of Information's intelligence report for the week ending 4 November 1940 which noted that large numbers of Coventrians had already evacuated to places as far distant as Kidderminster and Alcester, as well as nearby Warwick and Kenilworth. It was also claimed that 'about 20,000 people are said to go to the villages every night; many sleep in the fields or woods, and some in cars and charabancs which run special excursions for this purpose'.[45] As one of the country recipients of evacuees from the Coventry blitz, Mrs Milburn noted in her diary that fewer people arrived in her village than had been anticipated and provided for, while the Friends' Ambulance Unit expressed some surprise that 'the exodus had never been as large as had been expected'.[46]

In practice, evacuation, both before and after the 14 November raid, was a wise precaution since as a centre of munitions production the city was always likely to be vulnerable to air attack.

Moreover, the early raids in the summer and autumn of 1940 cast doubt upon the effectiveness of Coventry's air defences. In October 1940 the civil authorities complained that the anti-aircraft guns were located to the east and west of the city while experience showed that the raiders invariably approached from the south.[47] It was also rumoured that during the blitz the guns had exhausted their supplies of ammunition. MO reported that the anti-aircraft gunners attracted little criticism, performing as well as they could with the facilities at their disposal. One Coventry woman, however, took a less charitable view, recording in her diary, 'Out of 500 planes, marvellous overwhelming total of 2 shot down. Must have been an accident.'[48] Questions were also raised about the quantity and quality of shelter provision. Social and environmental conditions in the shelters attracted considerable adverse publicity and it was not until the beginning of 1941 that the local authority began seriously to discuss the introduction of special facilities for specific groups such as families and the elderly.[49] In addition, MO argued in its post-blitz report that more adequate provision of deep shelters would have helped to improve public confidence in Coventry's defensive arrangements. The deficiencies in the civil defence provision which the raid revealed probably had a similar effect in encouraging some people to regard sleeping out as a sensible precaution, while for others it was perhaps the only way of ensuring the sound night's sleep necessary to cope with the rigours of employment in the munitions factories. Following the raids of April 1941 the Ministry of Information reported: 'People were seen going to sleep in feeding centres and in the streets.'[50] Finally, and of paramount importance for many people, trekking was simply the inevitable consequence of the local authority's failure to provide adequately for the homeless.

Despite MO's dramatic assertions, there is no evidence of mass panic or a general collapse of civilian morale following the November blitz on Coventry. Most people were probably deeply shocked, upset, and afraid, and some temporarily lost their self-control, but these were understandable reactions to a highly traumatic experience and appear to have been within the normal boundaries of human behaviour. Soon after the raid the Communist Party's Midlands District Committee published a pamphlet calling for a negotiated peace, but this does not seem to have inspired any marked rise in anti-war feeling. Although Communist Party membership in Coventry increased after the November raid, the absolute numbers involved were tiny.[51] Some factories found it difficult to maintain a night shift but this may have been due as much to workers' reluctance to leave their families alone after dark, and concern over the quality of a firm's shelter arrangements, as any neuroticism derived from the threat of further raids. In general, manufacturing industry returned to production fairly quickly after the blitz and for a time problems of labour relations receded as a source of management concern. Interestingly, too, many workers who formally applied for transfer to employment elsewhere ultimately decided to remain in the city.

One significant consequence of the Coventry blitz was that it helped to promote official interest in the relationship between the Luftwaffe's bombing raids, civilian morale, and economic performance. Apart from reports on individual cities, comparative surveys were used to analyse the combination of circumstances which conditioned the psychological impact of air attack. This was partly because of the implications which could be drawn for the RAF's own bombing strategy, but also because civilian morale remained a problem in Coventry and elsewhere, even after the German onslaught began eventually to subside. Renewed concern over the state of morale in Coventry was provoked by a report emanating from the Ministry of Food in November 1941 which concluded that emotions were at a very low ebb with a high level of social introspection which approached collective paranoia. This report provides a useful starting point for an assessment of the range of factors which over the longer term affected civilian morale in Coventry and by implication in other large cities.

The Ministry of Food's report was compiled by A. Hope-Jones of its Special Enquiries and Reports Branch. According to Hope-Jones, Coventry's status as the first provincial centre to be blitzed had an enduring and damaging impact upon local morale for it created the expectation, which soon proved illusory, that the city would remain in the forefront of national attention. He noted that following the raid of 14 November 1940 Coventry attracted a high level of media interest and was widely used as an example of the nation's courage and determination to remain steadfast against the German advance. The arrival of royalty and leading politicians to view the wreckage and make their speeches added to the drama, but then 'the excitement died down, important visitors became fewer, and Coventry began to feel neglected'.[52] Sir Frank Tribe, Deputy Secretary at the Ministry of Labour, denied that Coventry had been neglected by the government but conceded that this was a widely held view in the city and expressed the opinion that 'it is a pity that it was so much "fussed" over when it was first blitzed'.[53] One senior regional official argued that any disillusionment among Coventry's population derived from the switch of media attention to other parts of the country as the Luftwaffe broadened the geographical bases of its attacks, with the result that people 'may feel rather out of the picture'.[54] These allegations suggest a degree of collective narcissism which is unlikely to have existed but which is difficult to refute. Perhaps the most pertinent conclusion to be drawn from this issue concerns the role of the media, particularly the popular press, in manipulating public opinion, and its potential for the achievement of unintended and undesirable results. Immediately after the raid MO condemned the 'extremely exaggerated accounts of "marvellous courage" etc. put out in the press' and stressed the need for 'immediate and factual coverage both of the damage and of the people'. It was further claimed that 'our evidence shows that the exaggerated treatment also makes people suspicious and has now been done so often that it encourages few'.[55]

If emotions in Coventry became deflated as the city ceased to be a focus of national interest this must have been compounded by the images of physical decay, which in many cases continued into the post-war period, and by the shanty town atmosphere created by the caravans and other forms of temporary accommodation which sprang up to house the homeless. An equally depressing sight must have been the brown paper which was used to cover blown out windows when other more permanent boarding materials ran out, and which 'was sodden and lying in the road by Saturday morning'.[56] Hope-Jones reported, 'The centre of the city is a depressing place, it was the only important shopping centre in Coventry, and it now presents a spectacle of gloom, which must have a bad psychological effect on the inhabitants.'[57] A senior regional official added that Coventry's bomb sites had not been properly cleared and that this, too, undermined civilian morale. Health also continued to be put at risk by environmental damage and by September 1943 there were widespread complaints of vermin in the city.[58] Labour shortages rendered it difficult to clear bomb sites, let alone contemplate a major rebuilding programme. However, the impression persists that more ought to have been achieved by the central and local authorities in removing debris and encouraging the erection of further shopping and other public facilities. Even small initiatives, such as the removal of pre-war notices which continued to tug at people's emotions until late in the war, could have had a favourable impact upon public attitudes.

A related problem identified by Hope-Jones concerned the extent to which the air raids had reduced the availability of leisure pursuits. He noted that Coventry had few organized entertainments and, although the cinemas were still open, performances were restricted to certain hours. Many of the pubs had been destroyed in the blitz and there was in any case a shortage of beer to be consumed. Sir Frank Tribe also recognized that opportunities for relaxation were at a premium in Coventry, though he claimed that the Ministry of Labour's local officer was attempting to promote works based sports and entertainments, pointing out that ENSA concerts had already been held in forty-two local factories. In Birmingham, the council sponsored variety shows, band concerts, and plays but the local authority in Coventry made no similar effort to tackle the leisure-time issue. Yet MO's report on Tube Investments' Aston factory in 1942 suggested that many of the firm's female workers perceived Birmingham to be rather dull, preferring instead an occasional outing to the nearby Aston Hippodrome. This was probably explained by the inconvenience of travelling to the city centre, especially after a long and tiring day's work, as well as the paucity of the entertainment.

The Hope-Jones report was prompted by concern over shopping difficulties in Coventry, especially with regard to food. In part, this involved the overall level of stocks in the city, but it also encompassed the broader question of shopping practices among female munitions workers. Hope-Jones concluded that Coventry did not qualify for special treatment since it received its appropriate allocation of rationed foods, while in his view those not on ration were readily available in the city. He admitted that long hours of work created a shopping problem for many women but argued that any increase in temporary food stores would only promote further unrest since it would not lead to a corresponding rise in total supplies. For Hope-Jones the problem was primarily one of improving morale: 'the basic need called for by the situation is that of brightening up life in Coventry.'[59] The shopping issue was thus viewed as largely beyond the scope of the Ministry of Food since it was merely another expression of the public's low psychological condition.

The view among regional officials was that in comparison with other Midland cities Coventry was particularly well provisioned and that it also benefited from several factory and other canteens which contributed significant additional food supplies. There was, however, a shopping problem in the sense that pay day generated long queues, especially at food shops. This was mainly attributable to the large number of working women in the city whose shopping was necessarily concentrated in the limited free time available to them at the end of the week. It was also exacerbated by the diminution in the number of retail outlets following the November blitz and by restricted bus services, caused in part by conductresses absenting themselves from work in order to do the family shopping. The relatively high level of absenteeism among the city's female munitions workers appears to have been closely related to the shopping problem, a connection which was recognized by those employers who made special arrangements to allow women time off to complete their weekly purchases.

In practice, the shopping issue and its relationship to civilian morale reached beyond the availability of food, and the logistics of obtaining it, to include the more general question of frustrated consumerism. MO's enquiries among Coventry retailers in November 1941 revealed that the level of demand for some goods remained exceptionally strong. Products with a relatively high income elasticity of demand, such as books and jewellery, sold well, while a local tobacconist reported long queues outside his premises, opining, 'I suppose people smoke more at night times because they have nothing else to do.' Despite increases in the price of admission, cinema audiences reached pre-war levels and, according to one theatre manager, 'It doesn't seem to matter what we show – they don't seem to mind what they see so long as it is a film.' Much of this expenditure was generated by women munitions workers who, for example, were said to represent a large part of the custom for hairdressing services. There was, however, much frustration caused by supply deficiencies. One chemist reported that 'people are ruder than they used to be before the war. They don't seem to understand that we can't get the supplies for them', adding that 'they would pay anything for the stuff if we could get it'. This last sentiment was echoed by the jeweller who pointed out, 'We can sell whatever we get.'[60] At the root of the shopping problem in Coventry was the high level of earnings obtained by a substantial proportion of the working population, combined with an exceptionally low propensity to save and limited outlets for expenditure. As Hope-Jones noted:

> The Coventry worker has a great deal of money in his pockets, with no more opportunity than anyone else to satisfy his desires. Rationing operates and price control prevents the best known symptoms of the inflationary disease from appearing but the social pressures set up in Coventry are, nevertheless, the result of an inflationary condition.[61]

High wartime incomes helped to reinforce the materialist culture which had developed during the 1930s when Coventry's economy boomed. Although the city was affected by the onset of the world depression in 1929, its impact was relatively mild and by the mid-1930s the growth of the motor vehicle, aircraft, and engineering industries meant that unemployment was low and wages exceptionally high. This was likely to have stimulated people's material expectations, but it is also possible that it helped to increase the level of shock when the blitz interrupted normal economic and social routines. One MO report prepared for the Admiralty claimed that following the raids of December 1940 morale in Liverpool was surprisingly high and attributed this in large measure to the 'peacetime conditioning of toughness and hardness' caused by unemployment and poverty.[62] It was also argued that this resilience to adversity was reinforced by Liverpool's seafaring traditions. The validity of these comments and their implications for the situation in Coventry are impossible to assess, particularly since many of that city's inhabitants had migrated from relatively depressed areas such as Merseyside. It is also worth remembering that Liverpool's high percentage of Catholics probably helped to give the city a distinctive element of familial support.

However, MO's investigators drew a number of other conclusions which have clear relevance to Coventry. For example, it was noted that morale in Liverpool was helped by the fact that the city's public utilities remained relatively untouched by the raids. This, of course, contrasted sharply with the dramatic fall in the availability and quality of most public services in Coventry following the November blitz. Another important point of comparison between the two cities is that, unlike Coventry, Liverpool's streets were often crowded with soldiers and sailors whose very presence was said to spread cheerfulness and confidence among local people. Significantly, perhaps, Hope-Jones noted in November 1941 that in Coventry one saw few uniforms, no bands or parades, and no recruiting drives. Interestingly, an event of this type was in fact held later that month which included a procession with a military band, tanks, and armoured cars, but although this excited considerable interest there 'was no cheering'.[63] MO also recognized that bomb damage in Liverpool was geographically less concentrated than in many other cities and that this too was a significant factor in the maintenance of public morale. In contrasting the impact of the air raids upon Hull and Birmingham, another report a year later drew a similar conclusion when it emphasized the importance of physical size, noting that larger towns had a greater capacity for absorbing damage 'so that the effect on the life of the population is minimised'.[64]

Despite its methodological limitations, the Liverpool study is valuable in highlighting the relationship between a city's broad social and economic profile and the impact of air raids upon civilian morale. Housing and education were two issues of particular relevance to Coventry since the raids severely compounded what were already major social problems. Coventry's population increased by over 57,000 during the 1930s, stimulated in particular by a sharp influx of migrant workers attracted by employment in the expanding industries. House building proceeded rapidly during this period, especially from 1934, but even so demand consistently outstripped supply and the accommodation problem was said to have become an important factor in limiting the city's population growth. The housing shortage was exacerbated after 1939 by further increases in migration and wartime limitations upon building activity. The pressure of demand also helped to force up the price of accommodation, disadvantaging workers on relatively low incomes. Wages in the drop forging industry, for example, were lower than those found in the engineering and aircraft factories so drop forging workers often found it difficult to secure accommodation at a price they could afford, leading in 1942 to the opening of special hostels in Coventry, Birmingham, and Kidderminster. These problems were made worse by the destructive impact of the Coventry blitz. Significantly, the report on the Birmingham and Hull raids, referred to earlier, emphasized that damage to the housing stock was of primary importance in the relationship between air attack and civilian morale.

The availability and quality of housing was a special problem for migrant workers. One recruit to the Daimler works in Coventry recalled:

> I was in several digs there. One I stayed in was of a poor family and very dirty. The only thing I liked about it was the old man who was a good draughts player, and we played almost every night with him puffing away at a dirty little old pipe. . . . Well. I caught a bad illness at this lodging and found I'd got Rheumatic Fever – at least the doctor said they were the symptoms – and told me to get out of that house as soon as possible. He knew them.[65]

In the most extreme cases, the overcrowding problem caused beds to be shared in lodgings, derelict buildings to be brought into use, and a variety of other, even less comfortable, makeshift arrangements to be employed. Accommodating the young women migrants who arrived in the Midlands to work in the munitions and related industries raised special problems. At Tube Investments' factory in Aston it was found that the girls had a strong preference for living communally in hostels, the majority of them being 'discontented and unhappy' in their private billets.[66] Migrants of both sexes were in any case likely to experience a strong sense of disorientation, at least until they became more settled in their new environment, and housing was one of the key variables which played upon this.

Education was a special problem in Coventry during the interwar period, again related in large measure to the influx of new workers and their families. As one HMI noted in 1938, 'the rapid growth and development of the City made the P.E.S. accm. problems bewilderingly complex'.[67] As in other major cities, evacuation seriously disrupted the education programme, causing many parents to become anxious about the welfare of their offspring. In Coventry, however, the quality of the education service appears to have been seriously undermined by inadequate staffing levels caused in part by the city's vulnerability to air attack. Even when this threat receded the local education authority found it difficult to attract and retain staff. Although the authority had a recruitment quota of 38 new teachers for the school year 1942/3, only 17 were in fact obtained; as one Ministry of Education official observed, 'Young teachers avoid Coventry.'[68]

According to the Home Morale Emergency Committee, 'class feeling' was one of the most dangerous impediments to the maintenance of a favourable level of civilian morale.[69] Coventry was the scene of a fairly high level of social tension during the First World War, manifested by industrial and rent strikes, and disputes over food allocations. As Walter Citrine noted in January 1941, 'Coventry was a very difficult spot during the last war and a number of incidents took place there which I think would have been prevented if conditions had been more normal.'[70] In general, however, the interwar period was not characterized by particularly turbulent labour relations. This reflected the relatively slow development of organized labour as well as expanding employment opportunities and rising incomes. The craft traditions of the city's watchmaking and textile industries and the high level of inward migration may also have exercised a moderating influence upon trade union practices, while the local Labour Party provided a vehicle for the expression of political grievances. By 1939 relations between capital and labour were often highly strained but it could not be said that Coventry displayed a high degree of class antagonism.

A variety of other economic and social issues, from nursery provision to the nature of employment, interacted with the November blitz to influence the tenor of civilian morale in Coventry. It was noted, for example, that in the case of Birmingham and Hull, wage levels were a key determinant of the degree of permanent post-raid evacuation, a phenomenon with particularly important implications for Coventry. Although the blitz had an immediate and traumatic impact, it is clearly naïve to interpret public attitudes and emotions after 14 November without reference to the broader framework of historical change. The blitz did not precipitate a collapse of civilian morale in Coventry, but it did exacerbate underlying tensions, many of which remained irritants throughout the war and beyond.

7

The civil defence controversy

Britain's civil defence provision became an increasingly controversial issue during the late 1930s as growing international tension rendered the onset of hostilities more likely. The principal services which would be required in wartime were frequently vilified for their poor organization, inadequate resources, and lack of central direction. The Cinderella status of civil defence during this period reflected the Treasury's conservative budgetary policy but also the powerful interests of the fighting services and the costly programme of rearmament. Many local authorities, while loath to relinquish their particular responsibilities, were similarly reluctant to commit ratepayers' money to projects which seemed to offer little immediate return. Yet air power had transformed the conduct of war since 1918 and Britain's vulnerability to incursions by the Luftwaffe brought a number of important initiatives which by September 1939 had significantly strengthened the country's civil defences. The 'phoney war' facilitated the introduction of further improvements, but when the bombing raids began in the summer of 1940, to be followed by the intensity of the blitz, civil defence soon became a highly contentious and widely discussed topic as its many inadequacies were publicly exposed. Apart from the physical damage, which was greater than expected, the government was alarmed at the threat to civilian morale which the raids posed, but despite further reforms civil defence remained a sensitive matter. This was inevitable since for the civilian population as a whole it was the point at which the authorities responded to external attack, though genuine concern continued to be expressed at the quality of the provision, which remained patchy. The range of civil defence issues was fully represented in the Midlands, while the region's contribution to the armaments industry and its large and highly concentrated population ensured that these would remain the subject of continuing government attention and concern.

As O'Brien points out, civil defence as it emerged during the war is difficult to define because of the scale and complexity of its operations.[1] Its role was most obvious during and immediately after an air raid when the rescue and fire fighting services were alerted by the wardens and the control centres distributed in each locality, but it also included the provision of air raid warnings, shelters, the blackout, and a variety of measures designed to soften the after-effects of an enemy attack. Moreover, civil defence was itself part of a wider protective network which included the armed services, the Home Guard, and the Royal Observer Corps. It was an expensive scheme to operate and to administer, consuming almost £1 billion during the war period, most of which was borne by the Exchequer.[2] At its peak, civil defence employed almost 2 million men and women, over 80 per cent of whom were part-timers, generating a bureaucracy and degree of personal interference which at the beginning of the war in particular often attracted a high level of popular resentment.

The political, social, and economic characteristics of the Midland region, together with its size and geographical features, rendered civil defence a large and difficult task. It was reported in 1939, however, that most urban areas were fairly well prepared for a sudden emergency, with only West Bromwich and Stoke-on-Trent being viewed as serious recalcitrants.[3] The pressures engendered by the outbreak of war, and in particular the bombing raids of 1940/1, showed this to be an unduly optimistic assessment. Inadequate and inefficient services fuelled local criticism which occasionally developed into a more serious confrontation between the public and the local and regional authorities. With the Luftwaffe's attacks in the region so heavily concentrated upon the Coventry–Birmingham axis it was inevitable that these two cities should be at the centre of the civil defence controversy. The points of criticism varied over time and between different services, though at the beginning of 1942 one government report claimed that civil defence as a whole in Birmingham had proved itself badly organized to withstand a sustained aerial attack.[4] More recent comments on the emergency services in Coventry during the

November blitz have also pointed to a state of general unpreparedness.[5] Yet these judgements need to be treated with caution since in practice the level and operational efficiency of the different arms of civil defence varied considerably and should therefore be analysed within their local and regional contexts.

For most people the first indication that an air raid was imminent was the public warning system of sirens and hooters. Many of these were attached to public buildings but in the industrial areas the majority were often found at factories and workshops. By 1939 the system was largely complete in the major centres of population, though it remained imperfectly tested. The reason for this was that, in order to limit the adverse impact upon civilian morale and industrial production caused by the casual use of sirens, pre-war practice exercises were mainly restricted to telephone messages. This lack of practical testing was responsible for frequent technical and organizational failures when the system was subjected to actual air raid conditions, while false warnings and inadequate arrangements for sounding the 'all clear' also stimulated public concern and created further problems for the civil defence authorities.

In general the authorities in the Midland region were relatively quick to establish an aural warning provision. However, wartime conditions soon revealed a number of deficiencies, some of which remained well beyond the blitz period. As late as February 1943, for example, technical problems continued to frustrate the effective operation of sirens throughout the Dudley area.[6] The most serious and persistent complaints emanated from Birmingham. When the city's early warning system was given its first full test early in 1939 many people protested that the sirens were simply inaudible in their part of the city. The first bombing raids in the summer of 1940 provoked similar criticisms, which became linked with a more general attack upon the competence of the civil defence authorities. One report prepared for the Ministry of Home Security noted:

The morale of the population had been disturbed by the ease with which enemy planes penetrated the city defences during the summer months of 1940. These raids, though not considered heavy and restricted though they were generally to the Tyburn Road and Ward End districts of the city, nevertheless revealed certain grave deficiencies in the organisation of the local civil

147

defence services. Bombs were dropped from enemy raiding planes before a warning could be given. This failure to devise an effective and satisfactory warning system of the approach of raiding planes had in turn its repercussion on industry and the workpeople. It was the subject of representations to the civic authorities who in turn addressed communications to the then Home Secretary, Sir John Anderson, and the Air Ministry. A feeling of insecurity and defencelessness was thus engendered, and the failure of the civic authorities to deal promptly and adequately with the victims of the air attack in the Tyburn Road and Ward End districts who were bombed out of their homes, served to undermine the confidence of the people in the administration of their civil defence services.[7]

One specific example of the industrial problems raised in this report came from Vickers' Castle Bromwich plant where in August 1940 many workers were said to be reluctant to operate the night shift because of 'the complete failure of the official system of air raid warnings'. It was also pointed out by the firm's management that 'Each night tells the same tale; hostile aircraft fly over the Factory and bombs are heard dropping in the vicinity before the official warning is received.'[8] Improvements were made to the early warning system, including the installation of a remote control alarm mechanism which activated several sirens simultaneously. However, completion of this work was delayed for well over a year and even then problems continued to persist. In April 1942 a defective fuse caused the total malfunctioning of eleven out of twelve remote alarm networks, while perversely the twelfth gave the alert instead of the all clear.[9]

Public shelter provision was not accorded high government priority during the 1930s. The Anderson shelter, designed to accommodate up to six people, became the focus of Neville Chamberlain's policy of household defence. Alternative arrangements were necessary for the protection of larger numbers of people and for those whose homes were unsuitable for the Anderson, so local authorities were given authority to construct purpose-built facilities and convert existing buildings for public use. The Munich crisis brought a general acceleration of the public shelter programme, with the authorities in Birmingham reacting particularly quickly in selecting and strengthening basements capable of accommodating up to 10,000 people. In addition, some three miles of trenches were excavated to provide further minimum emergency protection for 20,000 of the city's inhabitants. These provisions were subsequently extended and in October 1939 the ARP Committee estimated that Birmingham's public shelters could hold around 90,000 people.[10] Yet by the summer of 1940 when the Luftwaffe began its attack on Birmingham, the council's public shelter programme was incomplete, a problem which grew worse as more people than expected used the communal facilities in preference to their own domestic protection. Moreover, the city had a relatively large number of basement shelters and, while many of these were very secure, some were subject to flooding and gas leaks. Despite these limitations, Birmingham's public shelters appear to have withstood the bombing relatively well. A report by the city engineer's office in February 1942 claimed that a 'feature of the raiding is the extraordinary lack of casualties in public shelters – although many public shelters have had near misses and in some cases almost direct hits, only in two such instances were the casualties more than nominal'.[11] However, a more comprehensive provision of deep shelters would almost certainly have significantly reduced the number of air raid casualties in Birmingham.

The evidence concerning the scale and efficiency of public shelter accommodation in Coventry is also rather mixed. By the November blitz the local authority had provided seventy-nine shelters for public use, just over half of which took the form of trenches with most of the remainder being housed in reinforced basements. Only six surface shelters were available for those people who were on the streets and caught unexpectedly by the raids. According to Longmate, the shelters survived the blitz relatively well and he suggests that had the public not made such effective use of them the number of casualties would have been much greater.[12] Although some direct hits were sustained with the inevitable fatalities, there were also a number of fortuitous escapes. One notable example involved the reinforced basement beneath Owen Owen's department store in the city centre where several hundred people were sheltering when a large bomb descended through the building before exploding on the ground floor. Remarkably, no one was seriously injured.

Despite the apparent success of Coventry's shelters during the November raids, there are indications that more could and ought to have been done to meet local needs. One official report reaching the Ministry of Home Security in November 1940 was highly critical of the relative lack of deep shelters, while immediately after the blitz Mass Observation made the point that 'people would have felt very much better if there had been some way of going underground'. This particular report claimed more generally that 'shelters in Coventry were found to be quite inadequate both in quality and quantity'.[13] It seems likely, too, that the exceptionally high level of trekking from Coventry to the surrounding villages was in part an indication of the public's lack of confidence in the city's public shelters. As the Friends' Ambulance Unit explained, 'it is obvious that literally anyone who could get out of Coventry at the time of the raids did so', adding that not 'even the Coventry ARP officials seem to expect the people to stay in the city's air raid shelters'.[14] By the summer of 1942 MO was able to describe Coventry's public shelters as 'reasonably adequate', though the issue continued to cause concern both locally and among central government officials.[15] Contingency plans were discussed for tunnelled sheltering to the north of the city but the decline in enemy action caused these to be dropped and the problem as a whole to recede into the background of civil defence concerns.

Once the public alarm sounded the air raid wardens were responsible for ensuring an orderly retreat to the public shelters. They also enforced the blackout regulations, administered first aid, and even extinguished small fires, but their principal task was to report the immediate impact of bomb damage so that the authority's Control Centre could alert the appropriate emergency services. The government's pre-war civil defence survey suggested that in general the wardens' service in the Midlands was making satisfactory progress, though it remained handicapped by a shortage of full-time personnel. The organization of this service was necessarily complex. The scheme approved in Coventry in March 1937, for example, divided the city into six zones covering a total of 412 wardens' posts, with the Control Centre located beneath the Council House. Similar plans for Birmingham were delayed until the following year and even then the service operated under a number of important resource constraints. By the raids of April 1941, however, the city had over 10,000 wardens on duty who were said to have functioned very efficiently.[16] At the same period, around 2,500 wardens patrolled the Coventry area and according to the Deputy Regional Commissioner 'their work was done efficiently and without regard to personal risk'.[17]

If the wardens largely escaped adverse comment, the same cannot be said of the rescue and after-care services. The heavy rescue parties had the task of digging out individuals trapped in or beneath damaged buildings who could not be freed by the wardens, firemen, or local civilians. They were mainly labourers or skilled men employed in the construction industry and on some occasions, such as the BSA disaster, were called in from areas well outside the Midland region. The work was among the most physically demanding and emotionally taxing of all the civil defence functions with the crews risking considerable personal danger from falling masonry, ruptured electricity cables, escaping gas, steam, and hot water. Criticism of the Birmingham heavy rescue teams concerned their speed of response rather than their operational efficiency, though it was also said that the latter was impaired by fatigue and inadequate equipment. The central problem, however, was that the service was simply too small to cope with the demands placed upon it during a major air attack, which could involve attending six or more incidents in a single night. As one official noted, even with interregional co-operation 'Birmingham has too few rescue parties for a heavy raid.'[18] This meant that assistance was not only slow to arrive, but efficiency could be impaired because of insufficient rest periods. Following the raid on 19 November 1940 the Deputy Regional Commissioner reported that 'the rescue personnel in Birmingham are suffering from strain caused by having continuously to handle so many mutilated bodies. The men are said to be going "crackers".'[19]

The Coventry rescue squads attracted similarly adverse comment. One official from the Ministry of Home Security reported after the Coventry raid of 22 October 1940: 'The personnel of the rescue squads were undoubtedly exhausted by the long and continuous work of the previous days.' However, he also observed, 'There was apparently no person in charge of the work which was not being carried out on any systematic scheme.'[20] Incompetent organization was again highlighted in a paper from the Regional Commissioner's office following the blitz of 14 November when it was noted, 'Lack of technical direction generally has hindered progress considerably, many party leaders not having any idea as to how to tackle a difficult job.'[21] It was also pointed out that the rescue teams were inadequately equipped, particularly in respect of mobile cranes capable of lifting heavy debris.

The Luftwaffe's growing use of incendiary bombs elevated the country's fire fighting services to a position of particular importance, but the blitz period uncovered widespread deficiencies which in 1941 led to the creation of the National Fire Service. The first line of defence involved the employment of civilian fire watchers charged with spotting and extinguishing incendiary devices. This was a potentially valuable service since incendiary bombs could often be rendered harmless fairly easily providing that sand and water were applied soon after impact. Apart from saving valuable property, this helped to release the fire brigade for other duties. During the April raids, for example, the Coventry brigade answered only a small number of calls in the residential areas of the city due in part to the promptness of the watchers in extinguishing small fires. Yet although in general this part of the fire service appears to have operated relatively well, there were significant weaknesses, particularly in staffing levels. Recruitment was eventually sufficient to provide a reasonable degree of protection – some 31,000 fire watchers were enrolled in Coventry by April 1941 – but to begin with it was held back by the low priority status which the service attracted nationally. This meant that some areas were poorly served by fire watchers including, in the case of Birmingham, the city centre where the Luftwaffe concentrated much of its activity. One interesting side-effect of the local authority's attempt to increase the number of fire watchers by compulsion was to lead 'to a stampede of women teachers from Birmingham' with disastrous results for the education service.[22] Inadequate supplies of equipment, especially stirrup pumps, was another problem which appears to have had a general impact in restricting the efficiency of the fire watchers.

In 1939 most local authority fire brigades were fairly small scale operations which, while normally sufficient for routine incidents, were incapable of dealing with a prolonged attack involving incendiary bombs. The Coventry brigade, for example, coped well with the early raids on the city but it later became overwhelmed by the scale of the Luftwaffe's main onslaught. The Auxiliary Fire Service (AFS) was designed in 1938 to bring the professional grades up to strength through the recruitment of non-regular officers and the deployment of additional equipment and fire stations. Birmingham and Coventry both responded relatively quickly to this initiative, though by the outbreak of war there was still much to be achieved.

This was partly a question of resources. Although it was unfeasible to retain on standby the personnel necessary to combat successfully a major raid, it seems clear that the fire service, particularly in Birmingham, was much under-resourced with the inevitable result that it 'often had more calls than it could deal with'.[23] When trailer pumps were delivered for use by the city's AFS in 1939, they arrived without towing vehicles so that makeshift arrangements had to be introduced to haul them to where they were most required. Apart from exacerbating the general shortage of ARP vehicles in Birmingham, the failure to supply purpose-built machines almost certainly weakened the service's effective operation. Even before the heaviest raids began, a shortage of pumps meant that crews on their way to one incident were sometimes redirected to another, more serious, fire. Staffing remained a major problem, with manpower shortages during the blitz matched only by those which dogged the rescue squads, so that efficiency again suffered as firemen worked excessively long hours in very dangerous conditions, sometimes 'collapsing in the stations from sheer fatigue'.[24]

The Birmingham fire service, like that in other parts of the country, also suffered from poor management. This became obvious during the raids in November 1940, bringing the resignation of the brigade's chief officer. Apart from its organizational deficiencies, the Birmingham fire service was handicapped by the limitations of the reinforcements drafted in from other areas. The pumps were often old, slow, and subject to breakdown, and by the time they arrived many of the part-time AFS crews had to return home in order to clock on for work. Water was another problem, particularly when the mains became fractured by explosive bombs. The emergency tanks installed in Birmingham to provide for this contingency proved woefully inadequate to the demands made upon them. Interruptions to the water supply meant that on the night of 23 November 1940 the city was almost defenceless against an incendiary attack so that had the German air force returned it seems likely that most of the city would have been razed by fire.

During the night of 14 November 1940, and after a brave

struggle, Coventry's firemen eventually lost control of the situation, so great was the conflagration and so inadequate their resources. The main problem was that the water supply failed, though even before that the breakdown of the telephone system made it difficult for the brigade to function effectively. When outside assistance arrived it was found that equipment often failed to match, with some hoses being rendered useless because it was not possible to attach them to the city's hydrants. Yet the organization of the Coventry brigade did not attract the same level of criticism as its Birmingham counterpart and indeed a good deal of local opposition developed in the following year when control was transferred to that city following the creation of the National Fire Service. The November blitz was a disaster for Coventry but it was unexpected, where by contrast the attack on Birmingham a few days later was anticipated and public opinion appears to have been convinced that more effective civil defence preparations ought to have been made. Birmingham was also unfortunate in being subjected to a series of raids in December which stretched the resources of the city's fire service even further. Coventry's pre-war planning appears to have been fairly satisfactory. The AFS, for example, was largely up to strength and had undergone a period of intensive training, while in Birmingham it was not until the 'phoney war' period that the fire service appears to have attained a reasonably acceptable standard. Coventry was spatially and in terms of building construction highly vulnerable to incendiary bombs, but its relatively compact nature meant that resources could be more easily concentrated in particular areas than was the case in Birmingham. It also seems possible that the high number of works' fire brigades, together with the growing roll of fire watchers, helped to limit the impact of the Luftwaffe's later attacks on Coventry.

Many of the most critical comments concerning the civil defence provision in the Midlands involved the after-care services. To some extent this may have reflected people's willingness to attack the impersonal hand of local authority bureaucracy and a corresponding reluctance to challenge the frequently heroic efforts of the emergency services. Nevertheless, the arrangements for tackling the problems of physical hardship and emotional distress which appeared in the immediate aftermath of a raid do appear to have been inadequate in a number of ways, especially during 1940. In particular, there was a lack of information concerning the type of assistance available and its location, and also more general news on the local and national situation. This, it was suggested, depressed morale at the very time that the energies of the civilian population needed to be mobilized for the process of reconstruction. Thus MO claimed that following the Coventry blitz 'Ordinary people had no idea what they should do, and this helplessness and impotence only accelerated depression.'[25] As we have seen, MO also argued that this apparent failure of communications brought some people close to panic, threatening a further escalation of the public order problem and a simultaneous fall in industrial production. The confusion following a major raid inevitably rendered communications difficult, while the security issue was also important. However, the authorities in Coventry do seem to have been surprisingly unambitious in devising ways of maintaining contact with the general public. Perhaps MO had part of the solution when, in reporting on the Coventry blitz, it argued,

> If, on Friday morning, soon after they came out of their shelters, mobile canteens which had been waiting outside the town had come moving in through the streets, with loud-speaker vans giving advice, directing people to the still operating Rest Centres; if there had been social workers with arm bands, moving through the streets giving advice on special points; if the Mayor had got a roneoed news sheet, perhaps only to every fifth household by tea-time – then Coventry would have felt that the experience it had been through was more worth while and one which was directly associated with *winning* the war, instead of continuing it and sticking it.[26]

According to another MO report in July 1941, the view in Coventry was that 'nothing much apart from issuing posters can be done until people have recovered from their blitz-shocked conditions'.[27] A more systematic arrangement for the dissemination of information might well have been a significant contributor to the post-blitz recovery process.

A similar information gap existed in Birmingham and, following the early raids on the city, the issue developed into a highly charged political controversy involving the Unionists and the Labour Party. Harry Wickham, the secretary of the Birmingham Labour Party, alleged that in November 1940 'hundreds of people bombed out from the suburbs and the city and without any knowledge or information as to where they could present themselves for relief, wandered aimlessly round the city'.[28] It was also claimed that the public were not provided with sufficient information concerning the availability of food, shelter, and even fresh water supplies. Local officials were condemned for failing to demonstrate flexibility in accommodating the needs of distressed people. According to one report, 'the offices of the PAC closed promptly at 12 noon on Saturday the 23rd November, and people seeking, but not gaining relief before the offices closed, were told to come back on the following Monday'.[29] In these circumstances, the Labour Party headquarters in Corporation Street were said to have been besieged for several hours 'by anxious people seeking information, guidance and relief from their hardships'.[30] These criticisms probably reflected longstanding political tensions on the city council, but the subsequent improvements to the administration of the after-care services suggest that they were of some substance.

The potential scope of the after-care services was very large and ranged from highly specific needs, such as food and shelter, to less tangible matters affecting morale and mental health. Homelessness was one of the most serious welfare problems which accompanied the air raids. The task of providing immediate relief fell to the rest centres, which were under the control of the local authorities but staffed by volunteers. These centres attracted widespread criticism for the quality and availability of the assistance they provided. For example, it was said that following the Birmingham raids of 21–2 November 1940 'hundreds of people bombed out of their homes who had taken refuge in a rest centre at Garrison Lane, were without food of any sort until 4 p.m. the following day'. Yet perhaps these were relatively fortunate victims of the Luftwaffe's attack since other people were apparently left 'to fend for themselves, finding sleep and temporary refuge in shelters'.[31] During the November blitz the rest centres in Coventry provided a useful service with members of the Women's Voluntary Service and Women's Co-operative Guild dispensing clothing and hot drinks, though efficiency was said to have been undermined by poor organization, including an absence of information on the next stage of the rehabilitation process. The rest centres were intended to provide short-term comfort, but in London many of the homeless remained in them for several weeks. Conversely,

Coventry's population was reluctant to take advantage of the centres, preferring instead to seek temporary accommodation with neighbours until something more permanent could be arranged. The region's Deputy Commissioner expressed surprise that despite widespread damage to dwellings, little advantage had been taken of Coventry's rest centres during the raids of April 1941. Lack of confidence was perhaps the most critical factor in this, for earlier attacks had revealed their vulnerability to bomb damage, particularly since they lacked shelter accommodation.

The effectiveness of the civil defence provision was influenced by several factors but particularly the level of resources and the quality of management. Adequate staffing was a major frustration for all the principal emergency services but it also affected many marginal activities such as fire watching. The pre-war image of civil defence as poorly financed and badly organized deterred many potential recruits but some of these deficiencies were reduced or eliminated when training improved and control was seen to be more effective. For example, the professionalism of the wardens' service in Birmingham appeared to be strengthened when in May 1939 the Chief Constable was allocated overall responsibility for its operation. Nevertheless, the period of inactivity during the 'phoney war', together with continuing shortages of basic equipment, weakened the credibility and status of civil defence, sometimes even subjecting its volunteers to public ridicule. Yet civil defence duties could be extremely onerous, both physically and emotionally, as well as dangerous, and it seems likely that, with the onset of the raids, these considerations also affected recruitment. By the end of April 1941 some 49 members of Birmingham's rescue squads had been killed as a result of air attack and another 252 injured, though the wardens actually suffered the highest number of casualties among civil defence personnel as a whole.[32] Fire fighting was another high risk activity which required volunteers of exceptional character. The dangers endured by the most vulnerable groups of civil defence workers were compounded by staff shortages and poor equipment. By December 1940 the Birmingham wardens had still not been issued with their full complement of steel helmets and respirators 'with the consequence that many wardens were without adequate protection during the severe raiding period'.[33]

In their attempt to maintain or raise staffing levels, civil defence authorities in the West Midlands were handicapped by competition for labour from the region's armaments industries where rates of pay were often too attractive to be ignored. This was certainly an embarrassment in Birmingham where the rescue squads, for example, were consistently under-strength 'partly because of the great amount of munitions work and building work in the Midlands'.[34] Moreover, civil defence and manufacturing industry shared the problem of retaining personnel at a time when an increasing number of men were being drafted into the armed services. In the case of volunteers, civil defence had to compete with other, sometimes more attractive and less hazardous activities, including the Home Guard which in Birmingham was particularly successful in attracting wardens and others to its ranks. The situation eventually became so serious that the city was selected as one of only a handful of areas to receive special sanction for the recruitment of additional full-time civil defence officers.

Inevitably, the efficiency of civil defence, especially during emergencies, was influenced by the long hours worked by volunteers in their full-time occupations. This was a national concern but one which was particularly significant in the West Midlands where the incidence of air raids was high and labour was concentrated in industries where long hours of work quickly became normal practice after the outbreak of war. The ability to respond successfully to air attack was also influenced by the degree and quality of civil defence training. Before the war, this was something which, in the Midlands as elsewhere, was inconsistent, varying geographically and between the different services. Volunteers were sometimes reluctant to participate in training programmes, with older people deterred perhaps by anything which appeared physically demanding. Even the Munich crisis failed to break the widespread apathy towards the ARP which was found in the region's major industrial districts. One probable reason for this lack of interest was the mobile nature of the workforce which militated against involvement in local activities of this kind. The early concentration upon anti-gas techniques may have alarmed some potential volunteers fearful of the type of duties that they would be expected to perform, while at the same time directing resources into what was to prove a marginal activity. More significantly, however, training varied according to the attitudes of the responsible authorities, as the earlier example of the AFS illustrates. Training facilities were gradually improved as the war approached, but as late as March 1942 civil defence personnel in Birmingham were officially reported as having received only a minimum level of instruction. Birmingham later became one of the first cities to establish a civil defence training school, initially for the rescue squads, but this was not until late in the war when the danger of air attack had subsided.[35]

The implementation of a civil defence programme was essentially the responsibility of the local authorities, but the finance and overall pattern of development was conditioned by the policies adopted by central government. Inadequate funding dangerously impeded pre-war preparations for civil defence and even after September 1939 the build-up of equipment and manpower was painfully slow, reflecting the low priority which the service attracted. Even such modest aids as stirrup pumps, used to extinguish small fires and allocated first to wardens' posts, remained in short supply until well after the blitz period. Limited budgets also meant that research and development for civil defence purposes were kept to a minimum so that, for example, policy on air raid shelters suffered from a lack of recent experimental data.[36]

When representatives of Coventry's National Emergency Committee met with the Ministry of Home Security's Parliamentary Secretary in July 1940 they emphasized the highly adverse impact which the city's tight labour market was exerting upon the development of the local civil defence provision. It was pointed out that the AFS, rescue squad, and wardens' service were all dangerously understaffed because of the difficulty of attracting recruits at the comparatively modest remuneration which they could offer, as well as the continuing influence of the call-up. It was also alleged that there was a shortage of raw materials and labour for shelter construction. Although 350 bricklayers were already working on building more shelters, it was claimed that another '500 more are required to complete the programme laid down by the Ministry within a reasonable time'.[37] The Ministry of Home Security recognized that civil defence raised special difficulties in Coventry, but while officials indicated that a plan for compulsory service was under active consideration, they were unable to offer any immediate tangible assistance.

The government's own assessment of the probability of war and its views on the nature of modern warfare also conditioned the local character of civil defence. Pre-war planning was dominated by the threat of aerial attack and was based on the belief that physical damage would be severe and civilian casualties heavy.[38] It was also assumed that the raids would be directed mainly towards London and would involve high explosive and gas bombs. In reality, however, at the outbreak of war the Germans had no plans to bomb Britain, while one of the strategies behind the blitz when it finally arrived was to employ incendiary bombs in an attack upon several key industrial targets. The blitz also proved far less devastating than had been anticipated. Experience demonstrated that arrangements for dealing with fires, the rescue of survivors from damaged buildings, and the after-care needs of blitzed communities were important local authority functions which had been neglected because of the holocaust assumptions which lay behind civil defence planning in the 1930s. For example, Norman Tiptaft, chairman of Birmingham's ARP Committee, later admitted that the number of air raid casualties was far below what had been expected and that practical help for groups such as the homeless was at first inadequate.[39] Rather than arranging for mass burials, the local authorities were more often called upon to alleviate the less extreme manifestations of air attack such as emotional anxiety and disorientation. MO noted that the apparatus for dealing with the very large group 'who are merely immensely upset is, as yet, barely in existence'.[40]

In commenting upon their wartime experience of civil defence, local authority leaders readily emphasized the constraints imposed upon them by central government. Norman Tiptaft claimed that Whitehall officialdom retarded the pace of local preparations, observing in particular that the 'financial arrangements were badly organised'.[41] He also believed that the manpower problem was unnecessarily severe because compulsory civil defence duties were introduced too late. On the same theme it does appear incongruous that the Ministry of Labour withheld its agreement to a substantial increase in Birmingham's rescue service until April 1943 when the air raids had largely come to an end. Perhaps the most scathing comments were made by George Hodgkinson, vice-chairman and later chairman of Coventry's National Emergency Committee, who claimed that 'preparations for civilian defence were a sequence of misjudgements and miscalculations coupled with inertia in high places, of wishful thinking where there should have been practical ideas'.[42] Hodgkinson was particularly critical of government arrangements for protecting the civilian population against air attack, arguing that properly excavated deep shelters provided the only effective security against high explosive bombs. The government's preference for the domestic Morrison and Anderson shelters reflected the belief that the population ought to be dispersed and that public shelters would generate a siege mentality and also create health and public order problems, though in practice policy was also critically influenced by the national shortage of building materials and skilled labour. In reality, however, there was little pressure upon the government to modify its position since before the blitz public demand for deep shelters was relatively muted.

Criticism of government policy and its implementation by such public figures as Tiptaft and Hodgkinson were often soundly based but they also obscure the ineptness and inertia of local government itself. Lack of forward planning, together with poor post-raid organization and speed of reaction, were common problems and appear particularly difficult to explain in view of the government's warnings in the 1930s of the likely impact of aerial attack. Even the respite provided by the 'phoney war' was not used to initiate a general improvement in the level and quality of the civil defence provision and, although changes were made after November 1940, this was poor consolation to those who had already suffered unnecessary hardship.

Several factors contributed to the limited response of local government to the Luftwaffe's challenge. A report prepared for the Home Office in May 1942 identified complacency and lack of vision as key elements in the slow progress made by civil defence in Birmingham up to the raids of November 1940. It was argued that the

> long lull which followed the outbreak of war, together with the favourable geographical position of Birmingham in relation to the actual scene of warfare, would seem generally to have encouraged a false sense of security which reflected itself in the inability of the Civic Authorities rapidly and effectively to counter the initial effects of enemy air attack on the city.[43]

The authors of Birmingham's official history for this period explain this inertia in stronger terms, suggesting that there was 'even hostility' towards civil defence.[44] This, they argue, was partly for reasons of economy, but also because it was felt that Neville

Chamberlain's policy of appeasement would succeed in averting hostilities. Despite pressure from the Home Office, the council's Unionist majority was strong enough to retain its limited perception of civil defence until the raids of 1940 revealed how great the deficiencies really were and helped to mobilize public opinion in support of more positive measures.

The effectiveness of civil defence was also determined by the competence of local government administrators, both elected representatives and paid officers. Although this is difficult to define and quantify, there are reasons for believing that civil defence was sometimes seriously weakened by inept management as well as inappropriate policy decisions. The Hope-Jones report of November 1941 claimed that local government in Coventry was 'a weak and feeble thing', adding that the city was 'not adequately served by its local administration'.[45] It has been suggested that the City Council was hampered by a lack of collective initiative, relying heavily upon Home Office Circulars and Regulations, and certainly the minutes of the National Emergency Committee for 1940 do suggest a surprising degree of complacency and attention to administrative minutiae.[46] It was to be expected that the air raids would place enormous pressure on local authority services but in Coventry the November blitz disclosed such inadequacies that for a time the situation became unmanageable. George Hodgkinson later admitted that 'everything imaginable had gone wrong'.[47] Important civil defence officials who were supposed to be directing operations, including the Town Clerk, could not be located, while deputies had not been appointed to assume the responsibilities of injured senior personnel. Damage to telephone lines caused a breakdown in communications, and without proper support arrangements the ARP Control Room was rendered inoperable. The post-raid situation was so chaotic that it was even proposed that the city should be placed under martial law. This was avoided, but only perhaps because staff from the regional office of the Ministry of Home Security became closely involved in the immediate process of reconstruction. In the longer term, civil defence in Coventry was strengthened by the appointment of a senior officer from the Regional Commissioner's staff in Birmingham.

The effective operation of civil defence was often restricted by weak co-ordination between the responsible authorities. The failure to develop appropriate links between the fire services in different areas was perhaps the most important example of this for it rendered abortive many of the combined attempts to fight the numerous serious conflagrations which occurred in the industrial West Midlands. At a different level, the general introduction of a remote warning system in Birmingham was retarded because of a difference of opinion between the Chief Constable and the local authority. The Chief Constable argued that a fault in the network could activate all the alarms and therefore he preferred the police stations to function independently using the telephone system.[48] The debate dragged on for several months before the Chief Constable eventually capitulated and the remote control apparatus was installed, though, as we have seen, events were later to justify his doubts over the reliability of the technology involved. On a similar theme, the officer responsible for the introduction of the Royal Observer Corps' early warning arrangement for factories found progress impeded by the local authorities' reluctance to devote the necessary resources to its implementation. The early raids on Birmingham drew attention to a number of weaknesses in the local authority's organization of civil defence, particularly its after-care provision. The problem, which again was fundamentally one of co-ordination, provoked such a public outcry that overall responsibility in this field was eventually centralized under the ARP department, with beneficial results. In the Midlands, as elsewhere, the Regional Commissioner possessed extensive reserve powers but these could be drawn upon only in the most extreme circumstances so that both the planning and implementation of civil defence remained largely under the control of the local authorities. Although significant organizational initiatives were taken, particularly the creation of the National Fire Service in 1941, the principle of local autonomy was retained. This was an important aspect of the democratic political framework but it meant that self-interest, both within and between local authorities, was preserved, together with a complex management structure.

Civil defence was sometimes weakened by poor field management. The outstanding example was the Birmingham fire service, particularly before revised operational procedures were introduced following the resignation of the chief officer towards the end of 1940. The November raids of that year exposed several weaknesses in the way the service functioned, including a damaging lack of co-ordination between the brigade and the AFS. The new acting fire

chief recounted that on one occasion a 'serious unattended fire was
in progress in full view of an AFS station, whilst two pumps and
crews were available. The Station Officer in charge said that the
reason why he had not attended the fire was because he had not
been ordered to do so.'[49] In order to help prevent a recurrence of
this and similar perversities, political responsibility for the two
branches of the fire service was placed under one committee, while
the operational chain of command was strengthened and training
methods standardized under the supervision of one senior officer.
Initiatives were also introduced to improve fire-fighting techniques
and to maintain equipment in a better state of readiness. Although
the management of the fire service appears to have been
significantly strengthened by the end of 1940, it remained
handicapped by influences over which it had little or no control,
particularly staff shortages and water supply failures. For example,
it was reported that during the raid of 9 April 1941 'water supplies
were so badly affected that practically all our water for the
numerous fires had to be obtained either from bomb craters, or by
relay work, often from long distances'.[50]

The wardens' service was regarded as one of the best managed
aspects of civil defence in Birmingham, though it too had its
limitations. For instance, one official observer noted how during a
Home Guard exercise 'I stopped by three wardens on a main road
and asked to which district it led and the one very readily and
naively shouted "Walsall Sir".' The same individual went on to
recall that wardens

> were everywhere well in evidence but it did seem that many who
> must have been very close indeed to the attacking force were
> entirely unaware of its proximity. I appreciate that wardens
> represent Civil Defence but in my opinion they should be made
> aware of the presence of the enemy if only to warn house holders
> and to prevent possible temporary panic.[51]

Although it would be unwise to generalize from these incidents,
they do appear to reflect adversely on training, standing order
procedures, and co-ordination between the different bodies responsible for home security. Internal dissension was also said to have
been especially pronounced within the wardens' service. The scale
of the operation and its often stressful nature contributed to this,
though the leadership could also adopt a relatively authoritarian

style of management, as Dick Etheridge, a shop steward at Austin's Longbridge works, discovered when his helmet was stolen and he was forced to sign a letter of responsibility and pay for a replacement.[52]

Civil defence in Birmingham and Coventry exhibited similar characteristics. Much of the emphasis was upon the creation of suitable organizational structures rather than the input of capital in the form of shelters, rest centres, and equipment for the emergency services. The Luftwaffe's attacks revealed the limitations of the region's civil defence arrangements, though it is clear that had the blitz arrived a year earlier the devastation would have been far more severe. The raids of November 1940 provoked a public outcry in Birmingham which led to changes in the city's civil defence services. These developments were not paralleled in Coventry where the political and public response to the early attacks was relatively muted. The Birmingham Labour Party became an important vehicle for the expression of public concern on the civil defence issue, though the frequency of the raids also helped to create a climate conducive to change. Despite the severity of the raids, experience showed that they were not as devastating as had been predicted. This was partly because of poor German military strategy, but it also reflected the ability of even a limited civil defence provision to contain the impact of aerial bombardment. The raids on Coventry and Birmingham demonstrated that with more resources and better management civil defence was capable of providing significantly improved protection for the civilian population as a whole. The social and economic benefits of this might well have outweighed the burden of the additional expenditure.

Conclusion

Regional studies necessarily provide a limited view of economic change. Nevertheless, the example of the Midland region does yield a number of important insights into Britain's industrial economy immediately before and during the Second World War. It also provides some indication of the ways in which the war influenced the shape of Britain's economic development after 1945. The social response to war is in many respects more difficult to evaluate, certainly to quantify, though again local trends and phenomena help to inform our interpretation of the national situation. This study has not attempted to compile a full economic and social history of the Midland region during the war period but rather has concentrated upon a number of themes selected for their general importance and controversial nature.

The introduction of the shadow factory programme ensured that the Midlands was one of the first regional economies to be significantly affected by rearmament. It also represented an important stage in the developing relationship between industry and government, not least in undermining the doctrine of non-interference with normal commercial activity. Significantly, too, the success of the Midlands' first shadow factories served as a model of industrial organization which was emulated in other parts of the country. The regional engineering base responded to rearmament in a variety of other ways so that when the industrial concentration policy was introduced in 1940 it had less effect in the Midlands than in many other localities. Even so, the outbreak of war brought a dramatic change in the region's industrial profile, represented in particular by the switch in production of the motor companies away from cars and trucks, and towards aircraft, fighting and reconnaissance vehicles, armaments, and a miscellaneous collection of military and civil defence supplies. By the end of 1940 the regional economy, at least in respect of Birmingham and Coventry, had become intensively geared towards the war effort. The pace of change varied between industrial sectors and individual firms but this often reflected deficiencies in government procurement policy rather than the inadequacy of management. The principal impediment to change in the early period of war was a failure to co-ordinate effectively the factors of production, particularly supplies of raw materials and, in some cases, machine tools. As the war progressed, however, labour became the main problem, partly because of a reluctance among many local women to work in the munitions factories, but also because of the difficulty of recruiting workers from outside the region who were deterred by its housing problem and susceptibility to air attack.

One of the principal outcomes of this study is that it illustrates the difficulty of evaluating industrial efficiency during the war period. The monopsony role of government removed many of the constraints and incentives associated with the free market so that efficiency depended in large measure upon the discipline and commitment of management. Yet, as the chairman of Lucas pointed out in 1943,

> Whilst every endeavour is made to maintain proper economy of production, nevertheless, the very nature of the tasks, the necessary changes in programme and the whole atmosphere that surrounds control and direction from outside, result in a loss of efficiency as compared with normal business enterprise.[1]

In practice, however, management was left relatively free to organize production on a day to day basis so that some degree of innovation was possible, while the crucial area of labour relations remained largely under the control of individual firms. State bureaucracy was expanded to cope with the demands of the wartime economy but it was neither large enough nor sufficiently interventionist or inflexible to produce a totally regulated industrial sector.

The paucity of the data renders calculations of industrial efficiency at the level of the firm or region a somewhat futile exercise. Simple input–output analysis often reveals little about productivity changes because it cannot always take into account the numerous fluctuations in design and product mix which formed such an important part of the experience of most manufacturing activities. Indeed, in the aircraft industry this was probably the single most important variable which influenced the efficient utilization of capital and labour. Despite their lack of precision, other, non-quantitative forms of evidence do enable some significant conclusions to be drawn on the productivity issue. For example, although manufacturing techniques varied considerably between different firms, within the shadow factory programme an important element of standardization occurred which facilitated a general rise in levels of output. The least efficient firms were likely to have been found among the region's many small sub-contractors simply because of their limited ability to benefit from economies of scale. Even here, however, advantage could be taken of the growth in demand which allowed for more continuous output, while the flexibility of small manufacturing units provided the potential for a rapid response to changes in the government's supply policy.

The supply and quality of the workforce, together with its management, critically influenced the overall level of industrial output. From 1941 until the latter part of the war labour was a relatively scarce commodity within the industrial West Midlands. This provided certain natural limits to the growth of output, but more importantly it forced up earnings which, in some sectors of engineering, appears to have had the effect of depressing worker effort. In addition, many of the new recruits to the region's engineering firms were poorly trained or in other ways unsuitable for the tasks they were expected to perform. Yet these problems need to be balanced against the output obtained as a result of long working hours, the relaxation of trade union restrictive practices, and relatively settled industrial relations. No doubt some workers limited their efforts to the minimum acceptable level but there is no firm evidence that this was common practice in the Midlands, and in reality much would have depended upon the culture of the individual factory or workshop. Interestingly, although complaints of excessive wage levels were mainly directed towards the aero engine shadow factories, the evidence suggests that these undertakings were actually more efficient than the parent companies. Where wage levels were a problem, this was as much the fault of government for failing to come to grips with this aspect of the war economy, as of the trade unions and management.

CONCLUSION

For the Midlands, one of the most obvious economic effects of the war was the expansion of manufacturing capacity, particularly in respect of the shadow factories. By October 1945 approximately 5 million square feet of MAP owned factory space in the region had been taken up by firms exercising their pre-emptive rights.[2] Rovers became immediate beneficiaries, closing the bomb damaged Coventry works and moving to the comparative luxury of their former shadow factory at Solihull, while in the longer term Massey Ferguson, Peugeot, and Jaguar came to occupy premises which had once seen the assembly of Bristol aero engines or Spitfire fighter aircraft. One of the results of this, however, was to accelerate the process of industrial concentration so that the region's economic health came increasingly to rely upon a relatively narrow range of engineering industries. The contraction of the local aircraft industry in the 1960s and machine tools in the following decade meant that by the 1970s the West Midlands was in danger of becoming a depressed area. This was a particularly serious problem in Coventry since the city's economy was more specialized than that of Birmingham, lacking in particular a strong service sector.

Wartime military orders gave several of the Midlands' leading engineering firms the opportunity to gain experience of new engineering processes, engage in technical research, and introduce revised production methods. Jaguar, for example, extended its machining facilities and, with the help of equipment purchased from Standard, began eventually to produce its own power units, thus releasing the company from dependence upon outside suppliers and moving it into a new area of motor vehicle engineering. In some respects, however, the war led to an ossification of the local economy which ultimately exacerbated the problem of excessive product specialization. Relatively weak firms, such as Singer and Lea-Francis, which in other circumstances might have gone down, were supported by government contracts which enabled them to limp into the post-war era. The same could be said of more prestigious companies such as BSA and Rover, both of which were fortunate to survive the 1930s. The motor vehicle industry, in particular, entered the post-war period with a surplus of relatively small and under-capitalized companies, most of which eventually proved ill-equipped to cope with the rigours of foreign competition.

The trade unions emerged from the war in a greatly enhanced position. Membership had increased sharply in certain key industries while organizational arrangements had been greatly strengthened. Compared with the pre-war period, the motor vehicle industry in particular experienced a fundamental change in the conduct of its industrial relations. Influenced in part by their role on the Joint Production Committees, union officials expected to be consulted on a variety of issues, especially the determination of wage rates, hours, and general conditions of employment. The ratchet effect of the Coventry Tool Room Agreement, which remained operative until the early 1970s, exerted upward pressure upon wages, but this was reinforced after the war by the shortage of engineering labour which began to surface towards the end of 1945. The initiative on wages, labour recruitment, and working practices was taken by John Black. Almost as soon as the war ended Black produced a paper on the direction which he felt Standard's labour relations policy should follow. However, because of the company's relatively low level of output, his scheme to simplify wage agreements and motivate assembly line workers through the mechanism of bonus payments could not be introduced until 1948. The new arrangements provided for a reduction in the length of the working week and a substantial increase on bonus payments. As part of the deal, the number of gangs at the Canley works was significantly reduced, while all shop floor workers at the Banner Lane factory became part of one large gang. The essence of this agreement was that the gangs would assume a quasi-management role since bonus payments would be based on their output performance and prices negotiated directly with gang leaders. This arrangement, variants of which were adopted by most other car firms in the area, had a number of advantages for both employers and employees, but it came eventually to attract criticism because it was said to undermine management's control over labour costs and working practices.

The Midlands' contribution to the war effort is perhaps symbolized more by the destruction of Coventry cathedral during the blitz of 14 November 1940 than the output of its munitions factories. The impact of the air raids on Coventry and elsewhere remains a matter of debate, though it is only one aspect of the complex social profile of wartime Britain. However, it is a particularly significant topic since it raises fundamental questions of social cohesion which have important political and economic implications. There is no substantial evidence that Coventry's population reacted to the Luftwaffe's attacks with greater emotion and less self-control than that of Birmingham or any other British city. It is important to recognize, however, that the impact of each raid was not frozen into a short time period but lingered on and merged into a range of other variables which together influenced civilian morale and the public's ability to sustain the psychological traumas of a protracted war. In the longer term the real significance of Coventry's ordeal is perhaps less concerned with the reaction of local people and more with its propaganda value in helping to set the tone of Britain's war effort, both at home and abroad.

Notes

1 PRELUDE TO WAR: THE CREATION OF THE AIRCRAFT SHADOW FACTORIES

1. G. C. Peden, *British Rearmament and the Treasury: 1932–1939* (Scottish Academic Press, Edinburgh, 1979), p. 160.
2. J. A. Cross, *Lord Swinton* (Clarendon Press, Oxford, 1982), p. 135.
3. P. Fearon, 'The British airframe industry and the state', *Economic History Review*, 2nd series, vol. XXVII, no. 2 (1974).
4. W. Hornby, *Factories and Plant* (HMSO, London, 1958), pp. 218, 219.
5. Cross, *Lord Swinton*, p. 159.
6. Hornby, *Factories and Plant*, pp. 220, 256.
7. Churchill College Cambridge (CCC), Swinton Papers, II, 4/3, Progress Meeting, 28 April 1936.
8. CCC, Weir Papers, 19/1, Lord Weir to H. A. P. Disney, 29 May 1936.
9. CCC, Swinton Papers, II, 4/3, Progress Meeting, 28 April 1936.
10. Lord Swinton, *I Remember* (Hutchinson, London, 1946), p. 116.
11. CCC, Swinton Papers, II, 4/3, Progress Meeting, 12 May 1936.
12. CCC, Swinton Papers, II, 4/3, Progress Meeting, 21 April 1936.
13. CCC, Swinton Papers, II, 4/2, Progress Meeting, 21 January 1936.
14. CCC, Weir Papers, 19/1, C. Bullock to Swinton, n.d.
15. Public Record Office (PRO), Air 19/5, Shadow engine group, meeting with Swinton, 29 June 1936.
16. CCC, Swinton Papers, II, 4/3, Progress Meeting, 21 April 1936.
17. CCC, Weir Papers, 19/20, Daimler Motor Company to Swinton, 19 March 1936; Swinton Papers, II, 4/3, Progress Meeting, 10 March 1936.
18. CCC, Weir Papers, 19/15, Notes of a meeting between Swinton and representatives of the Bristol Aeroplane Company, 9 April 1936.
19. PRO, Air 19/5, Swinton to Sir Maurice Hankey, 21 December 1935. For Hankey's reply, see CCC, Weir Papers, 19/20, Hankey to Swinton, 8 January 1936.
20. Swinton, *I Remember*, p. 116.
21. PRO, Air 19/5, Shadow engine group, meeting with Swinton, 29 June 1936.

22. PRO, Air 19/11, No.1 Aero Engine Committee, meeting with Sir Samuel Hoare, 18 April 1940.
23. PRO, Air 19/3, Meeting between representatives of selected motor companies and Swinton, 7 April 1936.
24. PRO, Air 19/5, Shadow engine group, meeting with Swinton, 29 June 1936.
25. R. Church, *Herbert Austin* (Europa, London, 1979), pp. 158–60.
26. CCC, Swinton Papers, II, 4/3, Progress Meeting, 12 May 1936.
27. PRO, Air 19/3, Meeting between Swinton and Herbert Austin, 30 April 1936.
28. CCC, Swinton Papers, II, 4/2, Progress Meeting, 28 February 1936.
29. ibid.
30. Quoted by R. A. C. Parker, 'British rearmament 1936–9: Treasury, trade unions and skilled labour', *English Historical Review*, vol. XCVI, no. CCCLXXIX (1981), p. 333.
31. CCC, Swinton Papers, II, 4/3, Progress Meeting, 7 April 1936.
32. Church, *Herbert Austin*, p. 43.
33. Museum of British Road Transport, Coventry (MBRTC), Rootes at War MSS, nd., vol. 1, No. 1 Aero Engine Factory, p. 1.
34. D. Thoms and T. Donnelly, *The Motor Car Industry in Coventry Since the 1890s* (Croom Helm, London, 1985), p. 74.
35. ibid., pp. 75, 76.
36. PRO, Air 19/3, Report by F. W. Musson, 11 March 1936.
37. Thoms and Donnelly, *Motor Car Industry*, pp. 76, 77.
38. Church, *Herbert Austin*, p. 43.
39. CCC, Swinton Papers, II, 4/3, Progress Meeting, 12 May 1936.
40. R. Church and M. Miller, 'The big three: competition, management and marketing in the British motor industry, 1922–1939', in B. Supple (ed.), *Essays in British Business History* (Clarendon Press, Oxford, 1977), pp. 163, 180.
41. CCC, Swinton Papers, II, 4/2, Notes of a meeting between Swinton and Reginald Rootes, 3 March 1936.
42. Thoms and Donnelly, *Motor Car Industry*, pp. 97, 98.
43. PRO, Air 19/5, Report by H. A. P. Disney, 24 June 1936.
44. ibid.
45. CCC, Swinton Papers, II, 4/3, Progress Meeting, 31 March 1936.
46. Thoms and Donnelly, *Motor Car Industry*, p. 91.
47. PRO, Air 19/5, Report by H. A. P. Disney, 24 June 1936.
48. Thoms and Donnelly, *Motor Car Industry*, pp. 101, 102.
49. ibid., pp. 91–4.
50. PRO, Air 19/5, Report by H. A. P. Disney, 24 June 1936.
51. CCC, Swinton Papers, II, 4/3, Progress Meeting, 12 May 1936.
52. CCC, Weir Papers, 19/5, Chronological note of negotiations with Lord Nuffield, unsigned, n.d.
53. ibid.
54. ibid.
55. PRO, Air 19/1, Statement by Lord Nuffield to the Press Association, 22 October 1936.

56. Cross, *Lord Swinton*, p. 164.
57. PRO, Air 19/1, Statement by Lord Nuffield to the Press Association, 22 October 1936.
58. PRO, Air 19/1, Minute signed by H. A. P. Disney, 28 October 1936.
59. PRO, Air 19/1, A.M.S.O. to Swinton, 29 August 1936.
60. M. M. Postan, *British War Production* (HMSO, London, 1952), p. 16.
61. University of Warwick, Modern Records Centre (MRC), MSS 226/AU/1/1/2, Austin Board Minutes, 26 April 1939. I am grateful to BL Heritage Ltd for allowing me access to these minutes.
62. PRO, Avia 15/3765, H. A. P. Disney to C. R. Engelbach, 24 May 1937.
63. PRO, Avia 10/34, Minute signed by G. Durham, 14 February 1939.
64. Hornby, *Factories and Plant*, p. 256.
65. PRO, Avia 10/34, Minute signed by G. Durham, 14 February 1939.
66. CCC, Swinton Papers, II, 4/2, Progress Meeting, 28 February 1936.
67. ibid.
68. D. J. Smith, 'Shadow factories', *Aviation News*, June 1986, pp. 63, 64.
69. Hornby, *Factories and Plant*, p. 220.
70. J. D. Scott, *Vickers. A History* (Weidenfeld & Nicolson, London, 1962), p. 211.
71. PRO, Avia 15/3750, Sir John Simon to Kingsley Wood, 24 May 1938.
72. PRO, Air 19/1, Minute signed by D. S. P., 26 November 1939.
73. PRO, Air 19/1, Meeting between Kingsley Wood and Nuffield, 12 March 1940.
74. PRO, Air 19/1, Sir Charles Craven to Kingsley Wood, 18 March 1940.
75. ibid.
76. PRO, Avia 15/3750, Air Ministry Report for the Inter-Service Committee, 26 June 1939.
77. PRO, Avia 15/3750, W. L. Scott to A. Dunbar, 26 July 1940.
78. PRO, Avia 15/3750, J. D. Proper to D. S. A. M., 23 July 1940.
79. A. J. P. Taylor, *Beaverbrook* (Penguin, Harmondsworth, 1974), p. 547.
80. K. E. Richardson, *Twentieth Century Coventry* (Coventry City Council, Coventry, 1972), p. 68.
81. G. Robson, *The Rover Story* (Stephens, Cambridge, 1984), p. 38.
82. For the government file on this, see PRO, HO 192/1503.
83. P. W. S. Andrews and E. Brunner, *The Life of Lord Nuffield* (Blackwell, Oxford, 1959), p. 228.
84. Richardson, *Twentieth Century Coventry*, p. 68.
85. PRO, Avia 15/3765, Austin to S. A. M., 16 September 1936.
86. PRO, Avia 15/3765, Austin to H. A. P. Disney, 15 February 1937.
87. MBRTC, Rootes at War MSS, No. 2 Aero Engine Factory, p. 2.

2 THE GROWTH OF MANUFACTURING PRODUCTION

1. PRO, Avia 10/407, E. S. Lewis, Midland Aircraft Production, n.d.
2. For the scale and model distribution of aircraft production, see Hornby, *Factories and Plant*, pp. 395–403.

3. R. J. Wyatt, *The Austin 1905–1952* (David & Charles, Newton Abbot, 1981), p. 235.
4. MRC, MSS 180/MRB/3/3/9, Ministry of Aircraft Production, monthly report, region 9, October 1945, p. 1.
5. University of Cambridge Library (UCL), Vickers-Armstrong, tables showing output of Spitfire aircraft.
6. D. Seward, *'Bomber' Harris* (Cassell, London, 1984), p. 190.
7. Aston University, Rover Shadow Factory Management Committee Minutes, 3 May 1941. At the time of consultation these records were held by the University of Aston, but they have since been transferred to the Modern Records Centre, University of Warwick.
8. MRC, MSS 226/ST/1/1/9, Standard Board Minutes, various dates.
9. MRC, MSS 226/AU/1/1/2–3, Austin Board Minutes, various dates.
10. For a discussion of the Drakelow works, see Robson, *The Rover Story*, p. 40.
11. M. M. Postan, D. Hay, and J. D. Scott, *Design and Development of Weapons. Studies in Government and Industrial Organisation* (HMSO, London, 1964), p. 26.
12. PRO, Avia 15/320, Unsigned minute, 8 October 1941.
13. MBRTC, Rootes at War MSS, No. 1 Aero Engine Shadow Factory, p. 11.
14. MBRTC, Rootes at War MSS, Humber Aero Division, p. 1.
15. MRC, MSS 180/MRB/3/3/9, Ministry of Aircraft Production, monthly report, region 9, October 1945, p. 2.
16. E. Fairfax, *Calling All Arms* (Hutchinson, London, 1945), p. 95.
17. MRC, MSS 226/ST/1/1/9, Standard Board Minutes, 26 June 1941.
18. Richardson, *Twentieth Century Coventry*, p. 72.
19. T. H. Wisdom, *50 Years of Progress* (Automotive Products Group, Leamington Spa, n.d.), p. 8.
20. Lucas Ltd, Birmingham, Annual General Meeting, Minutes, 10 December 1945.
21. Wyatt, *The Austin*, p. 231.
22. Fairfax, *Calling All Arms*, pp. 89, 90.
23. MRC, MSS 180/MRB/3/4/28, Statistical tables, 27 February 1945.
24. *Rootes Gazette*, July 1944, p. 3.
25. ibid.
26. C. Barnett, *The Audit of War* (Macmillan, London, 1986), p. 161.
27. D. M. Ward, *The Other Battle* (Ben Johnson, York, 1946), p. 62.
28. PRO, Avia 10/407, E. S. Lewis, Midland Aircraft Production, n.d.
29. Coventry Record Office (CRO), Alfred Herbert, Departmental Board of Directors' Minutes, 6 August 1941.
30. Anon, *The War Record of the A. C. Wickman Limited Organisation* (the company, Coventry, n.d.), p. 15.
31. A. Sutcliffe and R. Smith, *Birmingham, 1939–1970* (Oxford University Press, Oxford, 1974), p. 45.
32. PRO, Cab 102/510, D. Mack Smith, Machine Tools 1940–44, p. 1.
33. MBRTC, Rootes at War MSS, Humber Aero Division, p. 1.
34. Sutcliffe and Smith, *Birmingham, 1939–1970*, p. 41.

35. Coventry and District Engineering Employers' Association, Minutes, 20 June 1938.
36. Thoms and Donnelly, *The Motor Car Industry in Coventry*, pp. 122, 123.
37. MRC, MSS 180/MRB/3/3/21, Report of Regional Controller, Ministry of Supply for Presentation to the Regional Board of Industry, 8 November 1945.
38. Sutcliffe and Smith, *Birmingham, 1939–1970*, p. 45.
39. See, PRO, Ed 60/557.
40. A. Muir, *75 Years* (Smith's Stamping, Coventry, 1958), p. 75.
41. P. Summerfield, *Women Workers in the Second World War* (Croom Helm, London, 1984), p. 38.
42. Sutcliffe and Smith, *Birmingham, 1939–1970*, p. 45.

3 THE MANAGEMENT OF RESOURCES

1. MRC, MSS 180/MRB/3/2, Bulletin from W. Citrine to trade union members of Regional Production Boards, 12 February 1942.
2. See in particular, Barnett, *The Audit of War*.
3. MRC, MSS 180/MRB/3/1, Midland Area Board, Minutes, 8 October 1940.
4. MBRTC, Rootes at War MSS, Humber-Hillman, p. 32.
5. Rover Board Minutes, 4 February 1941.
6. PRO, Avia 15/3765, H. Austin to W. Hallam, 24 June 1937.
7. Rover Shadow Factories, Management Committee Minutes, 18 January 1939. These records are now located at the Modern Records Centre, University of Warwick.
8. ibid., 29 September 1937.
9. MBRTC, Rootes at War MSS, Humber-Hillman, p. 6.
10. MRC, MSS 180/MRB/3/1, Midland Area Board, Minutes of a Special Meeting, 6 September 1940.
11. Lucas Ltd, File on wartime production of gun turrets, minutes of a meeting between representatives of the company and the Air Ministry, 23 April 1940.
12. MBRTC, Rootes at War MSS, Humber Aero Division, p. 4.
13. MRC, MSS 226/AU/1/1, Austin Board Minutes, 29 January 1941.
14. MRC, MSS 180/MRB/1/1, Midland Regional Board, Minutes, 7 December 1942.
15. In November 1938 Wilks informed Kingsley Wood, 'The Shadow Factories are still "news", and I am concerned because I fear that if I turn men away from our factory at a time when the Government are increasing production facilities and raising additional finance, the fact may be made use of politically.' PRO, Air 19/8, Wilks to Kingsley Wood, 30 November 1938.
16. Walton interview, March 1986.
17. Coventry Polytechnic audio tape collection, Alick Dick interview, 1984.
18. MRC, MSS 180/MRB/3/4, statistical summary, 27 February 1945.

19. MRC, MSS 180/MRB/3/4, some notes on the characteristic outlook and attitude of Midlands industry, G. B. King, 6 September 1945.
20. PRO, Avia 10/21, E. Lemon to G. S. Whitham, 8 June 1939.
21. PRO, Air 19/1, Charles Craven to Kingsley Wood, 18 March 1940.
22. Dick interview.
23. Walton interview.
24. MBRTC, Rootes at War MSS, No. 1 Aero Engine Shadow Factory, p. 3.
25. Cole interview.
26. CCC, Weir Papers, 19/21, H. A. P. Disney to Lord Weir, 14 July 1937.
27. CCC, Weir Papers, 19/1, H. A. P. Disney to Lord Weir, 2 July 1937.
28. MRC, MSS 226/AU/1/1, Austin Board Minutes, 29 January 1941.
29. University of Sussex (US), Mass Observation Archive (MOA), File Reports 1937–72, 1843, Report on Tube Investments Ltd, July/August 1942, p. 19.
30. CRO, 926/1/4/3, Alfred Herbert, Departmental Board of Directors' Minutes, 5 January 1944.
31. ibid.
32. US, MOA, Report on Tube Investments Ltd, p. 15.
33. S. Tolliday, 'Militancy and organization: women workers and trade unions in the motor trades in the 1930s', *Oral History Journal* (Autumn 1983), pp. 46, 47.
34. MRC, MSS 66/1/2/1/193, Coventry and District Engineering Employers' Association, Works Conferences, Minutes, 30 April 1943.
35. CRO, 926/1/4/3, Alfred Herbert, Departmental Board of Directors' Minutes, 20 August 1941.
36. MRC, MSS 226/ST/1/1/9, Standard Board Minutes, 20 November 1942.
37. UCL, Vickers-Armstrong Ltd, Sir Frederick Yapp File, 4/6, A. Dunbar to P. Hennesy, 15 November 1940.
38. PRO, Cab 102/406, Memorandum on Labour Welfare and Utilisation in the Aircraft Industry, J. B. Jeffreys, n.d., p. 10.
39. UCL, Vickers-Armstrong Ltd, Quarterly Reports on the Castle Bromwich Works, 203, 31 December 1941.
40. CRO, 926/1/4/3, Alfred Herbert, Departmental Board of Directors' Minutes, 22 May 1940.
41. UCL, Vickers-Armstrong Ltd, Sir Frederick Yapp File, 4/6, A. Dunbar to F. Yapp, 20 July 1940.
42. *Education*, 4 January 1935.
43. MRC, MSS 226/ST/1/1/9, Standard Board Minutes, 21 June 1941.
44. UCL, Vickers-Armstrong Ltd, Quarterly Reports, 199, 31 December 1940.
45. MRC, MSS 180/MRB/3/1/109, Midland Area Board, Draft Memorandum, n.d.
46. PRO, Lab 10/349, Chief Conciliation Officer, Midland Region, Weekly Reports, 21 December 1940.
47. UCL, Vickers-Armstrong Ltd, Quarterly Reports, 209, 30 June 1943.

48. MRC, MSS 66/1/1/1/65, CDEEA, Minutes, 18 November 1941.
49. For a discussion of these points, see Thoms and Donnelly, *The Motor Car Industry in Coventry*, pp. 135, 136. See also A. Shenfield and P. S. Florence, 'The economies and diseconomies of industrial concentration: the wartime experience of Coventry', *Review of Economic Studies* (1943–5).
50. MRC, MSS 66/1/2/1/10, CDEEA, Minutes, 16 January 1941.
51. US, MOA, Report on Tube Investments Ltd, p. 27.
52. ibid., pp. 25, 29.
53. ibid., pp. 88–92.
54. PRO, Lab 10/349, Chief Conciliation Officer, Midland Region, Weekly Reports, 10 February 1940.
55. A. Friedman, *Industry and Labour* (Macmillan, London, 1977), p. 204.
56. Coventry Polytechnic, audio tape collection, Jack Jones interview, 1984.
57. MRC, MSS 180/MRB/3/1/109, Midland Area Board, Draft Memorandum, n.d.
58. MRC, MSS 66/1/2/1/2, CDEEA, Minutes, 30 July 1940.
59. PRO, Lab 10/439, Chief Conciliation Officer, Midland Region, 23 December 1939.
60. S. Tolliday, 'Government, employers and shop floor organization in the British motor industry, 1939–69' in S. Tolliday and J. Zeitlin (eds), *Shop Floor Bargaining and the State*, (CUP, Cambridge, 1985), p. 112.
61. R. Croucher, *Engineers at War* (Merlin Press, London, 1982), pp. 111, 112.
62. Thoms and Donnelly, *The Motor Car Industry in Coventry*, p. 142.
63. Sutcliffe and Smith, *History of Birmingham*, p. 48.
64. PRO, Lab 10/444, Chief Conciliation Officer, Midland Region, Weekly Reports, 7 January 1944.
65. MRC, MSS 202/S/J/3/1/10, Report of the Shop Stewards' Committee at the Austin Longbridge Works, April 1944.
66. Tolliday, 'Government, employers and shop floor organization', p. 110.
67. Thoms and Donnelly, *The Motor Car Industry in Coventry*, pp. 143, 144.
68. PRO, Lab 10/254, Statement by Members of the Executive Committee of the Coventry Branches of the National Union of Sheet Metal Workers and Braziers, 20 May 1943; E. Bevin to W. J. Brown, 8 June 1943.
69. PRO, Lab 10/444, Chief Conciliation Officer, Midland Region, Weekly Reports, 5 May 1944.
70. Amalgamated Engineering Union, District Committee Minutes, 21 October 1941. At the time of consultation, these records were held by the union's District Office but they have since been transferred to the Coventry Record Office.
71. ibid., 28 October 1941.
72. Thoms and Donnelly, *The Motor Car Industry in Coventry*, pp. 145, 146.
73. PRO, Cab 102/406, Memorandum on Labour Welfare, Appendix B.

74. UCL, Vickers-Armstrong, Quarterly Reports, 207, 31 December 1942.
75. PRO, Cab 102/406, Memorandum on Labour Welfare, p. 54.
76. PRO, Lab 10/351, Industrial Relations Officer, Midland Region, Weekly Reports, 14 June 1941.
77. PRO, Lab 10/352, Chief Conciliation Officer, Midland Region, Weekly Reports, 19 September 1942.
78. J. Hinton, 'Coventry communism: a study of factory politics in the Second World War', *History Workshop Journal*, vol. 10 (1980), pp. 98, 99.
79. PRO, Lab 10/351, Chief Conciliation Officer, Midland Region, Weekly Reports, 9 August 1941.
80. PRO, Lab 10/352, Chief Conciliation Officer, Midland Region, Weekly Reports, 24 January 1942.
81. W. Lewchuk, *American Technology and the British Motor Vehicle Industry* (CUP, Cambridge, 1987), p. 190.
82. MRC, MSS 202/S/J/3/1/6, Report by the Shop Stewards' Committee on the Recent Dispute at the Austin Longbridge Works.
83. UCL, Vickers-Armstrong Ltd, Quarterly Reports, 203, 31 December 1941.
84. ibid., 209, 30 June 1943.
85. MBRTC, Rootes at War MSS, Humber-Hillman, p. 44.
86. PRO, Avia 9/57, Study of the Minutes of Joint Production Committees in 63 Aircraft Firms, 7 January 1943.
87. PRO, Lab 10/351, Chief Conciliation Officer, Midland Region, Weekly Reports, 1 March 1941.
88. PRO, Lab 10/352, Chief Conciliation Officer, Midland Region, Weekly Reports, 31 January 1942.
89. P. Inman, *Labour in the Munitions Industries* (HMSO, London, 1957), p. 325.
90. UCL, Vickers-Armstrong Ltd, Quarterly Reports, 202, 30 September 1941.
91. MRC, MSS 66/1/2/2/44, CDEEA, Minutes, 4 February 1944.

4   GOVERNMENT AND INDUSTRY: THE PROBLEMS
OF MONOPSONY

1. MRC, MSS 19A/3/3/24, K. R. Davis to G. D. Burton, 1 November 1935.
2. CRO, 985/1/1, Alvis Board Minutes, 14 June 1935.
3. RAF Museum, Hendon, Bulman Papers, unpublished autobiography, p. 297.
4. PRO, Air 19/6, T. G. John to H. A. P. Disney, 11 July 1936.
5. PRO, Air 6/25, Secretary of State's weekly progress meeting, 22 May 1936.
6. PRO, Air 19/6, Report by Sir Amos Ayre and S. R. Beale, 21 November 1938.

7. ibid.
8. PRO, Air 19/4, Report by N. Rowbotham, 29 July 1936, pp. 4, 5.
9. PRO, Air 19/6, T. G. John to Lord Swinton, 7 November 1936.
10. PRO, Air 19/6, Note by R. H. Verney, 8 January 1938.
11. ibid.
12. PRO, Air 19/6, Report by H. A. P. Disney, 23 December 1936.
13. PRO, Air 6/25, Secretary of State's weekly progress meeting, 5 November 1936.
14. PRO, Air 19/6, T. G. John to Sir Kingsley Wood, 21 November 1938.
15. PRO, Air 19/6, Notes of a telephone conversation between H. Balfour and T. G. John, 2 January 1939.
16. PRO, Air 19/6, T. G. John to Sir Kingsley Wood, 21 November 1938.
17. CRO, 985/1/1, Alvis Board Minutes, 19 May 1939.
18. CRO, 985/73/1, Alvis Mechanisation Board Minutes, 17 April 1940.
19. PRO, Avia 15/19, Sir Charles Latham to Harold Balfour, 6 October 1939.
20. PRO, Avia 22/174, T. C. L. Westbrook to Air Council, 30 November 1939.
21. PRO, Avia 15/19, Note by W. L. Scott, 19 October 1939.
22. PRO, Avia 15/19, Sir Charles Latham to Sir Edward Campbell, 20 October 1939.
23. PRO, Avia 15/19, H. Balfour to Sir Henry Self, 7 October 1939.
24. PRO, Avia 15/19, Air Ministry to General Manager, Lloyds Bank, London, 18 October 1939.
25. PRO, Avia 15/19, Air Council to T. C. L. Westbrook, 7 November 1939.
26. PRO, Avia 15/19, T. C. L. Westbrook to Air Council, 30 November 1939.
27. A. J. Robertson, 'Lord Beaverbrook and the supply of aircraft, 1940–1941', in A. Slaven and D. H. Aldcroft (eds), *Business, Banking and Urban History* (John Donald, Edinburgh, 1982), p. 83.
28. Midland Bank, Coventry, Ledger A-1, Manager to Head Office, 9 November 1939.
29. PRO, Cab 16/140, Memorandum by the Secretary of State for Air, 21 May 1936.
30. Cross, *Lord Swinton*, p. 167.
31. PRO, Cab 16/140, Memorandum by the Secretary of State for Air, 21 May 1936.
32. W. Ashworth, *Contracts and Finance* (HMSO, London, 1953), p. 90.
33. MRC, MSS 226/AU/1/1/2, Austin Board Minutes, 22 October 1941.
34. Ashworth, *Contracts and Finance*, pp. 91–4.
35. Rover Board Minutes, 12 June 1941. Spencer Wilks was reported to have observed 'that the procedure laid down by the Ministry under which they require estimates of expenditure to be submitted in minute detail before granting financial approval, not only seriously delayed getting into production at the Northern Dispersal Mills, but was . . . almost unworkable in practice'.
36. Ashworth, *Contracts and Finance*, p. 92.

37. PRO, Cab 102/406, Memorandum on Labour Welfare, p. 50.
38. ibid., p. 10.
39. PRO, Avia 10/40, Unsigned memorandum to the Secretary of State, 22 April 1940.
40. Rover Shadow Factory Management Committee Minutes, 16 April 1942.
41. CRO, 926/1/4/3, Alfred Herbert, Departmental Board of Directors' Minutes, 29 November 1939.
42. MBRTC, Rootes at War MSS, Humber Aero Division, p. 4.
43. UCL, Vickers-Armstrong Ltd, Quarterly Reports on the Castle Bromwich Works, 200, 31 March 1941.
44. ibid., 204, 31 March 1942.
45. PRO, Cab 21/702, Draft speech on defence and skilled labour position, 9 March 1936.
46. MRC, MSS 180/MRB/3/1, Midland Regional Board, Minutes, 2 October 1940.
47. MRC, MSS 180/MRB/3/2, Midland Regional Board, Minutes of the Executive Committee, 6 January 1942.
48. MRC, MSS 180/MRB/3/1, Midland Area Board, Minutes of a special meeting, 6 September 1940.
49. UCL, Vickers-Armstrong Ltd, Quarterly Reports on the Castle Bromwich Works, 209, 30 June 1943.
50. US, MOA, Report on Tube Investments Ltd, p. 26.
51. PRO, Cab 102/776, Report by W. E. Cavenagh on the Ministry of Labour and the Woman Worker's Child, n.d.
52. PRO, Lab 10/351, Industrial Relations Officer, Midland Region, Weekly Reports, 14 June 1941.
53. MRC, MSS 180/MRB/3/4, Memorandum on Post-War Reconstruction by the Coventry District Production Committee, 25 September 1944.
54. MRC, MSS 180/MRB/3/1, Midland Area Board, Minutes of the Executive Committee, 26 November 1940.
55. MRC, MSS 180/MRB/3/4, Future Regional Organisation, Report by the Regional Committee of the Ministry of Production, 3 November 1943.
56. MRC, MSS 226/ST/1/1/9, W. E. Rootes to Minister of Aircraft Production, 10 June 1941.
57. MRC, MSS 226/ST/1/1/9, Standard Board Minutes, 27 July 1943.
58. PRO, Avia 10/40, Unsigned memorandum to the Secretary of State, 22 April 1940.
59. MRC, MSS 180/MRB/1/2, Midland Regional Board, Minutes, 13 March 1944.
60. MRC, MSS 180/MRB/3/4, N. G. Lancaster to G. B. King, 29 September 1944.
61. MRC, MSS 226/AU/1/1/3, AGM, Report by L. P. Lord, 27 March 1946.
62. Lucas Ltd, King Street, Birmingham, AGM, Report by Sir Peter Bennett, 10 December 1945.

63. MRC, MSS 180/MRB/3/5, G. B. King to N. V. Kipping, 16 October 1944.
64. PRO, BT 170/72, Minutes of a meeting between Sir Stafford Cripps and representatives of Coventry trade union officials, 14 January 1946.
65. MRC, MSS 180/MRB/3/4, N. G. Lancaster to G. B. King, 29 September 1944.
66. PRO, BT 96/22, Sir Percival Liesching to Sir Arnold Overton, 7 July 1944.
67. ibid.
68. ibid.
69. PRO, BT 96/22, R. Pares to Wilson, 22 July 1944.
70. PRO, BT 96/22, Sir Arnold Overton to Preston, 27 July 1944.
71. MRC, MSS 226/AU/1/1/3, AGM, 27 March 1946.
72. MRC, MSS 226/AU/1/1/3, AGM, Report by L. P. Lord, 18 December 1946.
73. PRO, BT 96/22, CBS to President of the Board of Trade, 6 April 1945.
74. PRO, BT 96/22, HS to Sir William Palmer, 18 April 1945.

5 THE ECONOMIC IMPACT OF THE AIR RAIDS

1. T. Mason, 'Looking back on the blitz', in B. Lancaster and T. Mason (eds), *Life and Labour in a Twentieth Century City: The Experience of Coventry* (Cryfield Press, Coventry, 1986), p. 321.
2. T. H. O'Brien, *Civil Defence* (HMSO, London, 1955), p. 405.
3. PRO, HO 207/1069, Report on the shopping difficulties of women war workers in Coventry, A. Hope-Jones, 3 November 1941.
4. A. Calder, *The People's War* (Granada, St Albans, 1982), p. 234.
5. Richardson, *Twentieth Century Coventry*, p. 82.
6. See, in particular, A. Cave-Brown, *Bodyguard of Lies*, 4th edn (Comet, London, 1986); N. West, *Unreliable Witness* (Weidenfeld & Nicolson, London, 1984); R. Lewin, *Ultra Goes to War* (Hutchinson, London, 1978); F. H. Hinsley *et al.*, *British Intelligence in the Second World War*, Vol. 1 (HMSO, London, 1979).
7. Sutcliffe and Smith, *Birmingham 1939–1970*, p. 27.
8. ibid., p. 29.
9. Richardson, *Twentieth Century Coventry*, pp. 87, 88.
10. H. Klopper, *The Fight Against Fire. The History of the Birmingham Fire and Ambulance Service* (Birmingham Fire and Ambulance Service, Leamington Spa, 1954), p. 91.
11. CRO, 483, Report and Recommendations of the Coventry Reconstruction Co-ordinating Committee, 31 December 1940, p. 1.
12. MBRTC, Rootes at War MSS, Humber-Hillman, p. 15.
13. PRO, HO 192/1232, BSA works, damage report, unsigned, n.d.
14. PRO, HO 192/1169, Morris Engines, damage report, R. J. Johnson and W. H. Black, 18 September 1943.
15. PRO, Avia 22/174, Coventry Reconstruction Co-ordinating

Committee, Minutes, 19 November 1940, p. 2.
16. CRO, 926/1/4/3, Alfred Herbert, Departmental Board of Directors' Minutes, 19 March 1941.
17. CRO, 483, Report and Recommendations of the Coventry Reconstruction Co-ordinating Committee, 1 May 1941, p. 2.
18. Fairfax, *Calling All Arms*, p. 91.
19. MBRTC, Rootes at War MSS, Hillman-Humber, p. 16.
20. Robson, *The Rover Story*, p. 40.
21. MBRTC, Rootes at War MSS, No. 2 Aero Engine Shadow Factory, p. 3.
22. PRO, Avia 15/3750, Unsigned note, 17 February 1939.
23. MRC, MSS 19A/7/PR/29, Daimler works, damage report, unsigned, n.d.
24. CRO, 926/1/4/3, Alfred Herbert, Departmental Board of Directors' Minutes, 9 July 1941.
25. PRO, HO 192/1238, H. Manzoni to Ministry of Home Security, 5 February 1942.
26. PRO, HO 192/1232, Birmingham Economic and Social Survey, B. S. A. Small Heath Factory, unsigned, n.d., p. 2.
27. PRO, HO 192/1232, Report by the Ministry of Home Security on fire damage at the BSA Small Heath Works, 1.11.40–30.4.41.
28. PRO, Avia 22/174, Coventry Reconstruction Co-ordinating Committee, Minutes, 26 November 1940, p. 5.
29. ibid.
30. MBRTC, Rootes at War MSS, Hillman-Humber, p. 16.
31. ibid.
32. PRO, HO 199/442, Mass Observation, Report on Coventry, 18 November 1940, p. 4.
33. CRO, 483, Report and Recommendations of the Coventry Reconstruction Co-ordinating Committee, 31 December 1940, p. 6.
34. PRO, HO 207/1068, S. J. Grey, Report upon the Coventry raids of April 8/9 and 10/11, 1941, 26 April 1941, p. 3.
35. CRO, 483, Report and Recommendations of the Coventry Reconstruction Co-ordinating Committee, 31 December 1940, p. 12.
36. Quoted by N. Longmate, *Air Raid* (Hutchinson, London, 1976), p. 236.
37. UCL, Vickers-Armstrong Ltd, Sir Frederick Yapp File, 4/6, A. Dunbar to Sir Charles Craven, 20 August 1940.
38. MBRTC, Rootes at War MSS, Hillman-Humber, p. 17.
39. CRO, 926/1/4/3, Alfred Herbert, Departmental Board of Directors' Minutes, 5 January 1944.
40. PRO, HO 192/1242, Note by Councillor Sragg, 30 January 1942.
41. Cole interview, September 1987.
42. PRO, HO 192/1210, Birmingham Economic and Social Survey, PRB, 11 March 1942, p. 6.
43. MBRTC, Rootes at War MSS, Hillman-Humber, p. 15.
44. D. Wood, *Attack Warning Red. The Royal Observer Corps and the Defence of Britain 1925 to 1975* (Macdonald & Jane's, London, 1976), pp. 106, 107.

45. Forsyth Papers, Alarm Officer's Progress Report for the Month Ending March 31/41, Midland Region.
46. Rover Shadow Factory Management Committee Minutes, 16 April 1942.
47. MBRTC, Rootes at War MSS, Humber Aero Division, pp. 5–7.
48. CRO, 483, Report and Recommendations of the Coventry Reconstruction Co-ordinating Committee, 31 December 1940, p. 12.
49. CRO, 985/1/1, Alvis Board Minutes, 3 April 1943.
50. MBRTC, Rootes at War MSS, Humber-Hillman, p. 19.
51. PRO, HO 207/1067, Report by the City Engineer and Surveyor's Office, February 1942.

6 CIVILIAN MORALE: DID THE PEOPLE PANIC?

1. PRO, INF 1/292, Weekly reports, 14 January 1943.
2. Imperial War Museum (IWM), Bloomfield MSS.
3. I. McLaine, *Ministry of Morale* (Allen & Unwin, London, 1979), p. 119.
4. PRO, HO 192/1210, Report by T. H. Foster on morale in Birmingham, n.d.
5. IWM, Rice MSS.
6. G. Hodgkinson, *Sent to Coventry* (Maxwell, Bletchley, 1970), p. 153.
7. IWM, Bloomfield MSS.
8. IWM, Rice MSS.
9. Wood, *Attack Warning Red*, p. 104.
10. P. Donnelly (ed.), *Mrs Milburn's Diaries* (Harrap, London, 1979), p. 71.
11. PRO, HO 192/1164, Anon., Effects of the Coventry Raids, 5 July 1943.
12. PRO, INF 1/292, Special report on Coventry, 16 November 1940.
13. PRO, HO 199/442, Mass Observation, Report on Coventry, 18 November 1940, p. 1.
14. ibid.
15. Hodgkinson, *Sent to Coventry*, pp. 154, 155.
16. CRO, 501/1, no title, n.d., p. 4.
17. US, MOA, Town and District Survey, Box 4, 25 November 1940.
18. IWM, Hollingsworth Diary, 19 November 1940.
19. Medical Officer of Health for Coventry, Annual Report (1940), p. 3.
20. 'The police report that arising from raids since the 1st August, 1940, offences classified as "looting" are a disturbing feature. "Since the 1st August, 1940, the total of such offences is 128, but two thirds of these have been committed since the 20th November, and follow the severe raids of the 19th–20th. Of the 128 offences 53 have so far been detected and 84 prisoners, 31 adults and 53 juveniles, have been arrested. The circumstances vary from deliberate looting to thefts by juveniles which are more in the nature of pilfering." ' PRO, HO 192/1210, Birmingham Economic and Social Survey, PRB, 11 March 1942, p. 3.

21. PRO, HO 199/442, Mass Observation, Report on Coventry, p. 1.
22. ibid., p. 2
23. ibid.
24. ibid.
25. ibid.
26. PRO, HO 199/442, (Illeg) to Mabone, 21 January 1941.
27. PRO, HO 199/442, G. Gater to H. Morrison, 28 January 1941.
28. PRO, HO 199/442, (Illeg) to Mabone, 21 January 1941.
29. PRO, HO 199/442, Note by H. Scot, 27 December 1941.
30. McLaine, *Ministry of Morale*, p. 120.
31. Mason, 'Looking back on the blitz', in Lancaster and Mason (eds) *Life and Labour in a Twentieth Century City*, p. 327.
32. Forsyth interview, 17 February 1986.
33. PRO, HO 207/1068, Notes on a conversation with Captain Patterson, 16 November 1940 (unsigned).
34. PRO, HO 199/442, Mass Observation, Report on Coventry, p. 2.
35. PRO, INF 1/292, Weekly reports, 25 November 1940.
36. PRO, INF 1/292, Weekly reports, 4 December 1940.
37. PRO, INF 1/292, Weekly reports, 16 April 1941.
38. PRO, Ed 60/557, W. L. Chinn to Secretary, Board of Education, 13 December 1940.
39. PRO, HO 207/1069, Friends' Ambulance Unit, Report on the nightly exodus from Coventry, n.d.
40. ibid., p. 6.
41. PRO, Cab 102/725, Note by H. Beckwith, Evacuation Officer, Midland region, 29 December 1943.
42. McLaine, *Ministry of Morale*, p. 122.
43. PRO, Cab 102/731, Note by H. E. James, Ministry of Health, 22 May 1941.
44. US, MOA, Town and District Survey, Box 4, 22 November 1940.
45. PRO, INF 1/292, 4 November 1940.
46. PRO, HO 207/1069, Friends' Ambulance Unit, p. 5.
47. PRO, HO 207/1068, (Illeg) Report on Coventry, 24 October 1940.
48. IWM, Hollingsworth Diary, 17 November 1940.
49. CRO, SEC/MB/79/1, National Emergency Committee, Minutes, 9 January 1941.
50. PRO, INF 1/292, 16 April 1941.
51. Hinton, 'Coventry Communism', p. 95.
52. PRO, HO 207/1069, Ministry of Food, Report on the shopping difficulties of women war workers in Coventry, 3 November 1941.
53. PRO, HO 207/1069, Sir Frank Tribe to Sir Henry French, 3 December 1941.
54. PRO, HO 207/1069, Principal Officer, Midland Regional Office to J. H. Burrel, 24 December 1941.
55. PRO, HO 207/1069, Mass Observation, Report on Coventry, p. 4.
56. ibid.
57. PRO, HO 207/1069, Ministry of Food, Report on the shopping difficulties of women war workers.

58. CRO, 10/50, Fire Guard Organisation, 1939–43, unsigned note, 18 September 1943.
59. PRO, HO 207/1069, Ministry of Food, Report on the shopping difficulties of women war workers.
60. US, MOA, Town and District Survey, Box 4/G, 24/5 November 1941.
61. PRO, HO 207/1069, Ministry of Food, Report on the shopping difficulties of women war workers.
62. PRO, HO 199/442, MO Report on Liverpool, 10 January 1941.
63. US, MOA, Town and District Survey, Box 4/G, Women's War Work – Coventry, 25 November 1941.
64. PRO, HO 199/453, Report on the effect of air raids on Birmingham and Hull, 8 April 1942.
65. IWM, Clothier MSS.
66. US, MOA, Report on Tube Investments Ltd, p. 140.
67. PRO, Ed 60/557, T. W. Southern to G. L. Thornton, 13 October 1938.
68. PRO, Ed 60/557, Note by T. W. Southern, 27 February 1943.
69. McLaine, *Ministry of Morale*, p. 93.
70. PRO, Avia 15/354, W. Citrine to Kingsley Wood, 9 January 1940.

7   THE CIVIL DEFENCE CONTROVERSY

1. O'Brien, *Civil Defence*, p. xv.
2. ibid., p. 691.
3. PRO, HO 199/400, Civil defence report on region 9, 1939, p. 39.
4. PRO, HO 192/1210, Birmingham Economic and Social Survey, p. 2.
5. Mason, 'Looking back on the blitz', pp. 324–6.
6. PRO, HO 207/1067, H. E. Fenton to Ministry of Home Security, 24 March 1943.
7. PRO, HO 192/1210, Birmingham Economic and Social Survey, p. 1.
8. UCL, Vickers-Armstrong Ltd, A. Dunbar to Sir Charles Craven, 20 August 1940.
9. PRO, HO 207/1067, C. J. Mercer to E. S. Ritter, 9 June 1942.
10. Sutcliffe and Smith, *Birmingham 1939–1970*, p. 23.
11. PRO, HO 192/1238, Report by the City Engineer and Surveyor's Office, February 1942.
12. Longmate, *Air Raid*, p. 189.
13. PRO, HO 199/442, Mass Observation, Report on Coventry, p. 2.
14. PRO, HO 207/1069, Friends' Ambulance Unit, p. 8.
15. T. Harrison, *Living Through the Blitz* (Collins, London, 1976), p. 297.
16. PRO, HO 192/1238, T. H. Foster, Civil defence in Birmingham, n.d. (January 1942?)
17. PRO, HO 207/1068, Report upon the Coventry air raids of April 8/9th and 10/11th, 1941, p. 4.
18. PRO, HO 192/1238, T. H. Foster, Civil defence in Birmingham.
19. PRO, HO 192/1210, Birmingham Economic and Social Survey, p. 4.
20. PRO, HO 207/1068, (Illeg) Report on Coventry, 24 October 1940.

21. CRO 501/1, no title, n.d., pp. 2, 3.
22. PRO, Ed 60/556, F. T. Arnold to J. H. Burrows, 8 January 1943.
23. Klopper, *The Fight Against Fire*, p. 86.
24. ibid., p. 88.
25. PRO, HO 199/442, Report on Coventry, p. 2.
26. ibid., p. 5.
27. Quoted in Harrison, *Living Through the Blitz*, p. 297.
28. PRO, HO 192/1242, Comments by Harry Wickham and J. Simmonds, n.d.
29. PRO, HO 192/1210, Birmingham Economic and Social Survey, p. 4.
30. ibid.
31. ibid.
32. PRO, HO 192/1238, W. Mason to T. H. Foster, 29 December 1941.
33. PRO, HO 192/1238, T. H. Foster, Civil defence in Birmingham, n.d. (November 1941?).
34. PRO, HO 192/1238, Report by the City Engineer and Surveyor's Office, February 1942.
35. N. Tiptaft, *The Individualist* (the author, Birmingham, 1954), p. 180.
36. O'Brien, *Civil Defence*, p. 6.
37. MRC, MSS 11/3/3, Notes of a meeting between members of Coventry's National Emergency Committee and representatives of the Ministry of Home Security and the Ministry of Labour, 23 July 1940.
38. M. Balfour, *Propaganda in War 1939–1945* (Routledge & Kegan Paul, London, 1979), p. 154.
39. Tiptaft, *The Individualist*, p. 183.
40. PRO, HO 199/442, Mass Observation, Report on Coventry, p. 3.
41. Tiptaft, *The Individualist*, p. 184.
42. Hodgkinson, *Sent to Coventry*, p. 147.
43. PRO, HO 192/1210, Birmingham Economic and Social Survey, p. 1.
44. Sutcliffe and Smith, *Birmingham 1939–1970*, p. 23.
45. PRO, HO 207/1069, Ministry of Food, Report on the shopping difficulties of women war workers.
46. Amin Hamid Zein el Abdin, 'Administrative responses to the blitz on Coventry, 1940–41', unpublished MA dissertation, University of Warwick, 1976, p. 34.
47. Hodgkinson, *Sent to Coventry*, p. 156.
48. PRO, HO 207/1067, F. Wiltshire to Home Office, 4 October 1939.
49. Birmingham Reference Library (BRL), MSS 1303/54, Birmingham Fire Brigade, General Orders, Chief Officer to District, Divisional, Station and Section Officers, 5 December 1940.
50. BRL, MSS 1303/54, Birmingham Fire Brigade, General Orders, Fire Report on the Air Raid on Birmingham, 9/10 April 1941.
51. Forsyth Papers, R. Bryan to J. Forsyth, 11 August 1941.
52. MRC, MSS 202/S/J/3/1/3, W. Mason to R. Etheridge, 1 October 1942.

CONCLUSION

1. Lucas Ltd, Birmingham, Annual General Meeting, 6 December 1943.
2. MRC, MSS 180/MRB/3/3/9, Ministry of Aircraft Production, monthly report, region 9, p. 3.

Sources and select bibliography

MANUSCRIPT AND ORIGINAL SOURCES

Records in Public Depositories

Amalgamated Union of
  Engineering Workers
  Coventry Branch, Minutes
  (now transferred to Coventry
  Record Office)
Aston University
  Rover Motor Company,
  Directors' Minutes (now
  transferred to the Modern
  Records Centre, University of
  Warwick)
Birmingham Reference Library
  1303/54
    Birmingham Fire Brigade.
    General Orders
Churchill College, Cambridge
  Swinton Papers
  Weir Papers
Coventry Local Studies Library
  Chief Officer of the Fire Brigade,
    Annual Reports
  Medical Officer of Health,
    Annual Reports
Coventry Record Office
  10/50
    Fire Guard Organisation
  483
    Coventry Reconstruction Co-
    ordinating Committee,
    Minutes

501/1
  Civil Defence
926/1/4/3
  Alfred Herbert, Directors'
  Minutes
985/1/1
  Alvis, Directors' Minutes
985/73/1
  Alvis Straussler, Directors'
  Minutes
1049/1/2
  A. C. Wickman, Directors'
  Minutes
1060/1/3
  Armstrong-Siddeley Motors,
  Directors' Minutes
SEC/MB/79/1–3
  National Emergency
  Committee, Minutes
Imperial War Museum
  Diaries
    Bloomfield, Mrs M.
    Dunkley, F. J.
    Hollingsworth, Miss G. A.
  Memoirs
    Clothier, H. R.
    Platt, E.
    Rice, C. J.
Mass Observation Archive,
  University of Sussex

File Reports
1843
Surveys
Box 1, F
Box 4, C, G, H
Museum of British Road
Transport, Coventry
Rootes at War MSS
Public Record Office, Kew
Air
6/23, 6/24, 6/25, 6/26, 6/28,
19/1, 19/3, 19/4, 19/5, 19/6,
19/8, 19/10, 19/11, 46/35
Avia
9/34, 9/57, 10/16, 10/21,
10/34, 10/35, 10/40, 10/407,
15/19, 15/29, 15/99, 15/320,
15/354, 15/1503, 15/1806,
15/3749, 15/3750, 15/3751,
15/3765, 15/3766, 22/174
BT
64/3488, 96/22, 96/207A,
170/72
Cab
16/136, 16/140, 21/702,
102/57, 102/59, 102/406,
102/508, 102/509, 102/510,
102/725, 102/731, 102/776
Ed
53/608, 53/621, 53/636,
60/556, 60/557
HO
192/1164, 192/1169, 192/1171,
192/1210, 192/1232, 192/1238,
192/1242, 192/1248, 192/1414,
192/1503, 199/396, 199/400,
199/442, 199/453, 207/1066,
207/1067, 207/1068, 207/1069
INF

1/292
Lab
10/254, 10/349, 10/350,
10/351, 10/352, 10/444,
10/554, 22/174
RAF Museum, Hendon
Bulman Papers
University of Cambridge
Vickers-Armstrong Deposit
416
Sir Frederick Yapp File
198–217
Castle Bromwich Factory,
Quarterly Reports
University of Warwick: Modern
Records Centre
MSS 11
Air Raid Precautions in
Coventry, Miscellaneous
Papers
MSS 19A
BSA, Miscellaneous Papers
MSS 66
Coventry and District
Engineering Employers'
Association, Works
Conference Minutes
MSS 180/MRB
Midland Area and Regional
Boards, Minutes, Reports and
Correspondence
MSS 220/S/J
Papers of R. A. Etheridge
MSS 226/AU
Austin Motor Company,
Directors' Minutes, Reports
MSS 226/ST
Standard Motor Company,
Directors' Minutes, Reports

Records held privately

Coventry and District
Engineering Employers
Association
Executive Committee, Minutes
Forsyth Papers

Miscellaneous Papers Relating
to the ROC Watcher Scheme
and Civil Defence in
Birmingham and Coventry
Jaguar Cars Ltd

SOURCES AND SELECT BIBLIOGRAPHY

Directors' Minutes
Lucas Ltd, Birmingham
Miscellaneous Papers Relating
to the Firm's Wartime

Activities
Midland Bank, Coventry
Account Holders,
Correspondence

INTERVIEWS

Coventry Polytechnic
G. P. Bulman (Air Ministry),
A. Dick (Standard), J. Jones
(TGWU)

Private
R. B. Cole (Standard), B.
Jackman (Rover), J. Walton
(Rover), J. Forsyth (Royal
Observer Corps)

THESES AND DISSERTATIONS

Amin Hamid Zein el Abdin.
'Administrative responses to the
blitz on Coventry, 1940–41',
unpublished MA dissertation,
University of Warwick, 1976.
Claydon, T. 'The development of
trade unionism among British
automobile and aircraft
workers, c.1914–1946',
unpublished Ph.D. thesis,

University of Kent, 1981.
Lloyd, P. 'Evacuation of children
to the Southam rural district
1939–45', unpublished BA
dissertation, University of
Birmingham, 1983.
Winston, P. A. 'Government and
defence production, 1943–50',
unpublished Ph.D. thesis,
University of Cambridge, 1982.

BOOKS

Andrews, P. and Brunner, E. *The
Life of Lord Nuffield* (Blackwell,
Oxford, 1959).
Ashworth, W. *Contracts and Finance*
(HMSO, London, 1953).
Balfour, M. *Propaganda in War
1939–1945* (Routledge & Kegan
Paul, London, 1979).
Barnett, C. *The Audit of War*
(Macmillan, London, 1986).
Brennan, T. *Wolverhampton. Social
and Industry Survey 1945/46*
(Dobson, London, 1948).
Calder, A. *The People's War. Britain
1939–1945* (Granada, St Albans,
1982).
Cave-Brown, A. *Bodyguard of Lies*,
4th edn (Comet, London, 1986).

Church, R. *Herbert Austin: The
British Motor Industry to 1941*
(Europa, London, 1979).
Crosby, T. L. *The Impact of Civilian
Evacuation in the Second World War*
(Croom Helm, London, 1986).
Cross, J. A. *Lord Swinton*
(Clarendon Press, Oxford, 1982).
Croucher, R. *Engineers at War*
(Merlin Press, London, 1982).
Davy, J. *The Standard Car 1903–63*
(Sherbourne Press, Coventry,
1965).
Donnelly, P. (ed.) *Mrs Milburn's
Diaries* (Harrap, London, 1979).
Fairfax, E. *Calling All Arms*
(Hutchinson, London, 1945).
Friedman, A. *Industry and Labour*

(Macmillan, London, 1977).

Gosden, P. H. J. H. *Education in the Second World War* (Methuen, London, 1976).

Gunston, B. *By Jupiter. The Life of Sir Roy Fedden* (Royal Aeronautical Society, London, 1978).

Hancock, W. K. and Gowing, M. M. *British War Economy* (HMSO, London, 1949).

Harrison, T. *Living Through the Blitz* (Collins, London, 1976).

Hinsley, F. H. *et al. British Intelligence in the Second World War* (HMSO, London, 1979).

Hodgkinson, G. *Sent to Coventry* (Maxwell, Bletchley, 1970).

Hornby, W. *Factories and Plant* (HMSO, London, 1958).

Inman, P. *Labour in the Munitions Industries* (HMSO, London, 1957).

Jones, J. *Union Man* (Collins, London, 1986).

Klopper, H. *The Fight Against Fire. The History of the Birmingham Fire and Ambulance Service* (Birmingham Fire and Ambulance Service, Leamington Spa, 1954).

Lambert, Z. E. and Wyatt, R. J. *Lord Austin. The Man* (Sidgwick & Jackson, London, 1968).

Lancaster, B. and Mason, T. (eds) *Life and Labour in a Twentieth Century City: The Experience of Coventry* (Cryfield Press, Coventry, 1986).

Lewchuk, W. *American Technology and the British Vehicle Industry* (Cambridge University Press, Cambridge, 1987).

Lewin, R. *Ultra Goes to War*, (Hutchinson, London, 1978).

Lloyd, I. *Rolls Royce. The Merlin at War* (Macmillan, London, 1978).

Longmate, N. *Air Raid. The Bombing of Coventry, 1940* (Hutchinson, London, 1976).

McLaine, I. *Ministry of Morale* (Allen & Unwin, London, 1979).

Muir, A. *75 Years* (Smith's Stamping, Coventry, 1958).

O'Brien, T. H. *Civil Defence* (HMSO, London, 1955).

Overy, R. J. *The Air War 1939–1945* (Europa, London, 1980).

Overy, R. J. *William Morris, Viscount Nuffield* (Europa, London, 1976).

Parker, H. M. D. *Manpower. A Study of War-time Policy and Administration* (HMSO, London, 1957).

Peden, G. C. *British Rearmament and the Treasury: 1932–1939* (Scottish Academic Press, Edinburgh, 1979).

Pelling, H. *Britain and the Second World War* (Fontana, Glasgow, 1970).

Penrose, H. *British Aviation. The Ominous Skies 1935–1939* (HMSO, London, 1980).

Postan, M. M. *British War Production* (HMSO, London, 1952).

Postan, M. M., Hay, D., and Scott, J. D. *Design and Development of Weapons. Studies in Government and Industrial Organisation* (HMSO, London, 1964).

Richardson, K. E. *Twentieth Century Coventry* (Coventry City Council, Coventry, 1972).

Robson, G. *The Rover Story* (Stephens, Cambridge, 1984).

Scott, J. D. *Vickers. A History* (Weidenfeld & Nicolson, London, 1962).

Seward, D. *'Bomber' Harris* (Cassell, London, 1984).

Slaven, A. and Aldcroft D.H. (eds) *Business, Banking and Urban History* (John Donald, Edinburgh, 1982).

Stokes, R. *Dunlop in War and Peace* (Hutchinson, London, 1946).

Summerfield, P. *Women Workers in the Second World War* (Croom Helm, London, 1984).

Sutcliffe, A. and Smith, R. *Birmingham 1939–1970* (Oxford University Press, Oxford, 1974).

Swinton, Lord, *I Remember* (Hutchinson, London, 1946).

Taylor, A. J. P. *Beaverbrook* (Penguin, Harmondsworth, 1974).

Thoms, D. and Donnelly, T. *The Motor Car Industry in Coventry Since the 1890s* (Croom Helm, London, 1985).

Tiptaft, N. *The Individualist* (the author, Birmingham, 1954).

Titmuss, R. M. *Problems of Social Policy* (HMSO, London, 1950).

Tolliday, S. and Zeitlin, J. (eds) *Shop Floor Bargaining and the State* (Cambridge University Press, Cambridge, 1985).

Ward, D. *The Other Battle* (Ben Johnson, York, 1946).

West, N. *Unreliable Witness* (Weidenfeld & Nicolson, London, 1984).

Whyte, A. *Jaguar: The History of a Great British Car* (Jaguar Cars, Coventry, 1981).

Wisdom, T. H. *50 Years of Progress* (Automotive Products Group, Leamington Spa, n.d.).

Wood, D. *Attack Warning Red. The Royal Observer Corps and the Defence of Britain 1925–1975* (Macdonald & Jane's, London, 1976).

Wyatt, R. J. *The Austin 1905–1952* (David & Charles, Newton Abbot, 1981).

ARTICLES

Anon., 'The shadow factories', *Automobile Engineer*, vol. XXVII, no. 365 (1937).

Harrison, M. 'Resource mobilization for World War II: the USA, UK, USSR and Germany, 1938–1945', *Economic History Review*, 2nd Series, vol. XLI, no. 2 (1988).

Hart, R. A. and MacKay, D. I. 'Engineering earnings in Britain 1914–68', *Journal of the Royal Statistical Society*, vol. 138 (1975).

Hinton, J. 'Coventry Communism: a study of factory politics in the Second World War', *History Workshop Journal*, vol. 10 (1980).

Knowles, K. G. C. and Robinson, D. 'Wage movements in Coventry', *Bulletin of Oxford University Institute of Economics and Statistics*, vol. 51 (1969).

Shenfield, A. and Florence, P. S. 'Labour for the war industries: the experience of Coventry', *Review of Economic Studies* (1943–5).

Shenfield, A. and Florence, P. S. 'The economies and diseconomies of industrial concentration: the wartime experience of Coventry', *Review of Economic Studies* (1943–5).

Smith, D. J. 'Shadow factories', *Aviation News*, 13–26 June 1986.

Tolliday, S. 'Militancy and organization: women workers and trade unions in the motor trades in the 1930s', *Oral History Journal* (Autumn 1983).

SOURCES AND SELECT BIBLIOGRAPHY

NEWSPAPERS AND PERIODICALS

Automobile Engineer
Aviation News
Birmingham Gazette
Birmingham Post
Coventry Evening Telegraph

Fly Past
Rootes Gazette
Standard Car Review
The Times

Index

' by
e
,

4/91